Prepare for the NYSTCE: LAST and ATS-W

Joan U. Levy, Ph.D.

Norman Levy, Ph.D.

2nd Edition

NJL COLLEGE PREPARATION

PETERSON'S

A nelnet. COMPANY

About Peterson's, a Nelnet company

Peterson's (www.petersons.com) is a leading provider of education information and advice, with books and online resources focusing on education search, test preparation, and financial aid. Its Web site offers searchable databases and interactive tools for contacting educational institutions, online practice tests and instruction, and planning tools for securing financial aid. Peterson's serves 110 million education consumers annually.

For more information, contact Peterson's, 2000 Lenox Drive, Lawrenceville, NJ 08648; 800-338-3282; or find us on the World Wide Web at: www.petersons.com/about.

ISBN 13: 978-0-7689-1439-9
ISBN 10: 0-7689-1439-6

Printed in the United States of America

10 9 8 7 6 5 4 3 2   09 08 07

Second edition

CONTENTS

Introduction   Overview of the New York State
Teacher Certification Exam (NYSTCE) vii

Frequently Asked Questions ix

Top 10 Test Strategies xii

PART I: LAST REVIEW

Chapter 1: English Review 3

    Punctuation 3

    Capitalization 8

    Grammar and Usage 9

    Words Commonly Confused 14

    Sentence Structure 27

Chapter 2: Writing Review 33

    LAST–Writing 33

    How to Write the Essay 33

    Sample LAST Essay Questions 35

Chapter 3: Mathematics Review 37

    Use of Calculators 37

    Operations with Integers and Decimals 37

    Operations with Fractions 41

    Verbal Problems Involving Fractions 48

    Variation 53

    Finding Percents 59

    Verbal Problems Involving Percent 66

    Statistics and Probability 73

    Signed Numbers 84

    Linear Equations 86

    Literal Expressions 92

    Roots, Radicals, and Exponents 96

    Problem Solving in Algebra 99

    Geometry 110

Chapter 4: Science Review **117**

    Scientific Reasoning 117

    Graphs 122

    Research Summaries 123

Chapter 5: Practice Questions—LAST **139**

    Answer Key 148

PART II: LAST PRACTICE TESTS

Chapter 6: LAST—Practice Test 1 .... **153**

    Essay 169

    Answer Key 170

    Answers and Explanations 170

    Essay Response 174

Chapter 7: LAST—Practice Test 2 .... **177**

    Essay 192

    Answer Key 193

    Answers and Explanations 193

    Essay Response 197

PART III: ATS-W

Chapter 8: ATS-W Review **201**

    ATS-W Multiple-Choice Questions 201

    Written Assignment 203

    Overview of the Writing Process 203

    Writing Evaluation Checklist 206

Chapter 9: ATS-W—Practice Test 1 .... **209**

    Essay 228

    Answer Key 229

    Answers and Explanations 229

    Essay Response 237

Chapter 10: ATS-W—Practice Test 2 .... **241**

    Essay 261

    Answer Key 262

    Answers and Explanations 262

    Essay Response 270

About the Authors 271

DEDICATION

To Jessica Dawn and Joshua Seth,
two of the best reasons for writing this book.

ACKNOWLEDGMENTS

A work of this magnitude, scope, and complexity not only depends upon the expertise of its authors, but it also relies heavily on the assistance and advice of many other people. We want to thank the following people for their time, input, and suggestions:

— The staff of NJL College Preparation and National Learning Systems for their assistance in the preparation and proofreading of the manuscript.

— Arthur Getzel for his invaluable assistance on the ATS-W sections of the manuscript.

Petersons.com/publishing

Check our Web site at www.petersons.com/publishing to see if there is any new information regarding the test and any revisions or corrections to the content of this book. You should also carefully read the material you receive from the New York State Education Department and National Evaluation Systems, Inc. when you register for your test. We've made sure the information in this book is accurate and up-to-date; however, the test format or content may have changed since the time of publication.

INTRODUCTION

OVERVIEW OF THE NEW YORK STATE TEACHER CERTIFICATION EXAM (NYSTCE)

The NYSTCE is a testing program for prospective New York State teachers who wish to be granted a New York State certificate for teaching common branch subjects in pre-kindergarten through grade 6, or academic subjects at the secondary level for grades 7 through 12. Teachers must achieve qualifying scores on the NYSTCE as part of their requirements for certification.

The NYSTCE program includes the following components:

- Liberal Arts and Sciences Test (LAST)

- Elementary and Secondary Assessment of Teaching Skills–Written (ATS-W)

- Content Specialty Tests (CSTs)

- Assessment of Teaching Skills–Performance (ATS-P video)

- Communication and Quantitative Skills Test (CQST)

- Bilingual Education Assessments (BEAs)

The Liberal Arts and Sciences Test (LAST)

The Liberal Arts and Sciences Test consists of 80 multiple-choice questions and a written performance assessment. The test covers the following:

- Scientific and mathematical processes

- Historical and social science awareness

- Artistic expression and humanities

- Communication skills

- Written expression and analysis

The LAST is required for a provisional teaching certificate in New York State.

The Elementary and Secondary Assessment of Teaching Skills–Written (ATS-W)

Two versions of the Assessment of Teaching Skills–Written (ATS-W) exist. The elementary ATS-W is necessary for those who want a pre-kindergarten through grade 6 common branch subjects teaching certificate. The secondary ATS-W is necessary for those who want a certificate for a secondary academic subject. Those who seek certification in other titles are able to take either the elementary or the secondary ATS-W. The ATS-W is necessary for a provisional certificate.

The elementary and secondary versions of the ATS-W consist of 80 multiple-choice test questions and an extended written assignment. They include the following:

- Knowledge of the learner

- Instructional planning and assessment

- Instructional delivery

- The professional environment

Content Specialty Tests (CSTS)

Currently there are 21 Content Specialty Tests (CSTs). They include: Elementary Education, English, 11 other languages, English to Speakers of Other Languages, Mathematics, Biology, Chemistry, Earth Science, Physics, Social Studies, and the test for Early Childhood Annotation. Except for Greek, Hebrew, Cantonese, Mandarin, Russian, and Japanese, the CSTs are composed of multiple-choice test questions. All CSTs for languages except English include taped listening and speaking sections as well as writing sections. The CST in each area focuses on the subject that is being authorized to teach. CSTs are necessary for a permanent teaching certificate.

Language Proficiency Assessments (ELPA-C, ELPA-N, LPHAS)

The Language Proficiency Assessments are necessary for applicants for ESOL certificates and for bilingual education extension certificates. The English Language Proficiency Assessment for Classroom Personnel (ELPA-C) is necessary for those who seek a provisional New York State teaching certificate for teaching English to speakers of other languages and for those who seek a bilingual education extension to their teaching certificate. This assessment consists of taped listening and speaking components. The Target Language Proficiency Assessment (TLPA) and the English Language Proficiency Assessment for Non-classroom Personnel (ELPA-N) are necessary for those who seek a bilingual education extension to a certificate in pupil personnel services or school administration and supervision.

Assessment of Teaching Skills–Performance (ATS-P) (Video)

The Assessment of Teaching Skills–Performance (ATS-P) (Video) is necessary for those who seek a permanent New York State certificate for teaching in these specific areas:

- Common branch subjects (pre-kindergarten through grade 6)

- Grades 7–9 extension

- Early childhood annotation (pre-kindergarten through grade 3)

- Grades 7–12 academic subjects: English, mathematics, sciences, social studies

- Grades 5–6 extension

- Bilingual education (extension)

- English to speakers of other languages (ESOL)

The ATS-P is projected as a requirement for *all* permanent licenses in New York State in the future.

FREQUENTLY ASKED QUESTIONS

Who Is Required to Take the NYSTCE Examinations?

Beginning February 2, 2004, to obtain initial certification, teachers of early childhood and common branch subjects (pre-kindergarten through grade 6) and teachers of secondary academic subjects (grades 7–12) must achieve a passing score on the following:

- Liberal Arts and Sciences Test (LAST)
- Elementary or the secondary Assessment of Teaching Skills–Written (ATS-W)
- Content Speciality Test (CST) in the content area of certification

Bilingual Education Extension

To obtain a bilingual education extension to a teaching certificate, candidates must achieve a passing score on the Bilingual Education Assessment (BEA) in the target language of instruction.

When Should the Tests Be Taken?

The NYSTCE can be taken as early as the individual feels ready to take them. The LAST is often taken during the second or third year of college, and the ATS-W is taken during the last year of college. CSTs may also be taken in the third or last year of college, although they are not required until permanent certification is desired. The LPAs can be taken during the second or third year of college. This schedule allows a student to retake any of the necessary tests before completing the teacher preparation program. The tests can be retaken as often as needed until the prospective teacher passes the test. The ATS-P is recommended only after two years of classroom experience.

How Can I Register for the Tests?

Registration for the NYSTCE is done by submitting a registration form from the NYSTCE test booklet. There are four administrations of the LAST, ATS-W, and certain CSTs. Contact the National Evaluation Systems (NES) for registration, admission tickets, and test scores:

National Evaluation Systems
300 Gatehouse Road
Amherst, MA 01004-9008
Phone: (413) 256-2882 or (800) 309-5225 toll-free

Alternative testing arrangements are available for examinees who either cannot take the tests on Saturdays or whose disabilities require alternative testing arrangements.

What Are the Test Fees?

LAST: $70

ATS-W: $70

CST: $70

ATS-P: $145

ELPHA/TLPA: $70

Late Registration: $30

Special Summer Administration: $20

Additional Score Report: $15

Change of Registration: $20

Out of State Testing: $70

How Are the Tests Scored?

Scoring on the LAST and the ATS-W ranges from 100 to 300. Only items answered correctly add to your score; those omitted or answered incorrectly do not count. Passing each test requires a scaled score of 220 or better.

How Do I Receive My Scores?

Test scores are mailed to the examinee. The score reports include whether the examinee passed the test, his/her total test score, and a description of performance on the major content subtopics of the test.

The total test score is based upon performance on all sections of the test. Multiple-choice scores and scores on any performance assignment are joined to obtain the total score. The score is not compared with scores of any other examinees.

Scores are reported to the examinee, to the New York State Education Department, and to the New York State institution that was included on the registration form. Additional copies of score reports are available at $15.

Can the Tests Be Retaken?

Yes. If a candidate fails a test, he or she can retake the test without restriction until a passing grade is obtained. The *entire* test must be retaken, not merely the sub-area that proved too difficult.

If I Apply for NYSTCE Tests, Do I Also Apply Separately for Certification?

Yes. The test scores will automatically be reported to the Office of Teaching, but candidates must send a separate application for a certificate with supporting credentials to the Office of Teaching. Scores are held at the Office of Teaching for five years.

How Does Reciprocity Work with Other States?

The Interstate Certification Compact states that study in another state will satisfy New York's study and experience requirements. However, qualifying scores of the NYSTCE are an additional requirement for certification in New York State. Candidates who already have certification from a state that participates in the Interstate Certification Compact may obtain a conditional certificate, which is valid for two years. Candidates must then meet New York's testing requirements.

What If a Candidate Possesses Certification Based upon NTE (National Teacher Examination) Scores?

NYSTCEs are still required even if a candidate already passed the National Teacher Examination (NTE). All candidates for certification must take and pass NYSTCE tests.

When Are the Tests Given?

All tests, except for the ATS-P, are given in October, February, April, May, and July.

Where Can I Get Additional Information about Testing Requirements?

Office of Teaching
New York State Department of Education
Room 5N, Education Boulevard
Albany, NY 12234
Phone: (518) 474-3901
Web site: www.highered.nysed.gov/tcert

TOP 10 TEST STRATEGIES

1. **Fill in the correct oval.**

   Your score is based upon what you fill in on your answer sheet, so make sure that you fill in the answers properly.

2. **Answer everything.**

   You are graded on the number of answers that are correct. You are not penalized for wrong answers, so do not omit any question.

3. **Make an educated guess.**

   The process of elimination is the best way to improve your guess statistics. Check out the answer choices, and try to knock out any that are definitely wrong. Now, quickly take a closer look at the remaining choices and take your best guess.

4. **Don't read the directions.**

   This advice may seem somewhat surprising. After all, you are usually told to read directions carefully so that you understand what is required. However, by the time you take your LAST and ATS-W, you will have practiced solving so many model questions that you will already know what is required. So don't waste valuable time reading directions that you already know.

5. **Check your work.**

   If you have time at the end of a section, go over your work. Go back to items that you were unsure of, and check your answers.

6. **Keep moving.**

   If you've spent more than a minute on a question, chances are that you are just spinning your wheels and need to move on. But because there is no penalty for a wrong answer, you may as well fill in one of the ovals.

7. **Calm your test anxiety.**

   Don't let anyone kid you—everyone is at least a little nervous on exam day, and that's okay. But don't let it impede your performance. There is no one answer for everyone, but do what makes you feel less anxious. And relax—you can retake the test if you need to do so.

8. **Don't worry too much about time.**

   The LAST and ATS-W are 4 hours long. That should give you ample time to do the entire test and to check your work.

9. **Watch out for question traps.**

   The words *except, not,* or *least* may appear in some questions. Note that you are being asked for the answer that doesn't fit with the rest of the answer choices.

10. **Leave the most difficult questions for the end.**

    You gain the same points for difficult questions as for easy ones; therefore, it is in your best interest to answer the easier ones first and then tackle the harder ones later.

Part I
LAST REVIEW

Chapter 1

ENGLISH REVIEW

PUNCTUATION

Apostrophe

1. Use an apostrophe to show possession. Place the apostrophe according to this rule: "The apostrophe, when used to indicate possession, means *belonging to everything to the left of the apostrophe*."

   Examples: lady's = belonging to the lady

                   ladies' = belonging to the ladies

                   children's = belonging to the children

   Note: To test for correct placement of the apostrophe, read *of the*.

   Example: childrens' = of the childrens (obviously incorrect)

   The placement rule applies at all times, even in compound nouns separated by hyphens and in entities made up of two or more names.

   Examples: father-in-law's = belonging to a father-in-law

                   Lansdale, Jackson, and Roosevelt's law firm = the law firm belonging to Lansdale, Jackson, and Roosevelt

                   Brown and Son's delivery truck = the delivery truck of Brown and Son

2. Use an apostrophe in a contraction in place of the omitted letter or letters.

   Examples: haven't = have not

                   we're = we are

                   let's = let us

                   o'clock = of the clock

                   class of '90 = class of 1990

   Note: Do NOT begin a paragraph with a contraction.

3. Use an apostrophe to form plurals of numbers, letters, and phrases referred to as words.

   Examples: The Japanese child pronounced his *r*'s as *l*'s .

                   The solution of the puzzle involves crossing out all the 3's and 9's.

                   His speech was studded with *you know's.*

Colon

1. Use a colon after the salutation in a business letter.
   Example: Dear Board Member:

2. Use a colon to separate hours from minutes.
   Example: The eclipse occurred at 10:36 a.m.

3. Use of the colon is optional in the following cases:
   A. To introduce a list, especially after an expression such as "as follows"
   B. To introduce a long quotation
   C. To introduce a question
   Example: My favorite authors are: Frost, Yeats, and Poe.

Comma

1. Use a comma after the salutation of a personal letter.
   Example: Dear Mary,

2. Use a comma after the complimentary close of a letter.
   Example: Cordially yours,

3. Use a comma or a pair of commas to set off a noun of address.
   Example: When you finish your homework, Jeff, please take out the garbage.

4. Use a pair of commas to set off parenthetical expressions—words that interrupt the flow of the sentence, such as *however, though, for instance,* and *by the way.*
   Examples: We could not, however, get him to agree.
                      This book, I believe, is the best of its kind.

   Note: Test for placement of commas in a parenthetical expression by reading aloud. If you would pause before and after such an expression, then commas should set it off.

5. Use a comma between two or more adjectives that modify a noun equally.
   Example: The jolly, ruddy man stood at the top of the stairs.

   Note: If you can add the word *and* between the adjectives without changing the sense of the sentence, then use commas.

6. Use a comma to separate words, phrases, or clauses in a series. The use of a comma before *and* is optional. If the series ends in *etc.,* use a comma before *etc.* Do not use a comma after *etc.* in a series, even if the sentence continues.
   Examples: Coats, umbrellas, and boots should be placed in the closet at the end of the hall.
                      Pencils, scissors, paper clips, etc. belong in your top desk drawer.

7. Use a comma to separate a short direct quotation from the speaker.
   Examples: She said, "I must leave work on time today."
                      "Tomorrow I begin my summer job," he told us.

8. Use a comma after an introductory clause or phrase of five or more words.
   Example: Because the prisoner had a history of attempted jailbreaks, he was put under heavy guard.

9. Use a comma after a short introductory phrase whenever the comma would aid clarity.

    Examples: As a child she was a tomboy. (comma unnecessary)

    To Dan, Phil was friend as well as brother. (comma clarifies)

    In 1978, 300 people lost their lives in one air disaster. (comma clarifies)

    Note: A comma is not generally used before a subordinate clause that ends a sentence, though in long, unwieldy sentences such as this one, use of such comma is optional.

10. Use a comma before a coordinating conjunction, unless the two clauses are very short.

    Examples: The boy wanted to borrow a book from the library, but the librarian would not allow him to take it until he had paid his fines.

    Roy washed the dishes and Helen dried.

11. Use a pair of commas to set off a nonrestrictive adjective phrase or clause. A nonrestrictive phrase or clause is one that can be omitted without essentially changing the meaning of the sentence.

    Example: Our new sailboat, which has bright orange sails, is very seaworthy.

    Note: A restrictive phrase or clause is vital to the meaning of a sentence and cannot be omitted. Do NOT set it off with commas.

    Example: A sailboat without sails is useless.

12. Use a comma if the sentence might be subject to different interpretations without it.

    Examples: The banks which closed yesterday are in serious financial difficulty. (Some banks closed yesterday, and those banks are in trouble.)

    The banks, which closed yesterday, are in serious financial difficulty. (*All* banks closed yesterday, and *all* are in trouble.)

    My brother Bill is getting married. (The implication is that I have more than one brother.)

    My brother, Bill, is getting married. (Here, Bill is an appositive. Presumably, he is the only brother.)

13. Use a comma if a pause would make the sentence clearer and easier to read.

    Examples: Inside the people were dancing. (confusing)

    Inside, the people were dancing. (clearer)

    After all crime must be punished. (confusing)

    After all, crime must be punished. (clearer)

Dash

1. Use a dash—or parentheses—for emphasis or to set off an explanatory group of words.

    Example: The tools of his trade—probe, mirror, cotton swabs—were neatly arranged on the dentist's tray.

    Note: Unless the set-off expression ends a sentence, dashes, like parentheses, must be used in pairs.

2. Use a dash to break up a thought.

    Example: There are five—remember, I said five—good reasons to refuse their demands.

3. Use a dash to mark a sudden break in thought that leaves a sentence unfinished.

    Example: He opened the door a crack and saw—

Exclamation Mark

1. Use an exclamation mark only to express strong feeling or emotion, or to imply urgency.
   Examples: Congratulations! You broke the record.
                    Rush! Perishable contents.

Hyphen

1. Use a hyphen to divide a word at the end of a line. Always divide words between syllables.

2. Use a hyphen in numbers from *twenty-one* to *ninety-nine*.

3. Use a hyphen to join two words serving together as a single adjective before a noun.
   Examples: We left the highway and proceeded on a well-paved road.
                    That baby-faced man is considerably older than he appears to be.

4. Use a hyphen with the prefixes *ex-*, *self-*, *all-*, and the suffix *-elect*.
   Examples: ex-Senator, self-appointed, all-state, Governor-elect

5. Use a hyphen to avoid ambiguity.
   Example: After the custodian recovered the use of his right arm, he re-covered the
                    office chairs.

6. Use a hyphen to avoid an awkward union of letters.
   Examples: semi-independent, shell-like

Period

1. Use a period at the end of a sentence that makes a statement, gives a command, or makes a "polite request" in the form of a question that does not require an answer.
   Examples: I am preparing for my exam.
                    Proofread everything you type.
                    Would you please hold the script so that I may see if I have memorized my lines.

2. Use a period after the initial in a person's name.
   Example: Gen. Robert E. Lee led the Confederate forces.

3. Use periods after abbreviations.
   Examples: Tues., Mr., Mrs., Ms.

   Note: Do NOT use a period after postal service state name abbreviations such as AZ (for Arizona) or MI (for Michigan).

Question Mark

1. Use a question mark after a request for information.
   Example: At what time does the last bus leave?

   Note: A question must end with a question mark even if the question does not encompass the entire sentence.

   Example: "Daddy, are we there yet?" the child asked.

Quotation Marks

1. Use quotation marks to enclose all directly quoted material. Words not quoted must remain outside the quotation marks.
   Example: "If it is hot on Sunday," she said, "we will go to the beach."
   Note: Do NOT enclose an indirect quote in quotation marks.
   Example: She said that we might go to the beach on Sunday.

2. Use quotation marks around words used in an unusual way.
   Example: A surfer who "hangs ten" is performing a tricky maneuver on a surfboard, not staging a mass execution.

3. Use quotation marks to enclose the title of a short story, essay, short poem, song, article, or chapter titles of books.
   Example: Robert Louis Stevenson wrote a plaintive poem called "Bed in Summer."
   Note: Titles of books and plays are NOT enclosed in quotation marks; they are printed in italics. In a handwritten or typed manuscript, underscore titles of books and plays.
   Example: The song "Tradition" is from *Fiddler on the Roof.*

Placement of Quotation Marks

1. A period ALWAYS goes inside the quotation marks, whether the quotation marks are used to denote quoted material, to set off titles, or to isolate words used in a special sense.
   Examples: The principal said, "Cars parked in the fire lane will be ticketed."
   The first chapter of *The Andromeda Strain* is entitled "The Country of Lost Borders."
   Pornography is sold under the euphemism "adult books."

2. A comma ALWAYS goes inside the quotation marks.
   Examples: "We really must go home," said the dinner guests.
   If your skills become "rusty," you must study before you take the exam.
   Three stories in Kurt Vonnegut's *Welcome to the Monkey House* are "Harrison Bergeron," "Next Door," and "Epicac."

3. A question mark goes inside the quotation marks if it is part of the quotation. If the whole sentence containing the quotation is a question, the question mark goes outside the quotation marks.
   Examples: He asked, "Was the airplane on time?"
   What did you really mean when you said "I do"?

4. An exclamation mark goes inside the quotation marks if the quoted words are an exclamation, and it goes outside if the entire sentence—including the quoted words—is an exclamation.
   Examples: The sentry shouted, "Drop your gun!"
   Save us from our "friends"!

5. A colon and a semicolon ALWAYS go outside the quotation marks.
   Example: He said, "War is destructive"; she added, "Peace is constructive."

6. When a multiple-paragraph passage is quoted, each paragraph of the quotation must begin with quotation marks, but ending quotation marks are used only at the end of the last quoted paragraph.

Semicolon

1. Use a semicolon to separate a series of phrases or clauses, each of which contains commas.

   Example: The old gentleman's heirs were Margaret Whitlock, his half-sister; James Bagley, the butler; William Frame, companion to his late cousin, Robert Bone; and his favorite charity, the Salvation Army.

2. Use a semicolon to avoid confusion with numbers.

   Example: Add the following: $1.25; $7.50; and $12.89.

3. You may use a semicolon to join two short, related independent clauses.

   Example: Anne is working at the front desk on Monday; Ernie will take over on Tuesday.

   Note: Two main clauses must be separated by a conjunction or by a semicolon, *or* they must be written as two sentences. A semicolon never precedes a coordinating conjunction. The same two clauses may be written in any one of three ways:

   Examples: Autumn had come and the trees were almost bare.

   Autumn had come; the trees were almost bare.

   Autumn had come. The trees were almost bare.

4. You may use a semicolon to separate two independent clauses that are joined by an adverb such as *however, therefore, otherwise,* or *nevertheless*. The adverb must be followed by a comma.

   Example: You may use a semicolon to separate this clause from the next; however, you will not be incorrect if you choose to write two separate sentences.

   Note: If you are uncertain about how to use the semicolon to connect independent clauses, write two sentences instead.

CAPITALIZATION

1. Capitalize the first word of a sentence.

   Example: With cooperation, depression can be avoided.

2. Capitalize all proper nouns.

   Examples: America, Santa Fe Chief, General Motors, Abraham Lincoln

3. Capitalize days of the week and months.

   Example: The check was mailed on Thursday.

   Note: The seasons are not capitalized.

   Example: In Florida, winter is mild.

4. Capitalize the word *dear* when it is the first word in the salutation of a letter.

   Examples: Dear Mr. Jones:

   My dear Mr. Jones:

5. Capitalize the first word of the complimentary close of a letter.

   Examples: Truly yours,

   Very truly yours,

6. Capitalize the first and all other important words in a title.
   Example: The Art of Salesmanship

7. Capitalize a word used as part of a proper name.
   Examples: Elm Street (*But:* That street is narrow.)
   Morningside Terrace (*But:* We have a terrace apartment.)

8. Capitalize titles when they refer to a particular official or family member.
   Examples: The report was read by Secretary Marshall. (*But:* Miss Shaw, our secretary, is ill.)
   Let's visit Uncle Harry. (*But:* I have three uncles.)

9. Capitalize points of a compass when they refer to particular regions of the country.
   Example: We're going to the South next week. (*But:* New York is south of Albany.)
   Note: Write: the Far West, the Pacific Coast, the Middle East, etc.

10. Capitalize the first word of a direct quotation.
    Example: It was Alexander Pope who wrote, "A little teaming is a dangerous thing."
    Note: When a direct quotation sentence is broken, the first word of the second half of the sentence is not capitalized.
    Example: "Don't phone," Lily told me, "because they're not in yet."

GRAMMAR AND USAGE

Parts of Speech

A **noun** is the name of a person, place, thing, or idea: *teacher, city, desk, democracy*
A **pronoun** substitutes for a noun: *he, they, ours, those*
An **adjective** describes a noun: *warm, quick, tall, blue*
A **verb** expresses action or state of being: *yell, interpret, feel, are*
An **adverb** modifies a verb, an adjective, or another adverb: *quickly, loudly, very*
A **conjunction** joins words, sentences, and phrases: *and, but, or*
A **preposition** shows position in time or space: *in, during, after, behind*

Nouns

There are different kinds of nouns:
   Common nouns are general: *house, girl, street, city*
   Proper nouns are specific: *White House, Jane, Main Street, New York*
   Collective nouns name groups: *team, jury, class, Congress*
Nouns have *cases*:
   Nominative: the subject, noun of address, or predicate noun
   Objective: the direct object, indirect object, or object of the preposition
   Possessive: the form that shows possession

Pronouns

A **pronoun** must agree with its antecedent (the noun to which it refers) in gender, person, and number.

Examples: The *girls* handed in *their* assignments.

The *boy* left *his* jacket at school.

There are several kinds of pronouns. (Pronouns also have cases.)

Demonstrative pronoun: *this, that, these, those*

Indefinite pronoun: *all, any, nobody*

Interrogative pronoun: *who, which, what*

Personal pronoun: *he, she, they, we, you, them*

NOMINATIVE PRONOUNS			
	Case	**Objective**	**Possessive**
Singular	1st person	I	me my, mine
2nd person	you	you	your, yours
3rd person	he, she, it	him, her, it	his, her, hers
Plural	1st person	we	us our, ours
2nd person	you	you	your, yours
3rd person	they	them	their, theirs

Adjectives

Adjectives answer the questions "Which one?", "What kind?", and "How many?"
There are three uses of adjectives:

A **noun modifier** is usually placed directly before the noun it describes.

Example: He is a *tall* man.

A **predicate adjective** follows an inactive verb and modifies the subject.

Examples: He is *happy*.

I feel *terrible*.

Article and noun marker are other names for these adjectives: *the, a, an.*

Adverbs

Adverbs answer the questions *"Why?"*, *"How?"*, *"Where?"*, *"When?"*, and *"To what degree?"*
Adverbs are used to modify:

Verbs: He walked *quickly*.

Adjectives: The water was *extremely* cold.

Other adverbs: She whispered *very* softly.

Adverbs should *not* be used to modify nouns.

Roundup of Grammar Rules

Case of Nouns and Pronouns

1. The subject of a verb is in the nominative case even if the verb is understood and not expressed.

    Example: They are as old as we. (as we are)

2. The word *who* is in the nominative case. *Whom* is in the objective case.

    Examples: The trapeze artist who ran away with the clown broke the lion tamer's heart. (*Who* is the subject of the verb *ran*.)

    The trapeze artist whom he loved ran away with the circus clown. (*Whom* is the object of the verb *loved*.)

3. The word *whoever* is in the nominative case. *Whomever* is in the objective case.

    Examples: Whoever comes to the door is welcome to join in the party. (*Whoever* is the subject of the verb *comes*.)

    Invite whomever you wish to accompany you. (*Whomever* is the object of the verb *invite*.)

4. Nouns or pronouns connected by a form of the verb *to be* should always be in the nominative case.

    Example: It is I. (not *me*)

5. The object of a preposition or a transitive verb should use a pronoun in the objective case.

    Examples: It would be impossible for me to do that job alone. (*Me* is the object of the preposition *for*.)

    The attendant gave *me* the keys to the locker. (*Me* is the indirect object of the verb *gave*.)

    Note: When the first-person pronoun (I or me) is used in conjunction with one or more proper names, you may confirm the choice of *I* or *me* by eliminating the proper names and reading the sentence with the pronoun alone.

    Examples: John, George, Marylou, and (I or me) went to the movies last night. (By eliminating the names, you can readily choose that *I went to the movies* is correct.)

    It would be very difficult for Mac and (I or me) to attend the wedding. (Without *Mac,* it is clear that it is *difficult for me* to attend.)

6. A noun or pronoun modifying a gerund should be in the possessive case.

    Example: Is there any criticism of *Arthur's* going? (*Going* is a gerund. It must be modified by *Arthur's,* not by *Arthur*.)

7. Do not use the possessive case when referring to an inanimate object.

    Example: He had difficulty with the *store's* management. (WRONG) *But:* He had difficulty with the management of the store.

Agreement

8. *Each, either, neither, anyone, anybody, somebody, someone, every, everyone, one, no one,* and *nobody* are singular pronouns. Each of these words takes a singular verb and a singular pronoun.

   Examples: *Neither likes* the pets of the other.

   Everyone must wait *his* turn.

   Each of the patients *carries* insurance.

   Neither of the women *has* completed *her* assignment.

9. When the correlative conjunctions *both/and* and *not only/but also* are used, the number of the verb agrees with the number of the last subject.

   Example: Neither John nor *Greg eats* meat.

   Either the cat or the *mice take* charge in the barn.

10. A subject consisting of two or more nouns joined by a coordinating conjunction takes a plural verb.

    Example: Paul *and* Sue *were* the last to arrive.

11. The number of the verb is not affected by the addition to the subject of words introduced by *with, together with, no less than, as well as,* etc.

    Example: The *captain,* together with the rest of the team, *was delighted* by the victory celebration.

12. A verb agrees in number with its subject. A verb should not be made to agree with a noun that is part of a phrase following the subject.

    Examples: *Mount Snow,* one of my favorite ski areas, *is* in Vermont.

    The *mountains* of Colorado, like those of Switzerland, *offer* excellent skiing.

13. A verb should agree in number with the subject, not with the predicate noun or pronoun.

    Examples: Poor study *habits are* the leading cause of unsatisfactory achievement in school.

    The leading *cause* of unsatisfactory achievement in school *is* poor study habits.

14. A pronoun agrees with its antecedent in person, number, and gender.

    Example: Because you were absent on Tuesday, you will have to ask Mary or Beth for *her* notes on the lecture. (Use *her,* not their, because two singular antecedents joined by *or* take a singular pronoun.)

15. In sentences beginning with *there is* and *there are,* the verb should agree in number with the noun that follows it.

    Examples: There *isn't* an unbroken *bone* in her body. (The singular subject *bone* takes the singular verb *is.*)

    There *are* many *choices* to be made. (The plural subject *choices* takes the plural verb *are.*)

Double Negatives

16. *Hardly, scarcely, barely, only,* and *but* (when it means *only*) are negative words. Do NOT use another negative in conjunction with any of these words.

> *Not:* He didn't have *but* one hat. (WRONG)
>
> *But:* He had *but* one hat. *Or:* He had *only* one hat.
>
> *Not: I can't hardly* read the small print. (WRONG)
>
> *But: I can hardly* read the small print. *Or: I can't* read the small print.

Like *and* As

17. *As* is a conjunction introducing a subordinate clause. *Like* is a preposition. The object of a preposition is a noun or phrase.

> *Examples:*   The infant was wrinkled and red, *as* newborns usually are. (*Newborns* is the subject of the clause; *are* is its verb.)
>
> He behaves *like* a fool.
>
> The gambler accepts only hard currency *like* gold coins.

Subjunctive

18. When expressing a condition contrary to fact or a wish, use the subjunctive form *were*.

> *Example:*   I wish I *were* a movie star.

Exercise: Grammar and Usage

> *Directions:* For each sentence, choose the word in parentheses that is correct, and circle the word.

1. To (who, whom) shall I give the package?
2. Who is it? It is (me, I).
3. It is (my, me) understanding of the situation that the class was cancelled.
4. Each of the girls (was, were) pleased with the results.
5. Neither Jessica nor Joan (were, was) accepted to the college of her choice.
6. Either Josh or his sisters (were, was) coming over tonight.
7. Howard, together with his friends, (is, are) on the track team.
8. Cleveland, one of the Great Lakes ports, (is, are) home to the Rock 'n' Roll Hall of Fame.
9. If I (were, was) rich, I'd travel extensively.
10. (Whoever, Whomever) gets there first should reserve five seats.

Answers and Explanations

1. **The correct answer is *whom*.** Rule 2 states that *whom* is in the objective case (object of the preposition *to*).

2. **The correct answer is *I*.** Rule 4 tells us that the verb *to be* takes nominative pronouns. It is a form of *to be*.

3. **The correct answer is *my*.** Rule 6 states that a gerund, *understanding*, requires the possessive pronoun *my*.

4. **The correct answer is *was*.** Rule 8 states that *each* is singular and requires the singular verb *was*.

5. **The correct answer is *was*.** Rule 9 tells us that singular subjects joined by *nor* take a singular verb, *was*.

6. **The correct answer is *were*.** Rule 9 states that in an *either/or* construction, the verb agrees with the nearest subject.

7. **The correct answer is *is*.** Rule 11 states that the subject of the sentence remains singular and needs the singular verb *is*.

8. **The correct answer is *is*.** Rule 12 tells us that a verb must agree in number with its subject, regardless of any intervening phrase.

9. **The correct answer is *were*.** Rule 18 states that *were* expresses a wish.

10. **The correct answer is *Whoever*.** Rule 3 tells us that *whoever* is in the nominative case.

WORDS COMMONLY CONFUSED

accede—means to agree with.
concede—means to yield, but not necessarily in agreement.
exceed—means to be more than.

> We shall *accede* to your request for more evidence.

> To avoid delay, we shall *concede* that more evidence is necessary.

> Federal expenditures now *exceed* federal income.

accept—means to take when offered.
except—means excluding. (preposition)
except—means to leave out. (verb)

> We *accept* your invitation to the Halloween party.

> The entire class will be there *except* Bill and me.

> The coach refused to *except* any student from the eligibility requirements.

access—means availability.
excess—means too much.

> The lawyer was given *access* to the grand jury records.

> The expenditures this month are far in *excess* of income.

adapt—means to adjust or change.
adopt—means to take as one's own.
adept—means skillful.

> Children can *adapt* to changing conditions very easily.

> The half-starved stray cat was *adopted* by the kind woman.

> Proper instruction makes children *adept* in various games.

> **Note:** adapt to, adopt by, adept in, or adept at

adapted for—implies created suitability.

adapted from—implies changed to be made suitable.

adapted to—implies original or natural suitability.

> Atomic energy is constantly being *adapted for* new uses.
>
> Many of Richard Wagner's opera librettos were *adapted from* old Norse sagas.
>
> The gills of the fish are *adapted to* underwater breathing.

addition—means the act or process of adding.

edition—means a printing of a publication.

> In *addition* to a dictionary, he always used a thesaurus.
>
> The first *edition* of Shakespeare's plays appeared in 1623.

advantage—means a superior position.

benefit—means a favor conferred or earned (as a profit).

> He had an *advantage* in experience over his opponent.
>
> The rules were changed for his *benefit*.
>
> **Note:** to take advantage of, to have an advantage over

adverse—(pronounced AD-verse) means unfavorable.

averse—(pronounced a-VERSE) means disliking.

> He took the *adverse* decision poorly.
>
> Many students are *averse* to criticism by their classmates.

advise—means to give advice. *Advise* is losing favor as a synonym for notify.

> *Acceptable:* The teacher will *advise* the student in habits of study.
>
> *Unacceptable:* We are *advising* you of a delivery under separate cover. (SAY: notifying)

affect—means to influence. (verb)

effect—means an influence. (noun)

effect—means to bring about. (verb)

> Your education must *affect* your future.
>
> The *effect* of the last war is still being felt.

> A diploma *effected* a tremendous change in his attitude.
>
> **Note:** *Affect* also has a meaning of pretend.
>
> She had an *affected* manner.

after—is unnecessary with the past participle.

> *Correct:* After checking the timetable, I left for the station.
>
> *Incorrect:* After having checked (omit *after*) the timetable, I left for the station.

agree—use with a person in regards to a plan or opinion.

ain't—is an unacceptable contraction for *am not*, *are not*, or *is not*.

aisle—is a passageway between seats.

isle—is a small island. (Both words rhyme with *pile*.)

all ready—means everybody or everything ready.

already—means previously.

> They were *all ready* to write when the teacher arrived.
>
> They had *already* begun writing when the teacher arrived.

alright—is unacceptable.

all right—is acceptable.

all-round—means versatile or general.

all around—means all over a given area.

> Rafer Johnson, decathlon champion, is an *all-round* athlete.
>
> The police were lined up for miles *all around*.

all together—means everybody or everything together.

altogether—means completely.

> The boys and girls sang *all together*.
>
> This was *altogether* strange for a person of his type.

all ways—means in every possible way.

always—means at all times.

> He was in *all ways* acceptable to the voters.
>
> His reputation had *always* been spotless.

allude—means to make a reference to.
elude—means to escape from.

> Only incidentally does Coleridge *allude* to Shakespeare's puns.
>
> It is almost impossible for one to *elude* tax collectors.

allusion—means a reference.
illusion—means a deception of the eye or mind.

> The student made *allusions* to his teacher's habits.
>
> *Illusions* of the mind, unlike those of the eye, cannot be corrected with glasses.

alongside of—means side by side with.
alongside—means parallel to the side.

> Bill stood *alongside* of Henry.
>
> Park the car *alongside* the curb.

alot—is unacceptable. It should always be written as two words: a lot.

among—is used with more than two people or things.

> **Note:** *Amongst* should be avoided.

between—is used with two persons or things.

> The inheritance was equally divided *among* the four children. The business, however, was divided *between* the oldest and the youngest one.

amount—applies to quantities that cannot be counted one by one.
number—applies to quantities that can be counted one by one.

> A large *amount* of grain was delivered to the storehouse.
>
> A large *number* of bags of grain was delivered.

annual—means yearly.
biannual—means twice a year. (*Semiannual* means the same.)
biennial—means once in two years or every two years.

anywheres—is unacceptable.
anywhere—is acceptable.

> SAY: We can't find it *anywhere*.
>
> ALSO SAY: nowhere (NOT nowheres), somewhere (NOT somewheres)

aren't I—is colloquial. Its use is to be discouraged.

> SAY: *Am* I not entitled to an explanation? preferred to *Aren't I* . . .

as—is followed by a verb. (conjunction)
like—is NOT followed by a verb. (preposition)

> Do as I do, not *as* I say.
>
> Try not to behave *like* a child.
>
> *Unacceptable:* He acts like I do.

as far as—expresses distance.
so far as—indicates a limitation.

> We hiked *as far as* the next guest house.
>
> *So far as* we know, the barn was adequate for a night's stay.

as good as—should be used for comparisons only.

> This motel is *as good as* the next one.
>
> **Note:** *As good as* does NOT mean practically.
>
> *Unacceptable:* They *as good as* promised us a place in the hall.
>
> *Acceptable:* They *practically* promised us a place in the hall.

as if—is correctly used in the expression, "He talked *as if* his jaw hurt him."

> *Unacceptable:* "He talked *like* his jaw hurt him."

as . . . as—used for comparison in positive statements.
not so . . . as—used for comparison in negative statements.

> *Correct:* She was *as* clever *as* her sister.
>
> *Correct:* He was *not so* deft *as* his father.

ascent—is the act of rising.
assent—means approval.

> The *ascent* to the top of the mountain was perilous.
>
> Congress gave its *assent* to the president's emergency directive.

assay—means to try or experiment.
essay—means an effort or the result of an effort.

> We shall *assay* the ascent of the mountain tomorrow.
>
> The candidate's views were expressed in a well-written *essay*.

attend to—means to take care of.
tend to—means to be inclined to.

> One of the clerks will *attend to* the mail in my absence.
>
> Inactive people *tend to* gain weight.

back—should NOT be used with such words as *refer* and *return* because the prefix *re* means back.

> *Unacceptable:* Refer *back* to the text, if you have difficulty recalling the facts.

backward/backwards—both are acceptable and may be used interchangeably as adverbs.

> We tried to run *backward* (or *backwards*).
>
> *Backward* as an adjective means slow in learning. (Do NOT use *backwards* in this case.)
>
> A *backward* pupil should be given every encouragement.

badly—an adverb meaning unfavorably. It should NOT be used synonymously with *very much*.

> *Correct:* Joshua hurt himself *badly*.
>
> *Incorrect:* Pearl wanted to go to the play *badly*. (Use *very much* instead.)

being as/being that—both expressions are nonstandard. *Since* or *because* should be used in their place.

> *Correct: Since* Harold was here first, he got the best seats.
>
> *Incorrect: Being that* Dawn was in his class, the teacher recognized her.

berth—is a resting place.
birth—means the beginning of life.

> The new liner was given a wide *berth* in the harbor.
>
> He was a fortunate man from *birth*.

beside—means close to.
besides—refers to something that has been added.
He lived *beside* the stream.
He found wild flowers and weeds *besides*.

better—means recovering.
well—means completely recovered.

> He is *better* now than he was a week ago.
>
> In a few more weeks, he will be *well*.

blame—should NOT be used with *on*.

> *Correct:* Don't *blame* her for the accident.
>
> *Incorrect:* Don't *blame* the accident *on* her.

both—means two considered together.
each—means one of two or more.

> *Both* of the applicants qualified for the position.
>
> *Each* applicant was given a generous reference.
>
> **Note:** Avoid using expressions such as these:
>
> *Both* girls had a new typewriter. (Use *each girl* instead.)
>
> *Both* girls tried to outdo the other. (Use *each girl* instead.)
>
> They are *both* alike. (Omit *both*.)

breath—means an intake of air.
breathe—means to draw air in and give it out.
breadth—means width.

> Before you dive in, take a very deep *breath*.
>
> It is difficult to *breathe* under water.
>
> In a square, the *breadth* should be equal to the length.

bring—means to carry toward the person who is speaking.

take—means to carry away from the speaker.

> *Bring* the books here.
>
> *Take* your raincoat with you when you go out.

broke—is the past tense of *break*.

broke—is unacceptable to mean without money.

> He *broke* his arm.
>
> "Go for *broke*" is a slang expression widely used in gambling circles.

bunch—refers to things.

group—refers to people or things.

> This looks like a delicious *bunch* of bananas.
>
> What a well-behaved *group* of children!
>
> **Note:** The colloquial use of *bunch* applied to people is to be discouraged.
>
> A *bunch* of boys were whooping it up. (*Number* is preferable.)

calendar—is a system of time.

calender—is a smoothing and glazing machine.

colander—is a kind of sieve.

> In this part of the world, most people prefer the 12-month *calendar*.
>
> In ceramic work, the potting wheel and the *calender* are indispensable.
>
> Garden-picked vegetables should be washed in a *colander* before cooking.

can—means physically able.

may—implies permission.

> I *can* lift this chair over my head.
>
> You *may* leave after you finish your work.

cannot help—must be followed by an *-ing* form.

> We *cannot help feeling* (NOT *feel*) distressed about this.
>
> **Note:** *cannot help but* is unacceptable.

can't hardly/can't scarcely—are double negatives. They are unacceptable.

> SAY: The child *can hardly* (or *can scarcely*) walk in those shoes.

capital—is the city.

capitol—is the building.

> Paris is the *capital* of France.
>
> The *Capitol* in Washington is occupied by the Congress. (The Washington *Capitol* is always capitalized.)
>
> **Note:** *Capital* also means wealth.

cease—means to end.

seize—means to take hold of.

> Will you please *cease* making those sounds?
>
> *Seize* him by the collar as he comes around the corner.

cent—means a coin.

scent—means an odor.

sent—is the past tense of *send*.

> The one-*cent* postal card is a thing of the past.
>
> The *scent* of roses is pleasing.
>
> We were *sent* to the rear of the balcony.

certainly—(and *surely*) is an adverb.

sure—is an adjective.

> He was *certainly* learning fast.
>
> *Unacceptable:* He sure was learning fast.

cite—means to quote.

sight—means seeing.

site—means a place for a building.

> He was fond of *citing* from the Scriptures.
>
> The *sight* of the wreck was appalling.
>
> The Board of Education is seeking a *site* for the new school.

coarse—means vulgar or harsh.

course—means a path or a study.

> He was shunned because of his *coarse* behavior.
>
> The ship took its usual *course*.
>
> Which history *course* are you taking?

come to be—should NOT be replaced with the expression *become to be*, because *become* means *come to be*.

> True freedom will *come to be* when all tyrants have been overthrown.

comic—means intentionally funny.
comical—means unintentionally funny.

> A clown is a *comic* figure.
> The peculiar hat she wore gave her a *comical* appearance.

compare to—means to liken to something that has a different form.
compare with—means to compare persons or things of the same kind.
contrast with—means to show the difference between two things.

> A minister is sometimes *compared to* a shepherd.
> Shakespeare's plays are often *compared with* those of Marlowe.
> The writer *contrasted* the sensitivity of the dancer *with* the grossness of the pugilist.

complement—means a completing part.
compliment—is an expression of admiration.

> His wit was a *complement* to her beauty.
> He *complimented* her attractive hairstyle.

concur in—used for an opinion.
concur with—used with a person.

conscience—means sense of right.
conscientious—means showing care and precision.
conscious—means aware of one's self.

> Man's *conscience* prevents him from becoming completely selfish.
> He is *conscientious* about getting his work done on time.
> The injured man was completely *conscious*.

consensus of opinion—using of *opinion* is redundant.

considerable—is properly used only as an adjective, NOT as a noun.

consul—means a government representative.
council—means an assembly that meets for deliberation.
counsel—means advice.

> Americans abroad should keep in touch with their *consuls*.
> The City *Council* enacts local laws and regulations.
> The defendant heeded the *counsel* of his friends.

convenient to—should be followed by a person.
convenient for—should be followed by a purpose.

> Will these plans be *convenient to* you?
> You must agree that they are *convenient for* the occasion.

copy—is an imitation of an original work (not necessarily an exact imitation).
facsimile—is an exact imitation of an original work.

> The counterfeiters made a crude *copy* of the hundred-dollar bill.
> The official government engraver, however, prepared a *facsimile* of the bill.

could of—is unacceptable. (*Should of* is also unacceptable.)
could have—is acceptable. (*Should have* is also acceptable.)

> *Acceptable:* You *could have* done better with more care.
> *Unacceptable:* I could of won.
> Also avoid: must of, would of

decent—means suitable.
descent—means going down.
dissent—means disagreement.

> The *decent* thing to do is to admit your fault.
> The *descent* into the cave was treacherous.
> Two of the nine justices filed a *dissenting* opinion.

deduction—means reasoning from the general (laws or principles) to the particular (facts).

induction—means reasoning from the particular (facts) to the general (laws or principles).

> All men are mortal. Since Brad is a man, he is mortal. (*deduction*)
>
> There are 10,000 oranges in this truckload. I have examined 100 from various parts of the load and find them all of the same quality. I conclude that the 10,000 oranges are of this quality. (*induction*)

delusion—means a wrong idea that probably will influence action.

illusion—means a wrong idea that probably will not influence action.

> People were under the *delusion* that the earth was flat.
>
> It is just an *illusion* that the earth is flat.

desert—(pronounced DEZZ–ert) means an arid area.

desert—(pronounced di–ZERT) means to abandon; also a reward or punishment.

dessert—(pronounced di–ZERT) means the final course of a meal.

> The Sahara is the world's most famous *desert*.
>
> A true friend will not *desert* you in times of trouble.
>
> Imprisonment was a just *desert* for his crime.
>
> We had chocolate cake for *dessert*.

differ—used with a person.

different—used with a thing. Do NOT use *different than*.

> Jessica *differed with* her mother on the importance of homework.
>
> Norm's interpretation was *different from* that of his colleague.

doubt that—is acceptable.

doubt whether—is unacceptable.

Acceptable: I *doubt that* you will pass this term.

Unacceptable: We *doubt whether* you will succeed.

dual—means relating to two.

duel—means a contest between two people.

> Dr. Jekyll had a *dual* personality.
>
> Alexander Hamilton was fatally injured in a *duel* with Aaron Burr.

due to—is unacceptable at the beginning of a sentence. Use *because of*, *on account of*, or some similar expression instead.

> *Unacceptable: Due to* the rain, the game was postponed.
>
> *Acceptable: Because of* the rain, the game was postponed.
>
> *Acceptable:* The postponement was *due to* the rain.

each other—refers to two people.

one another—refers to more than two people.

> The two girls have known *each other* for many years.
>
> Several of the girls have known *one another* for many years.

either . . . or—is used when referring to choices.

neither . . . nor—is the negative form.

> *Either* you *or* I will win the election.
>
> *Neither* Eric *nor* Alex is expected to have a chance.

eliminate—means to get rid of.

illuminate—means to supply with light.

> Let us try to *eliminate* the unnecessary steps.
>
> Several lamps were needed to *illuminate* the corridor.

emerge—means to rise out of.

immerge—means to sink into. (also *immerse*)

> The swimmer *emerged* from the pool.
>
> She *immerged* the dress in the hot, soapy water.

emigrate—means to leave one's country for another.

immigrate—means to enter another country.

> The Norwegians *emigrated* to America in the mid-1860s.
>
> Many of the Norwegian *immigrants* settled in the Midwest.

endorse on the back of—*on the back of* is redundant.

enthused—unacceptable diction. USE: *enthusiastic*.

equally as—*as* is unnecessary.

>My assignment is *equally good*.

everyone—is written as one word when it is a pronoun.

every one—(two words) is used when each individual is stressed.

>*Everyone* present voted for the proposal.

>*Every* one of the voters accepted the proposal.

>**Note:** *Everybody* is written as one word.

everywheres—is unacceptable.

everywhere—is acceptable.

>We searched *everywhere* for the missing book.

>**Note:** *Everyplace* (one word) is likewise unacceptable.

feel bad—means to feel ill.

feel badly—means to have a poor sense of touch.

>I *feel bad* about the accident I saw.

>The numbness in his fingers caused him to *feel badly*.

feel good—means to be happy.

feel well—means to be in good health.

>I *feel* very *good* about my recent promotion.

>Spring weather always made him *feel well*.

flout—means to insult.

flaunt—means to make a display of.

>He *flouted the* authority of the principal.

>Hester Prynne flaunted her scarlet "A."

formally—means in a formal way.

formerly—means at an earlier time.

>The letter of reference was *formally* written.

>He was *formerly* a delegate to the convention.

former—means the first of two.

latter—means the second of two.

>The *former* half of the book was prose.

>The *latter* half of the book was poetry.

forth—means forward.

fourth—comes after *third*.

>They went *forth* like warriors of old.

>The *Fourth* of July is our Independence Day.

>**Note:** spelling of forty (40) and fourteen (14)

get—is a verb that strictly means to obtain.

>Please *get* my bag.

>There are many slang forms of *get* that should be avoided.

>*Avoid*: Do you *get* me? (SAY: Do you *understand* me?)

>*Avoid*: You can't *get away with* it. (SAY: You won't avoid punishment if you do it.)

>*Avoid*: *Get wise* to yourself. (SAY: Use common sense.)

>*Avoid*: We didn't *get to* go. (SAY: We didn't *manage to* go.)

got—means obtained.

>He *got* the tickets yesterday.

>*Avoid*: You've *got to* do it. (SAY: You *have to* do it.)

>*Avoid*: We *have got* no sympathy for them. (SAY: We *have* no sympathy for them.)

>*Avoid*: They *have got* a great deal of property. (SAY: They *have* a great deal of property.)

hanged—is used in reference to a person.

hung—is used in reference to a thing.

>The prisoner was *hanged* at dawn.

>The picture was *hung* above the fireplace.

however—means nevertheless.
how ever—means in what possible way.

>We are certain, *however*, that you will like this class.
>
>We are certain that, *how ever* you decide to study, you will succeed.

humans—is unacceptable usage. *Human beings* is the noun. *Human* is the adjective.

>Barney treated his antiques as if they were *human beings*.
>
>The malfunction was traced to *human* error.

if—introduces a condition.
whether—introduces a choice.

>I shall go to Europe *if* I win the prize.
>
>He asked me *whether* I intended to go to Europe (NOT *if*).

in—usually refers to a state of being. (no motion)
into—is used for motion from one place to another.

>The records are *in* that drawer.
>
>I put the records *into* that drawer.

in regards to—is unacceptable usage. USE: *in regard to* or *regarding*.

>*Regarding* your letter, I responded to it immediately,

irregardless—is unacceptable.
regardless—is acceptable.

>*Unacceptable: Irregardless* of the weather, I am going to the game.
>
>*Acceptable: Regardless* of his ability, he is not likely to win.
>
>**its**—means belonging to it.
>
>**it's**—means it is.
>
>The house lost *its* roof.
>
>*It's* an exposed house now.

kind of/sort of—are unacceptable expressions for *rather*. SAY: We are *rather* disappointed in you.

last—refers to the final member in a series.
latest—refers to the most recent in time.

latter—refers to the second of two.

>This is the *last* bulletin. There won't be any other bulletins.
>
>This is the *latest* bulletin. There will be other bulletins.
>
>Of the two most recent bulletins, the *latter is* more encouraging.

lay—means to place.
lie—means to recline.

>Note the forms of each verb:

Tense	Lay (Place)
Present	She *lays* the book on the desk.
Past	She *laid* the book on the desk.
Present Perfect	She *has laid* the book on the desk.

Tense	Lie (Recline)
Present	The child *lies* down.
Past	The child *lay* down.
Present Perfect	The child *has lain* down.

lightening—is the present participle of to *lighten*.
lightning—means the flashes of light accompanied by thunder.

>Leaving the extra food behind resulted in *lightening* the backpack.
>
>Summer thunderstorms produce startling *lightning* bolts.

lose out, win out—are unacceptable usage. USE: *lose* or *win*.

>If you cheat on the examination, you will certainly *lose* in the future.

many—refers to a number.
much—refers to a quantity in bulk.

>How *many* inches of rain fell last night?
>
>I don't know, but I would say *much* rain fell last night.

may—is used in the present tense.
might—is used in the past tense.

>We are hoping that he *may* come today.
>
>He *might* have done it if you had encouraged him.

noplace—as a solid word, is unacceptable for *no place* or *nowhere*.

>*Acceptable*: You now have *nowhere* to go.

number—is singular when the total is intended.

> The *number* (of pages in the book) is 50.

number—is plural when the individual units are referred to.

> A *number* of pages (in the book) were printed in italic type.

of any/of anyone—is unacceptable for all. SAY: His was the highest mark *of all*. (NOT *of any* or *of anyone*.)

off of—is unacceptable. SAY: He took the book off the table.

out loud—is unacceptable for *aloud*. SAY: He read *aloud* to his family every evening.

outdoor/out-of-door—is an adjective.
outdoors—is an adverb.

> We spent most of the summer at an *outdoor* music camp.
>
> Most of the time we played string quartets *outdoors*.
>
> **Note:** *Out-of-doors* is acceptable in either case.

people—comprise a united or collective group of individuals.
persons—are individuals that are separate and unrelated.

> The *people* of New York City have enthusiastically accepted "Shakespeare-in-the-Park" productions.
>
> Only five *persons* remained in the theater after the first act.

persecute—means to make life miserable for someone. (Persecution is illegal.)
prosecute—means to conduct a criminal investigation. (Prosecution is legal.)

> Some racial groups insist upon *persecuting* other groups.
>
> The District Attorney is *prosecuting* the racketeers.

precede—means to come before.
proceed—means to go ahead. (*Procedure* is the noun.)

supersede—means to replace.

> What were the circumstances that *preceded* the attack?
>
> We can *proceed* with our plan for resisting a second attack.
>
> It is then possible that Plan B will *supersede* Plan A.

principal—means chief or main (as an adjective); a leader (as a noun).
principle—means a fundamental truth or belief.

> His *principal* supporters came from among the peasants.
>
> The *principal* of the school asked for cooperation from the staff.
>
> Humility was the guiding *principle* of Buddha's life.
>
> **Note:** *Principal* may also mean a sum placed at interest.
>
> Part of his monthly payment was applied as interest on the *principal*.

reason is because—*because* is unnecessary. USE: *reason is that*.

> The *reason* for Shirley's lateness *is that* the bus broke down.

repeat again—is unnecessary. USE: *repeat*.

seldom ever—incorrect usage. USE: seldom *if* ever.

sit—means to take a seat (intransitive verb).
set—means to place (transitive verb).

> Note the forms of each verb:

Tense	Sit (Take a seat)
Present	He *sits* on a chair.
Past	He *sat* on the chair.
Present Perfect	He *has sat* on the chair.

Tense	Set (Place)
Present	He *sets* the lamp on the table.
Past	He *set* the lamp on the table.
Present Perfect	He *has set* the lamp on the table.

some time—means a portion of time.
sometime—means at an indefinite time in the future.

sometimes—means on occasion.

> I'll need *some time* to make a decision.
>
> Let us meet *sometime* after noon.
>
> *Sometimes* it is better to hesitate before signing a contract.

somewheres/someplace—are unacceptable.
somewhere—is acceptable.

stationary—means standing still.
stationery—means writing materials.

> In ancient times people thought the earth was *stationary*.
>
> We bought writing paper at the *stationery* store.

stayed—means remained.
stood—means remained upright or erect.

> The army *stayed* in the trenches for five days.
>
> The soldiers *stood* at attention for 1 hour.

sure/for surely—is unacceptable. SAY: *You surely* (NOT *sure*) are not going to write that!

take in—is unacceptable in the sense of deceive or attend. SAY: We were deceived (NOT *taken in*) by his oily manner.

> We should like to attend (NOT *take in*) a few plays during our vacation.

their—means belonging to them.
there—means in that place.
they're—means they are.

> We took *their* books home with us.
>
> You will find your books over *there* on the desk.
>
> *They're* going to the ballpark with us.

theirselves—is unacceptable for *themselves*. SAY: Most children of school age are able to care for *themselves* in many ways.

these kind—is unacceptable.
this kind—is acceptable.

> I am fond of *this kind* of apple.
>
> **Note:** *These kinds* of apples would also be acceptable.

through—is unacceptable to mean finished or completed. SAY: We'll finish (NOT *be through with*) the work by 5 o'clock.

try to—is acceptable.
try and—is unacceptable.

> *Try to* come (NOT: *Try and* come).
>
> **Note:** *Plan on going* is unacceptable. *Plan to go* is acceptable.

two—is the numeral 2.
to—means in the direction of.
too—means more than or also.

> There are *two* sides to every story.
>
> Three *two's* (or 2's) equal six.
>
> We shall go *to* school.
>
> We shall go, *too*.
>
> The weather is *too* hot for school.

wait on—is incorrect usage. USE: *wait for*.

> Sharon could not *wait for* her husband a moment longer.

was/were—If something is contrary to fact (not a fact), use *were* in every instance.

> I wish I *were* in Bermuda.
>
> *Unacceptable:* If he *was* sensible, he wouldn't act like that. (SAY: If he *were*. . .)

ways—is unacceptable for *way*. SAY: We climbed a little *way* (NOT *ways*) up the hill.

went and took/went and stole, etc.—is unacceptable. SAY: They *stole* (NOT *went and stole*) our tools.

when (and where)—should NOT be used to introduce a definition of a noun.

> SAY: A tornado is a twisting, high wind on land. (NOT: A tornado is *when* a twisting, high wind is on land.)
>
> A pool is a place for swimming. (NOT: A pool is *where* people swim.)

whereabouts—is unacceptable for *where*. SAY: *Where* do you live?

> **Note:** *Whereabouts* as a noun meaning a place is acceptable.
>
> Do you know his *whereabouts*?

whether—should NOT be preceded by *of* or *as to*.

SAY: The president will consider the question *whether* (NOT *of whether*) it is better to ask for or demand higher taxes now.

He inquired *whether* (NOT *as to whether*) we were going or not.

which—is used incorrectly in the following expressions:

He asked me to stay, *which* I did. (*Correct:* He asked me to stay, and I did.)

It has been a severe winter, *which* is unfortunate. (*Correct:* Unfortunately, it has been a severe winter.)

You did not write; besides *which*, you have not telephoned. (*Correct:* OMIT *which*.)

Which must be preceded by a noun that it modifies.

SAY: Jessica said that I was always late, a statement *which* is not true.

while—is unacceptable for *and* or *though*. SAY: The library is situated on the south side; (OMIT *while*) the laboratory is on the north side.

Though (NOT *while*) I disagree with you, I shall not interfere with your right to express your opinion.

Though (NOT *while*) I am in my office every day, you do not attempt to see me.

who/whom—The following is a method (without going into grammar rules) for determining when to use who or whom.

"Tell me (*who, whom*) you think should represent our company."

Step 1: Change the *who-whom* part of the sentence to its natural order.

"You think (*who, whom*) should represent our company?"

Step 2: Substitute *he* for *who*, *him* for *whom*.

"You think (*he, him*) should represent our company?" (You would say *he* in this case.)

Therefore: "Tell me *who* you think should represent our company?" is correct.

who is/who am—Note these constructions:

It is I *who am* the most experienced.

It is he *who is*. . .

It is he or I *who am*. . .

It is I or he *who is*. . .

It is he and I *who are*. . .

whose—means of whom.

who's—means who is.

Whose notebook is this?

Who's in the next office?

would of—is incorrect usage. USE: *would have*.

If I had known the answer, I *would have* responded.

you all—is unacceptable for *you* (plural). SAY: We welcome *you*, the delegates from Ethiopia.

You are *all* welcome, delegates of Ethiopia.

Exercise: Confusing Words

> *Directions:* Mark each sentence **Correct** or **Incorrect**. Correct all incorrect sentences.

1. *Try and* come over to my apartment tonight.
2. Their *principal* means of attack was by air.
3. Of the three dresses, she preferred the *latter*.
4. My grandparents *emigrated* to the United States from Poland.
5. We have never been *formally* introduced.
6. Can you *cite* any of Shakespeare's soliloquies?
7. I *differ from* you in many respects.
8. Salt and pepper *complement* the meal.
9. The *reason* Josh cannot come is *because* he is being punished.
10. Jessica is *as* pretty *as* Dawn.
11. Karen *laid* down when she was ill.
12. His *principal* means of support was his salary.
13. To *whom* do you wish to speak?
14. The drapes were *hung* on the rod.
15. Did you heed her excellent *advise?*

Answers and Explanations

1. **(Incorrect)** The correct expression is *try to*.
2. **(Correct)** *Principal* means main.
3. **(Incorrect)** *Latter* compares two items only. For three or more items, use *last*.
4. **(Incorrect)** *Emigrate* means to leave a country. *Immigrate* means to enter a new country.
5. **(Correct)** *Formally* means in a formal way.
6. **(Correct)** *Cite* means to quote.
7. **(Correct)** One *differs from* another.
8. **(Correct)** *Complement* means goes together with.
9. **(Incorrect)** *Reason is because* is incorrect usage. The *reason is that* he is being punished.
10. **(Correct)** In a positive comparison, *as . . . as* is used.
11. **(Incorrect)** The past tense of *lie* is *lay*.
12. **(Correct)** *Principal* means main.
13. **(Correct)** *Whom* is the object of the preposition *to*.
14. **(Correct)** Objects are *hung*. People are *hanged*.
15. **(Incorrect)** *Advise* is a verb. *Advice* is a noun.

SENTENCE STRUCTURE

Subjects

1. Every sentence must have a subject. The subject may be a noun, a pronoun, or a word or group of words functioning as a noun.

   Examples: *Fish* swim. (noun)

   Boats are sailed. (noun)

   She is young. (pronoun)

   Running is good exercise. (gerund)

   To argue is pointless. (infinitive)

   That he was tired was evident. (noun clause)

   Note: In commands, the subject is usually not expressed but is understood to be *you*.

   Example: Mind your own business.

Verbs

2. Every sentence must contain a verb. A group of words, no matter how long, without a verb is a sentence fragment, not a sentence. A verb may consist of one, two, three, or four words.

   Examples: The boy *studies* hard.

   The boy *will study* hard.

   The boy *has been studying* hard.

   The boy *should have been* studying hard.

   Note: The words that make up a single verb may be separated.

   Examples: It *is* not *snowing*.

   It *will* almost certainly *snow* tomorrow.

Phrases and Clauses

3. A phrase cannot stand by itself as a sentence. A phrase is any group of related words that has no subject or predicate and that is used as a single part of speech. Phrases may be built around prepositions, participles, gerunds, or infinitives.

   Examples: The boy *with curly hair is* my brother. (prepositional phrase used as an adjective modifying *boy*)

   My favorite cousin lives *on a farm*. (prepositional phrase used as an adverb modifying *lives*)

   Beyond the double white line is out of bounds. (prepositional phrase used as a noun, the subject of the sentence)

   A thunderstorm *preceding a cold front* is often welcome. (participial phrase used as an adjective modifying *thunderstorm*)

   We eagerly awaited the pay envelopes *brought by the messenger*. (participial phrase used as an adjective modifying *envelopes*)

Running a day camp is an exhausting job. (gerund phrase used as a noun, subject of the sentence)

The director is paid well *for running the day camp*. (gerund phrase used as a noun, the object of the preposition *for*)

To breathe unpolluted air should be every person's birthright. (infinitive phrase used as a noun, the subject of the sentence)

The child began *to unwrap his gift*. (infinitive phrase used as a noun, the object of the verb *began*)

The boy ran away from home *to become a Marine*. (infinitive phrase used as an adverb modifying *ran away*)

4. A main, independent, or principal clause can stand alone as a complete sentence. A main clause has a subject and a verb. It may stand by itself or be introduced by a coordinating conjunction.

Example: The sky darkened ominously, and rain began to fall. (two independent clauses joined by a coordinating conjunction)

A subordinate or dependent clause must never stand alone. It is not a complete sentence but is a sentence fragment, despite the fact that it has a subject and a verb. A subordinate clause usually is introduced by a subordinating conjunction. Subordinated clauses may act as adverbs, adjectives, or nouns. Subordinate adverbial clauses are generally introduced by the subordinating conjunctions *when, while, because, as soon as, if, after, although, as before, since, than, though, until*, and *unless*.

Examples: *While* we were waiting for the local train, the express roared past.

The woman applied for a new job *because* she wanted to earn more money.

Although a subordinate clause contains both a subject and a verb, it cannot stand alone because it is introduced by a subordinating word.

Subordinate adjective clauses may be introduced by the pronouns *who, which*, and *that*.

Examples: The play *that* he liked best was a mystery.

I have a neighbor *who* served in the Peace Corps.

Subordinate noun clauses may be introduced by *who, what*, or *that*.

Examples: The stationmaster says *that* the train will be late.

I asked the waiter *what* the stew contained.

I wish I knew *who* backed into my car.

5. Two independent clauses cannot share one sentence without some form of connective. If they do, they form a run-on sentence. Two independent clauses may be joined by a coordinating conjunction, by a comma followed by a coordinating conjunction, or by a semicolon. Two main clauses may NEVER be joined by a comma without a coordinating conjunction. This error is called a comma splice.

Examples: A college education has never been more important than it is today it has never cost more. (WRONG: run-on sentence)

A college education has never been more important than it is today, it has never cost more. (WRONG: comma splice)

To correct a run-on sentence:

A. **Divide it into two separate sentences, adding a transitional word if necessary.**

Example: A college education has never been more important than it is today. Also, it has never cost more.

B. **Join the two independent clauses with a comma and a conjunction.**

Example: A college education has never been more important than it is today, and it has never cost more.

C. **Join the dependent clauses with a semicolon.**

Example: A college education has never been more important than it is today; it has never cost more.

D. **Make one clause subordinate to the other.**

Example: While a college education has never been more important than it is today, it has also never cost more.

6. Phrases should be placed near the words they modify.

Not: We need someone to keep the records *with bookkeeping experience*. (The records cannot have bookkeeping experience.)

But: We need someone *with bookkeeping experience* to keep the records.

7. Relative clauses should be placed immediately after the words they modify.

Not: The report must be typewritten, *which is due tomorrow*.

But: The report, *which is due tomorrow,* must be typewritten.

Modifiers

8. Adjectives modify only nouns and pronouns. Adverbs modify verbs, adjectives, and other adverbs.

Examples: One can swim in a lake as *easy* as in a pool. (WRONG)

One can swim in a lake as *easily* as in a pool. (The adverb *easily* must modify the verb *can swim*.)

I was *real* happy. (WRONG)

I was *really* happy. (The adverb *really* must be used to modify the adjective *happy*.)

Sometimes context determines the use of adjective or adverb.

Examples: The old man looked *angry*. (*Angry* is an adjective describing the old man [angry old man].)

The old man looked *angrily* out the window. (*Angrily* is an adverb describing the man's manner of looking out the window.)

9. Adverbs should be placed near the words they modify.

Not: The man was *only* willing to contribute one dollar.

But: The man was willing to contribute *only* one dollar.

10. A modifier must modify something.

Not: Running for the bus, her shoe fell off. (The phrase *running for the bus* has nothing to modify. Obviously a *shoe* cannot *run*.)

But: Running for the bus, she lost her shoe.

Or: As she was running for the bus, her shoe fell off. (Either way, the addition of the pronoun *she* tells who did the running.)

Pronoun Antecedents

11. The antecedent of a pronoun must be a specific word, not an idea expressed in a phrase or clause.

    Not: Although the doctor operated at once, *it* was not a success and the patient died. (There is no specific noun to which *it* can refer.)

    But: Although the doctor performed the operation at once, *it* was not a success and the patient died. (*It* correctly refers to the nearest noun, *operation.*)

Parallelism

12. Express ideas that balance each other in the same grammatical structure.

    Not: Skiing and *to skate* are both winter sports.

    But: Skiing and *skating* are both winter sports.

    Not: She spends all her time eating, asleep, and on her studies.

    But: She spends all her time *eating, sleeping,* and *studying.*

    Not: The work is neither difficult, nor do I find it interesting.

    But: The work is neither *difficult* nor *interesting.*

Point of View

13. Avoid needless shifts in point of view. A change from one tense or mood to another, from one subject or voice to another, or from one person to another destroys parallelism within the sentence.

    Not: After he *rescued* the kitten, he *rushes* down the ladder to find its owner. (shift from past tense to present tense)

    But: After he *rescued* the kitten, he *rushed* down the ladder to find its owner.

    Not: Mary especially likes math, but *history* is also enjoyed by her. (shift from active to passive voice)

    But: Mary especially likes math, but *she* also enjoys history.

    Not: First stand at attention, and then you should salute the flag. (shift from imperative to indicative mood)

    But: First stand at attention, and then salute the flag.

    Not: One should listen to the weather forecast so that they may anticipate a hurricane. (shift from singular to plural subject)

    But: One (or He) should listen to the weather forecast so that one (or he) may anticipate a hurricane.

Wordiness

14. Avoid unnecessary repetition and superfluous words.

    Not: She *began to get started* knitting the sweater.

    But: She *began* knitting the sweater.

    Not: This skirt *is longer in length* than that one.

    But: This skirt *is longer* than that one.

Comparisons

15. Make comparisons logical and complete.

Not: Wilmington is larger than any city in Delaware. (not logical because Wilmington is a city in Delaware)

But: Wilmington is larger than any *other* city in Delaware.

Not: He is as fat, if not fatter, than his uncle. (not complete because *as fat* is completed by *as,* not *than*)

But: He is as fat *as,* if not fatter than, his uncle.

Exercise: Sentence Structure

Directions: Mark each sentence **Correct** or **Incorrect**. Correct all incorrect sentences.

1. She likes tennis, golf, and to go swimming.
2. He could not deliver the supplies. Because the roads had not yet been plowed.
3. If you want to succeed, one must be willing to work hard.
4. Jeff is taller than any boy in his class.
5. To get to school we nearly walked 2 miles.
6. The heroine was unbelievable naive.
7. Drive carefully. There may be ice on the roads.
8. Leaning out the window, the garden could be seen below.
9. The hotel room was clean and comfortable that we had reserved.
10. This book is heavier in weight than that one.

Answers and Explanations

1. **(Incorrect)** She likes tennis, golf, and *swimming*. Rule 12 states that parallel ideas should be expressed in the same grammatical structure.

2. **(Incorrect)** He could not deliver the supplies *because* the roads had not yet been plowed. Rule 4 states that a subordinate clause cannot stand alone.

3. **(Incorrect)** If you want to succeed, you must be willing to work hard. Rule 13 cautions against shifts in point of view.

4. **(Incorrect)** Jeff is taller than any *other* boy in his class. Rule 15 states that comparisons must be logical. Jeff cannot be compared to himself; therefore, he must be separated from the rest of the boys by the use of the word *other*.

5. **(Incorrect)** To get to school, we walked *nearly 2 miles*. Rule 9 explains that adverbs must be placed near the words they modify. *Nearly* modifies *2 miles*, not *walked*.

6. **(Incorrect)** The heroine was *unbelievably* naive. Rule 8 indicates that an adverb is needed to modify the adjective *naive*.

7. **(Correct)** Rules 1 and 2 verify that each statement is a complete sentence.

8. **(Incorrect)** Leaning out the window, *she could see* the garden below. Rule 10 states that every modifier must modify something. Without the addition of *she, leaning out the window* has nothing to modify.

9. **(Incorrect)** The hotel room *that we had reserved* was clean and comfortable. Rule 6 states that phrases must be placed near the words they modify.

10. **(Incorrect)** This book *is heavier* than that one. Rule 14 warns against using unnecessary words. *Heavier in weight* is redundant.

Chapter 2
WRITING REVIEW

LAST–WRITING

LAST writing assignments are scored from a low of 0 to a high of 3. They are scored holistically, meaning the rater gives a total score based on the nature of the essay as a whole. Raters are trained by the National Evaluation Systems to evaluate the responses according to their guidelines listed below:

0 Represents a poorly written, incomplete assignment. It does not answer the question well and contains many errors in grammar, spelling, and/or punctuation.

1 Represents an unfinished, poorly written essay. It does not completely answer the question and may contain grammar, spelling, and/or punctuation errors.

2 Represents a complete essay that is fairly well-developed. It may not completely respond to the entire question, and explanations may not be completely supported. It may have some errors in grammar, punctuation, and/or spelling.

3 Represents a complete, well-developed essay that responds to the topic and provides clear explanations. It does not contain errors in grammar, punctuation, or spelling.

HOW TO WRITE THE ESSAY

Nothing strikes fear in the hearts of most students as much as writing an essay, especially one that constitutes a part of the grade on an important examination. However, essay writing does not have to be frightening or terribly difficult.

The key to writing a good essay is *organization*. The LAST essay is a persuasive essay. It is meant to espouse a point of view and give evidence to support that point of view. Therefore, certain techniques should be used in writing the essay.

Steps in Writing a Persuasive Essay

1.   **Choose Your Point of View**

Most LAST essays ask you to agree or disagree with a given topic or to state your opinion on some material that is provided. Your first step is to read the assignment carefully and decide your own point of view.

2.   **Prepare an Outline**

Some people believe that an outline wastes valuable test time on an examination. On the contrary, an outline can actually save you time by organizing your thoughts in an orderly fashion before you begin to write your essay.

The outline functions as a rough guide to your presentation of material. It helps you include relevant material in appropriate places and provide a cogent, well-presented argument. The outline should be organized loosely as follows:

I.   **Introduction**
   A.   Introduce the topic.
   B.   State the thesis (your point of view in the argument). The thesis is *essential* in a good persuasive essay.

II. **Body**
   A.   Provide specific examples or reasons to support your thesis.
   B.   Utilize positive as well as negative verification for the argument. Show not only why this is plausible, but also why other interpretations are not.

III. **Conclusion**
   A.   Summarize the information.
   B.   Restate the thesis.

3.   **Write the Essay**

Once you write the outline, the actual essay writing should be fairly straightforward. You should have all your information and should know where you want to put each piece of supporting evidence. The thesis should be clear, and the examples and/or arguments should follow in logical order.

Each discrete example belongs in its own paragraph; transitional words—*in addition, another, however, furthermore, moreover, therefore, thus, consequently, hence,* etc.—can be used to make one paragraph flow into the next one.

4.   **Proofread the Essay**

This is a crucial step in writing a good essay. Make sure to take the time to read over the essay carefully. Use the following checklist:

   A.   **Is everything spelled correctly?**
Nothing looks worse on an essay than misspelled words. If you don't know how a word is spelled, use another in its place!

   B.   **Are the sentences varied in sentence structure?**
Try to use simple sentences, compound sentences, complex sentences, questions, and declarative statements. Make the essay interesting to the reader.

   C.   **Is the essay grammatically correct?**
Check subject-verb agreement, tense, plurals, etc.

   D.   **Are the essay's arguments well presented?**
Are they convincing? Do they support the thesis and argue their case well? Are any essential parts of the argument omitted?

Proofreading need not take a long time, but it can make the difference between a good essay and a superb one. Don't forget this essential step!

SAMPLE LAST ESSAY QUESTIONS

1. Some people contend that children learn more about life from the television programs they watch than from their parents. The television hero becomes the role model, and children often imitate the violence and hostility depicted on the television screen.

   Do you agree or disagree? Explain and illustrate your answer from your own experience or from your observation of others.

2. Although some people feel that there should be strict gun control laws, these laws would certainly curtail the freedom of the majority and prove ineffective. Violence comes about because our society has many violent members, not because we have allowed people to possess weapons. Actually, allowing our citizens to possess guns would offer a means of protection and preserve law and order.

   The passage states that gun control laws are valueless and can even prove harmful. Do you agree or disagree? Explain and illustrate your answer.

3. The public schools have been criticized for being too lenient with students who break rules concerning proper dress and behavior. Some critics of the system say that students should be given strict punishment when they are found guilty of violating school rules.

   Do you agree or disagree? Explain and illustrate your answer from your own experience, your observation of others, or your reading.

Chapter 3

MATHEMATICS REVIEW

USE OF CALCULATORS

You are permitted to use the following graphic calculators during your test:

CASIO   FX7400G

             FX7400GPLUS

             CFX-9850G

             CFX-9850Ga

             CFX-9850Ga-PLUS

             CFX-9850GB-PLUS

SHARP   EL-9300

             EL9600

             EL-9600c

TEXAS INSTRUMENTS

    TI-82

    TI-83

    TI-83 Plus

    TI-83 Plus Silver

HEWLETT-PACKARD

    HP 40G

OPERATIONS WITH INTEGERS AND DECIMALS

The four basic arithmetic operations are:

- Addition
- Subtraction
- Multiplication
- Division

The results of these operations are called the sum, difference, product, and quotient, respectively. Because these words are often used in math problems, you should be thoroughly familiar with them.

When adding integers and/or decimals, remember to keep your columns aligned and to write all digits in their proper column according to place value.

Q Add: 43.75, 0.631, and 5

The correct answer is 49.381.

$$\begin{array}{r} 43.75 \\ 0.631 \\ \underline{5.} \\ 49.381 \end{array}$$

When subtracting integers and/or decimals, it is important to place numbers in their proper columns. Be particularly careful in subtracting a "longer" decimal from a "shorter" one.

Q Subtract: 0.2567 from 3.8

The correct answer is 3.5433.

$$\begin{array}{r} 3.8000 \\ \underline{-0.2567} \\ 3.5433 \end{array}$$

To perform this subtraction, zeros must be added to the top number to extend it to equal length with the bottom number. The zeros in this case are only place-fillers and in no way change the value of the number.

When multiplying integers, pay particular attention to zeros.

Q Find the product of 403 and 30.

The correct answer is 12,090.

$$\begin{array}{r} 403 \\ \underline{\times\,30} \\ 12{,}090 \end{array}$$

When multiplying decimals, remember that the number of decimal places in the product must be equal to the sum of the number of decimal places in the numbers being multiplied.

Q Find the product of 4.03 and 0.3.

The correct answer is 1.209.

$$\begin{array}{r} 4.03 \\ \underline{\times\,0.3} \\ 1.209 \end{array}$$

When dividing, it is also important to watch for zeros.

Q Divide: 4,935 by 7

The correct answer is 705. $7\overline{)4{,}935}$ with quotient 705

Because 7 divides into 49 evenly, there is no remainder to carry to the next digit. Since we cannot divide 3 by 7, we write a 0 in the quotient and try to divide 35 by 7. It divides evenly, so we have no remainder.

When dividing decimals, remember that we always wish to divide by an integer. If the divisor is a decimal, we must multiply by a power of 10 to make it an integer. Multiplying by 10 moves a decimal point one place to the right. Multiplying by 100 moves it two places to the right, and so forth. However, remember to do the same to the dividend. Division can always be written as a fraction in which the number we are dividing by becomes the denominator when we remove a decimal point from the divisor.

 Divide: 4.935 by .07

The correct answer is 70.5. $.07 \overline{)4.935} \rightarrow 07 \overline{)493.5}$ with quotient 70.5

Exercise: Operations with Integers and Decimals

> *Directions:* Work out each problem in the space provided.

Add:

1. 6 + 37 + 42.083 + 125

2. 0.007 + 32.4 + 1.234 + 7.3

3. 0.37 + 0.037 + 0.0037 + 37

Subtract:

4. 3,701 − 371

5. 1,000 − 112

6. 40.37 − 6.983

Multiply:

7. 3,147 by 206

8. 2.137 by 0.11

9. 0.45 by 0.06

Divide:

10. 12.894 by 42

11. 34.68 by 3.4

12. 0.175 by 25

Answers and Explanations

1. The correct answer is 210.083.

```
    6.000
   37.000
   42.083
  125.000
  210.083
```

2. The correct answer is 40.941.

```
   0.007
  32.4
   1.234
   7.3
  40.941
```

3. The correct answer is 37.4107.

```
  0.37
  0.037
  0.0037
 37.
 37.4107
```

4. The correct answer is 3,330.

```
  3,701
 −  371
  3,330
```

5. The correct answer is 888.

```
  1,000
 − 112
    888
```

6. The correct answer is 33.387.

```
  40.370
 − 6.983
  33.387
```

7. The correct answer is 648,282.

```
    3,147
  × 206
   18882
   62940
  648,282
```

8. The correct answer is 0.23507.

```
    2.137
  × 0.11
    2137
    2137
   0.23507
```

9. The correct answer is 0.0270.

```
    0.45
  × 0.06
   0.0270
```

10. The correct answer is 0.307.

$$
\begin{array}{r}
0.307 \\
42\overline{)12.894} \\
126 \\
294 \\
294 \\
0
\end{array}
$$

11. The correct answer is 10.2.

$$
\begin{array}{r}
10.2 \\
3.\underline{4}\overline{)34.\underline{68}} \\
34 \\
68 \\
68 \\
0
\end{array}
$$

12. The correct answer is 0.007.

$$
\begin{array}{r}
0.007 \\
25\overline{)0.175} \\
175 \\
0
\end{array}
$$

OPERATIONS WITH FRACTIONS

A **fraction** is part of a unit. A fraction has a **numerator** and a **denominator**.

In the fraction $\frac{3}{4}$, 3 is the numerator and 4 is the denominator.

In any fraction, the numerator is being divided by the denominator.

The fraction $\frac{2}{7}$ indicates that 2 is being divided by 7.

In a fraction problem, the whole quantity is 1, which may be expressed by a fraction in which the numerator and denominator are the same number.

If the problem involves $\frac{1}{8}$ of a quantity, then the whole quantity is $\frac{8}{8}$, or 1.

A **mixed number** is an integer together with a fraction, such as $2\frac{3}{5}$, $7\frac{5}{8}$, $3\frac{1}{3}$, etc. The integer is the integral part, and the fraction is the fractional part.

A positive **improper fraction** is one in which the numerator is equal to or greater than the denominator, such as $\frac{9}{5}$, $\frac{7}{3}$, $\frac{53}{2}$, or $\frac{7}{7}$.

To rewrite a mixed number as an improper fraction, follow these 3 steps:

- **Multiply** the denominator of the fraction by the integer.
- **Add** the numerator to this product.
- **Place** this sum over the denominator of the fraction.

Q Rewrite $3\frac{4}{7}$ as an improper fraction.

The correct answer is $\frac{25}{7}$. $7 \times 3 = 21$
$$21 + 4 = 25$$
$$3\frac{4}{7} = \frac{25}{7}$$

To rewrite an improper fraction as a mixed number, follow these 2 steps:

- **Divide** the numerator by the denominator. The quotient, disregarding the remainder, is the integral part of the mixed number.
- **Place** the remainder, if any, over the denominator. This is the fractional part of the mixed number.

Q Rewrite $\frac{36}{13}$ as a mixed number.

The correct answer is $2\frac{10}{13}$.
$$13\overline{)36}$$
with quotient 2,
$$\underline{26}$$
$$10 \quad \text{remainder}$$

$$\frac{36}{13} = 2\frac{10}{13}$$

The numerator and denominator of a fraction may be changed by multiplying both by the same number, without affecting the value of the fraction.

The value of the fraction will not be altered if both the numerator and the denominator are multiplied by 2, to yield $\frac{3}{5} \times \frac{2}{2} = \frac{6}{10}$.

The numerator and the denominator of a fraction may be changed by dividing both by the same number, without affecting the value of the fraction. This process is called **simplifying the fraction**. A fraction that has been simplified as much as possible is said to be in **simplest form**.

The value of the fraction $\frac{3}{12}$ will not be altered if both the numerator and the denominator are each divided by 3, to yield $\frac{1}{4}$.

If $\frac{6}{30}$ is simplified to simplest form (by dividing both the numerator and the denominator by 6), the result is $\frac{1}{5}$.

Adding and Subtracting Fractions

To add or subtract fractions, you must remember that the numbers must have the same (common) denominator.

Q Add: $\frac{1}{3} + \frac{2}{5} + \frac{3}{4}$

The correct answer is $1\frac{29}{60}$. The least number into which 3, 5, and 4 all divide evenly is 60.

Therefore, we must use 60 as our common denominator. To add our fractions, we divide 60 by each denominator and multiply the result by the given numerator:

$$\frac{20 + 24 + 45}{60} = \frac{89}{60} \text{ or } 1\frac{29}{60}$$

To add or subtract two fractions quickly, remember that a sum can be found by adding the two cross products and putting this answer over the denominator product:

$$\frac{a}{b} \times \frac{c}{d} = \frac{ad+bc}{bd}$$

A similar shortcut applies to subtraction:

$$\frac{a}{b} - \frac{c}{d} = \frac{ad-bc}{bd}$$

$$\frac{3}{4} - \frac{5}{7} = \frac{21-20}{28} = \frac{1}{28}$$

All fractions should be left in their simplest form. That is, there should be no factor common to both the numerator and the denominator. Often in multiple-choice questions you may find that the answer you have correctly computed is not among the choices, but an equivalent fraction is. Be careful!

In simplifying fractions involving great numbers, it is helpful to be able to tell whether a factor is common to both numerator and denominator before a lengthy trial division. Certain tests for divisibility help with this.

To test if a number is divisible by:	Check to see:
2	if it is even
3	if the sum of the digits is divisible by 3
4	if the number formed by the last two digits is divisible by 4
5	if it ends in 5 or 0
6	if it is even and the sum of the digits is divisible by 3
8	if the number formed by the last three digits is divisible by 8
9	if the sum of the digits is divisible by 9
10	if it ends in 0

Q Simplify to simplest form: $\dfrac{3,525}{4,341}$

The correct answer is $\dfrac{1,175}{1,447}$. This fraction can be simplified using 3 because the sum of the digits of the numerator is 15 and of the denominator is 12, both divisible by 3.

Simplify this fraction:

$$\frac{3,525}{4,341} = \frac{1,175}{1,447}$$

The resulting fraction meets no further divisibility tests and, therefore, is likely to have no common factor.

To add or subtract mixed numbers, it is again important to remember common denominators. In "borrowing" in subtraction, you must "borrow" in terms of the common denominator.

Addition: $43\dfrac{2}{5}$ $43\dfrac{6}{15}$

          $\rightarrow$

$+\ 8\dfrac{1}{3}$ $+\ 8\dfrac{5}{15}$

                    $51\dfrac{11}{15}$

Subtraction: $43\dfrac{2}{5}$ $43\dfrac{6}{15}$ $42\dfrac{21}{15}$

          $\rightarrow$ $\rightarrow$

$-\ 6\dfrac{2}{3}$ $-\ 6\dfrac{10}{15}$ $-\ 6\dfrac{10}{15}$

                              $36\dfrac{11}{15}$

Multiplying and Dividing Fractions

To multiply fractions, always try to divide common factors where possible before actually multiplying. In multiplying mixed numbers, always rewrite them as improper fractions first.

Ⓠ Multiply: $\dfrac{2}{5}\cdot\dfrac{10}{11}\cdot\dfrac{99}{110}$

The correct answer is $\dfrac{18}{55}$.

$$\dfrac{2}{\cancel{5}}\cdot\dfrac{\cancel{10}^{\,2}}{\cancel{11}}\cdot\dfrac{\cancel{99}^{\,9}}{\cancel{110}_{\,55}}=\dfrac{18}{55}$$

Ⓠ Multiply: $4\dfrac{1}{2}\times1\dfrac{2}{3}\times5\dfrac{1}{5}$

The correct answer is 39.

$$\dfrac{\cancel{9}^{\,3}}{\cancel{2}}\times\dfrac{\cancel{5}}{\cancel{3}}\times\dfrac{\cancel{26}^{\,13}}{\cancel{5}}=39$$

To divide fractions or mixed numbers, remember to multiply by the reciprocal of the divisor (the number after the division sign).

Q Divide: $4\dfrac{1}{2} \div \dfrac{3}{4}$

The correct answer is 6.

$$\dfrac{\overset{3}{\cancel{9}}}{\cancel{2}} \cdot \dfrac{\overset{2}{\cancel{4}}}{\cancel{3}} = 6$$

Q Divide: $62\dfrac{1}{2} \div 5$

The correct answer is $12\dfrac{1}{2}$.

$$\dfrac{\overset{25}{\cancel{125}}}{2} \cdot \dfrac{1}{\cancel{5}} = 12\dfrac{1}{2}$$

To simplify complex fractions (fractions within fractions), multiply every term by the least number needed to clear all fractions in the given numerator and denominator.

Q $\dfrac{\dfrac{1}{2}+\dfrac{1}{3}}{\dfrac{1}{4}+\dfrac{1}{6}}$

The correct answer is 2. The least number that can be used to clear all fractions is 12. Multiplying each term by 12, we have this:

$$\dfrac{6+4}{3+2} = \dfrac{10}{5} = 2$$

Q $\dfrac{\dfrac{3}{4}+\dfrac{2}{3}}{1-\dfrac{1}{2}}$

The correct answer is $2\dfrac{5}{6}$. Again, we multiply by 12:

$$\dfrac{9+8}{12-6} = \dfrac{17}{6} = 2\dfrac{5}{6}$$

Exercise: Operations with Fractions

> *Directions:* Work out each problem in the space provided.

Add:

1. $12\frac{5}{6} + 2\frac{3}{8} + 21\frac{1}{4}$

2. $\frac{1}{2} + \frac{1}{3} + \frac{1}{4} + \frac{1}{5} + \frac{1}{6}$

Subtract:

3. $5\frac{3}{4}$ from $10\frac{1}{2}$

4. $17\frac{2}{3}$ from 50

5. $25\frac{3}{5}$ from $30\frac{9}{10}$

Multiply:

6. $5\frac{1}{4} \times 1\frac{5}{7}$

7. $\frac{3}{4} \times \frac{3}{4} \times \frac{3}{4}$

8. $12\frac{1}{2} \times 16$

Divide:

9. $\frac{1}{5}$ by 5

10. 5 by $\frac{1}{5}$

11. $3\frac{2}{3}$ by $1\frac{5}{6}$

Simplify:

12. $\dfrac{\frac{5}{6} - \frac{1}{3}}{2 + \frac{1}{5}}$

13. $\dfrac{3 + \frac{1}{4}}{5 - \frac{1}{2}}$

Answers and Explanations

1. The correct answer is $36\dfrac{11}{24}$.

$$12\dfrac{5}{6} = 12\dfrac{20}{24}$$

$$2\dfrac{3}{8} = 2\dfrac{9}{24}$$

$$+21\dfrac{1}{4} = 21\dfrac{6}{24}$$

$$35\dfrac{35}{24} = 36\dfrac{11}{24}$$

2. The correct answer is $1\dfrac{9}{20}$.

$$\dfrac{1}{2} = \dfrac{30}{60}$$

$$\dfrac{1}{3} = \dfrac{20}{60}$$

$$\dfrac{1}{4} = \dfrac{15}{60}$$

$$\dfrac{1}{5} = \dfrac{12}{60}$$

$$+\dfrac{1}{6} = \dfrac{10}{60}$$

$$\dfrac{87}{60} = 1\dfrac{27}{60} = 1\dfrac{9}{20}$$

3. The correct answer is $4\dfrac{3}{4}$.

$$10\dfrac{1}{2} = 10\dfrac{2}{4} = 9\dfrac{6}{4}$$

$$-5\dfrac{3}{4} = 5\dfrac{3}{4} = 5\dfrac{3}{4}$$

$$4\dfrac{3}{4}$$

4. The correct answer is $32\dfrac{1}{3}$.

$$50 = 49\dfrac{3}{3}$$

$$-17\dfrac{2}{3} = 17\dfrac{2}{3}$$

$$32\dfrac{1}{3}$$

5. The correct answer is $5\dfrac{3}{10}$.

$$30\dfrac{9}{10} = 30\dfrac{9}{10}$$

$$-25\dfrac{3}{5} = 25\dfrac{6}{10}$$

$$5\dfrac{3}{10}$$

6. The correct answer is 9.

$$\dfrac{\overset{3}{\cancel{21}}}{\cancel{4}} \times \dfrac{\overset{3}{\cancel{12}}}{\cancel{7}} = 9$$

7. The correct answer is $\dfrac{27}{64}$.

$$\dfrac{3}{4} \times \dfrac{3}{4} \times \dfrac{3}{4} = \dfrac{27}{64}$$

8. The correct answer is 200.

$$\dfrac{25}{\cancel{2}} \times \overset{8}{\cancel{16}} = 200$$

9. The correct answer is $\dfrac{1}{25}$. $\dfrac{1}{5} \times \dfrac{1}{5} = \dfrac{1}{25}$

10. The correct answer is 25. $5 \times 5 = 25$

11. The correct answer is 2. $\dfrac{\cancel{11}}{\cancel{3}} \cdot \dfrac{\overset{2}{\cancel{6}}}{\cancel{11}} = 2$

12. The correct answer is $\frac{5}{22}$. $\frac{25-10}{60+6}=\frac{15}{66}=\frac{5}{22}$ 13. The correct answer is $\frac{13}{18}$. $\frac{12+1}{20-2}=\frac{13}{18}$

Each term was multiplied by 30.　　　　Each term was multiplied by 4.

VERBAL PROBLEMS INVOLVING FRACTIONS

In dealing with fractional problems, we are usually dealing with a part of a whole.

Q A class has 12 boys and 18 girls. What part of the class is boys?

The correct answer is $\frac{2}{5}$. 12 out of 30 students, or $\frac{12}{30}=\frac{2}{5}$

Read all the questions carefully. Often a problem may refer to a previously mentioned part.

Q Of this year's seniors, $\frac{1}{4}$ have averages above 90, and $\frac{1}{2}$ of the remainder have averages between 80 and 90. What part of the senior class has a below 80 average?

The correct answer is $\frac{3}{8}$. $\frac{1}{4}$ have averages above 90.

$\frac{1}{2}$ of $\frac{3}{4}$, or $\frac{3}{8}$, have averages between 80 and 90.

$\frac{1}{4}+\frac{3}{8}$, or $\frac{5}{8}$, have averages above 80.

Therefore, $\frac{3}{8}$ of the class have averages below 80.

When a problem can easily be translated into an algebraic equation, remember that algebra is a very useful tool.

Q 14 is $\frac{2}{3}$ of what number?

The correct answer is 21. $14=\frac{2}{3}x$

Multiply each side by $\frac{3}{2}$.
$21=x$

If a problem is given with letters in place of numbers, the same reasoning must be used as if numbers were given. If you are not sure how to proceed, replace the letters with numbers to determine the steps that must be taken.

Q If John has p hours of homework and has worked for r hours, what part of his homework is yet to be done?

The correct answer is $\frac{p-r}{p}$. If John had 5 hours of homework and had worked for 3 hours, we would first find he had 5 − 3 hours, or 2 hours, yet to do. This represents $\frac{2}{5}$ of his work. Using letters, we have $\frac{p-r}{p}$.

Exercise: Verbal Problems Involving Fractions

Directions: Work out each problem in the space provided, then circle your answer.

1. A team played 30 games, of which it won 24.
   What part of the games played did it lose?

   (A) $\dfrac{4}{5}$

   (B) $\dfrac{1}{4}$

   (C) $\dfrac{1}{5}$

   (D) $\dfrac{3}{4}$

2. If a man's weekly salary is x and he saves y,
   what part of his weekly salary does he spend?

   (A) $\dfrac{x}{y}$

   (B) $\dfrac{x-y}{x}$

   (C) $\dfrac{x-y}{y}$

   (D) $\dfrac{y-x}{x}$

3. What part of an hour elapses between
   11:50 a.m. and 12:14 p.m.?

   (A) $\dfrac{2}{5}$

   (B) $\dfrac{7}{30}$

   (C) $\dfrac{17}{30}$

   (D) $\dfrac{1}{6}$

4. One-half of the employees of Acme Co. earn salaries greater than $18,000 annually. One-third of the remainder earns salaries between $15,000 and $18,000. What part of the staff earns less than $15,000?

   (A) $\dfrac{1}{6}$

   (B) $\dfrac{2}{3}$

   (C) $\dfrac{1}{2}$

   (D) $\dfrac{1}{3}$

5. David receives his allowance on Sunday. He spends $\dfrac{1}{4}$ of his allowance on Monday and $\dfrac{2}{3}$ of the remainder on Tuesday. What part of his allowance is left for the rest of the week?

   (A) $\dfrac{1}{3}$

   (B) $\dfrac{1}{12}$

   (C) $\dfrac{1}{4}$

   (D) $\dfrac{1}{2}$

6. 12 is $\dfrac{3}{4}$ of what number?

   (A) 16
   (B) 9
   (C) 36
   (D) 20

7. A piece of fabric is cut into three sections so that the first is three times as long as the second and the second section is three times as long as the third. What part of the entire piece is the smallest section?

   (A) $\dfrac{1}{12}$

   (B) $\dfrac{1}{9}$

(C) $\dfrac{1}{3}$

(D) $\dfrac{1}{13}$

8. What part of a gallon is one quart?

   (A) $\dfrac{1}{2}$

   (B) $\dfrac{1}{4}$

   (C) $\dfrac{2}{3}$

   (D) $\dfrac{1}{3}$

9. A factory employs m men and w women. What part of its employees are women?

   (A) $\dfrac{w}{m}$

   (B) $\dfrac{m+w}{w}$

   (C) $\dfrac{w}{m-w}$

   (D) $\dfrac{w}{m+w}$

10. A motion was passed by a vote of 5:3. What part of the votes cast was in favor of the motion?

    (A) $\dfrac{5}{8}$

    (B) $\dfrac{5}{3}$

    (C) $\dfrac{3}{5}$

    (D) $\dfrac{2}{5}$

Answers and Explanations

1. **The correct answer is (C).** The team lost 6 games out of 30. $\dfrac{6}{30} = \dfrac{1}{5}$

2. **The correct answer is (B).** The man spends $x - y$ out of x. $\dfrac{x-y}{x}$

3. **The correct answer is (A).** A total of 10 minutes elapse until noon, and another 14 after noon, making a total of 24 minutes. There are 60 minutes in an hour. $\dfrac{24}{60} = \dfrac{2}{5}$

4. **The correct answer is (D).** One half earn greater than \$18,000. One third of the other $\dfrac{1}{2}$, or $\dfrac{1}{6}$, earn between \$15,000 and \$18,000 inclusive. This accounts for $\dfrac{1}{2} + \dfrac{1}{6}$, or $\dfrac{3}{6} + \dfrac{1}{6} = \dfrac{4}{6} = \dfrac{2}{3}$ of staff, leaving $\dfrac{1}{3}$ to earn less than \$15,000.

5. **The correct answer is (C).** David spends $\dfrac{1}{4}$ on Monday and $\dfrac{2}{3}$ of the other $\dfrac{3}{4}$, or $\dfrac{1}{2}$, on Tuesday, leaving only $\dfrac{1}{4}$ for the rest of the week.

6. **The correct answer is (A).** $12 = \dfrac{3}{4}x$. Multiply each side by $\dfrac{4}{3}$: $16 = x$

7. **The correct answer is (D).** Let the third or shortest section $= x$. Then the second section $= 3x$. And the first section $= 9x$. The entire piece of fabric is then $13x$, and the shortest piece represents $\dfrac{x}{13x}$, or $\dfrac{1}{13}$, of the entire piece.

8. **The correct answer is (B).** There are 4 quarts in one gallon.

9. **The correct answer is (D).** The factory employs $m + w$ people, out of which w are women.

10. **The correct answer is (A).** For every 5 votes in favor, 3 were cast against; so, 5 out of every 8 votes cast were in favor of the motion.

VARIATION

Variation in mathematics refers to the interrelationship of variables in such a manner that a change of value for one variable produces a corresponding change in another. This section describes the three basic types of variation: direct, inverse, and joint.

Direct Variation

The expression "x varies directly as y" can be described by any of the following equations:

$$\frac{x}{y} = \text{constant} \quad \bigg| \quad \frac{x_1}{y_1} = \frac{x_2}{y_2} \quad \bigg| \quad \frac{x_1}{x_2} = \frac{y_1}{y_2}$$

Two quantities are said to vary directly if they change in the same direction. As one increases, the other increases and their ratio (quotient) is equal to a positive constant.

For example, the amount you must pay for milk varies directly with the number of quarts of milk you buy. The amount of sugar needed in a recipe varies directly with the amount of butter used. The number of inches between two cities on a map varies directly with the number of miles between these cities.

 If x varies directly as the square of y, and $x = 12$ when $y = 2$, what is the value of x when $y = 3$?

The correct answer is 27.

$$\frac{x_1}{y_1^{\,2}} = \frac{x_2}{y_2^{\,2}} \rightarrow \frac{x}{(3)^2} = \frac{12}{(2)^2}$$

$$\frac{x}{9} = \frac{12}{4}$$

$$\frac{x}{9} = 3$$

$$x = 27$$

Inverse Variation

The expression "x varies inversely as y" can be described by any of the following equations:

$$xy = \text{constant} \quad \bigg| \quad x_1 y_1 = x_2 y_2 \quad \bigg| \quad \frac{x_1}{x_2} = \frac{y_2}{y_1}$$

Two quantities are said to vary inversely if they change in opposite directions. As one *increases*, the other *decreases*.

For example, the number of people hired to paint a house varies inversely with the number of days the job will take. A doctor's stock of flu vaccine varies inversely with the number of patients he or she injects. The number of days a given supply of cat food lasts varies inversely with the number of cats being fed.

[Q] The time (t) to empty a container varies inversely as the square root of the number of men (m) working on the job. If it takes 3 hours for 16 men to do the job, how long will it take 4 men working at the same rate to empty the container?

The correct answer is 6.

$$t_1\sqrt{m_1} = t_2\sqrt{m_2}$$

$$3\sqrt{16} = t\sqrt{4}$$

$$3(4) = t(2)$$

$$12 = 2t$$

$$6 = t$$

Joint Variation

The expression "x varies jointly as y and z" can be described by any of the following equations:

$$\frac{y}{yz} = \text{constant} \quad \Big| \quad \frac{x_1}{y_1z_1} = \frac{x_2}{y_2z_2} \quad \Big| \quad \frac{x_1}{x_2} = \left(\frac{y_1}{y_2}\right)\left(\frac{z_1}{z_2}\right)$$

[Q] The area (A) of a triangle varies jointly as the base (b) and the height (h). If $A = 20$ when $b = 10$ and $h = 4$, find the value of A when $b = 6$ and $h = 7$.

The correct answer is 21.

$$\frac{A_1}{b_1h_1} = \frac{A_2}{b_2h_2}$$

$$\frac{20}{(10)(4)} = \frac{A_2}{(6)(7)}$$

$$\frac{20}{40} = \frac{A_2}{42}$$

$$\frac{1}{2} = \frac{A_2}{42}$$

$$21 = A_2$$

Exercise: Variation

Directions: Work out each problem in the space provided, then circle your answer.

1. If 60 feet of uniform wire weigh 80 pounds, what is the weight of 2 yards of the same wire?

   (A) $2\frac{2}{3}$ pounds

   (B) 6 pounds

   (C) 2,400 pounds

   (D) 8 pounds

2. A gear 50 inches in diameter turns a smaller gear 30 inches in diameter. If the larger gear makes 15 revolutions, how many revolutions does the smaller gear make in that time?

   (A) 9

   (B) 12

   (C) 20

   (D) 25

3. The number of men required to do a job varies inversely with the length of time. If x men can do a job in h days, how long would y men take to do the same job?

   (A) $\dfrac{x}{h}$

   (B) $\dfrac{xh}{y}$

   (C) $\dfrac{hy}{x}$

   (D) $\dfrac{xy}{h}$

4. If a furnace uses 40 gallons of oil in a week, how many gallons, to the nearest gallon, does it use in 10 days?

   (A) 57

   (B) 4

   (C) 28

   (D) 400

5. A recipe requires 13 oz. of sugar and 18 oz. of flour. If only 10 oz. of sugar are used, how much flour, to the nearest ounce, should be used?

(A) 13
(B) 23
(C) 24
(D) 14

6. If a car can be driven 25 miles on 2 gallons of gasoline, how many gallons will be needed for a trip of 150 miles?

(A) 12
(B) 3
(C) 6
(D) 7

7. A school has enough bread to last 30 children 4 days. If 10 more children are added, how many days will the bread last?

(A) $5\frac{1}{3}$

(B) $1\frac{1}{3}$

(C) $2\frac{2}{3}$

(D) 3

8. At c cents per pound, what is the cost of a ounces of salami?

(A) $\dfrac{c}{a}$

(B) $\dfrac{a}{c}$

(C) ac

(D) $\dfrac{ac}{16}$

9. If 3 miles are equivalent to 4.83 kilometers, then 11.27 kilometers are equivalent to how many miles?

   (A) $7\dfrac{1}{3}$

   (B) $2\dfrac{1}{3}$

   (C) 7

   (D) 5

10. If p pencils cost d dollars, how many pencils can be bought for c cents?

   (A) $\dfrac{100pc}{d}$

   (B) $\dfrac{pc}{100d}$

   (C) $\dfrac{pd}{c}$

   (D) $\dfrac{pc}{d}$

11. m varies directly as the square of t. If m is 7 when $t = 1$, what is the value of m when $t = 2$?

   (A) 28

   (B) 14

   (C) 7

   (D) $3\dfrac{1}{2}$

12. m varies jointly as r and s. If m is 8 when r and s are each 1, what is the value of m when r and s are each 2?

   (A) 64

   (B) 32

   (C) 16

   (D) 4

Answers and Explanations

1. **The correct answer is (D).** We are comparing *feet* with pounds; the more feet, the more pounds. This is direct variation. Remember to change yards to feet:

$$\frac{\overset{3}{\cancel{60}}}{\underset{4}{\cancel{80}}} = \frac{6}{x}$$

$$3x = 24$$

$$x = 8$$

2. **The correct answer is (D).** The larger a gear, the fewer times it revolves in a given period of time. This is inverse variation:

$$50 \cdot 15 = 30 \cdot x$$

$$750 = 30x$$

$$25 = x$$

3. **The correct answer is (B).** The more men, the fewer days. This is inverse variation:

$$x \cdot h = y \cdot ?$$

$$\frac{xh}{y} = ?$$

4. **The correct answer is (A).** The more days, the more oil. This is direct variation. Remember to change a week to days:

$$\frac{40}{7} = \frac{x}{10}$$

$$400 = 7x$$

$$57\frac{1}{7} = x$$

5. **The correct answer is (D).** The more sugar, the more flour. This is direct variation:

$$\frac{13}{18} = \frac{10}{x}$$

$$180 = 13x$$

$$13\frac{11}{13} = x$$

6. **The correct answer is (A).** The more miles, the more gasoline. This is direct variation:

$$\frac{25}{2} = \frac{150}{x}$$

$$300 = 25x$$

$$12 = x$$

7. **The correct answer is (D).** The more children, the fewer days. This is inverse variation:

$$30 \cdot 4 = 40 \cdot x$$

$$120 = 40x$$

$$3 = x$$

8. **The correct answer is (D).** The more salami, the more it will cost. This is direct variation. Remember to change a pound to 16 ounces:

$$\frac{c}{16} = \frac{x}{a}$$

$$x = \frac{ac}{16}$$

9. **The correct answer is (C).** The more miles, the more kilometers. This is direct variation:

$$\frac{\text{miles}}{\text{kilometers}} = \frac{\text{miles}}{\text{kilometers}}$$

$$\frac{3}{4.83} = \frac{x}{11.27}$$

$$4.83x = 33.81$$

$$x = 7$$

10. **The correct answer is (B).** The more pencils, the greater the cost. This is direct variation. Remember to change dollars to cents:

$$\frac{\text{pencils}}{\text{cents}} = \frac{\text{pencils}}{\text{cents}}$$

$$\frac{p}{100d} = \frac{x}{c}$$

$$\frac{pc}{100d} = x$$

11. **The correct answer is (A).** The expression "*m* varies directly as the square of *t*" can be expressed mathematically as:

$$\frac{m_1}{t_1^2} = \frac{m_2}{t_2^2}$$

$$\frac{7}{(1)^2} = \frac{m}{(2)^2}$$

$$\frac{7}{1} = \frac{m}{4}$$

$$28 = m$$

12. **The correct answer is (B).** The expression "*m* varies jointly as *r* and *s*" can be expressed mathematically as:

$$\frac{m_1}{r_1 s_1} = \frac{m_2}{r_2 s_2}$$

$$\frac{8}{(1)(1)} = \frac{m}{(2)(2)}$$

$$\frac{8}{1} = \frac{m}{4}$$

$$32 = m$$

FINDING PERCENTS

Percent means "out of 100." With this concept in mind, it then becomes very easy to rewrite a percent as an equivalent decimal or fraction:

$$5\% = \frac{5}{100} = 0.05$$

$$2.6\% = \frac{2.6}{100} = 0.026$$

$$c\% = \frac{c}{100} \text{ or } \frac{1}{100} \cdot c = 0.01c$$

$$\frac{1}{2}\% = \frac{\frac{1}{2}}{100} = \frac{1}{2} \cdot \frac{1}{100} = 0.5\left(\frac{1}{100}\right) = 0.005$$

To rewrite a percent as a decimal, we must remove the % sign and divide by 100. This has the effect of moving the decimal point two places to the left. For example:

$37\% = .37$

To rewrite a decimal as a percent, we must put in the % sign and multiply by 100. This has the effect of moving the decimal point two places to the right. For example:

$.043 = 4.3\%$

To rewrite a percent as a fraction, we must remove the % sign and divide by 100. This has the effect of putting the % over 100 and simplifying the resulting fraction. For example:

$$75\% = \frac{75}{100} = \frac{3}{4}$$

To rewrite a fraction as a percent, we must put in the % sign and multiply by 100. For example:

$$\frac{1}{8} = \frac{1}{8} \cdot 100\% = \frac{100}{8}\% = 12\frac{1}{2}\%$$

Certain fractional equivalents of common percents occur frequently enough that they should be memorized. Learning the values in the following table will make your work with percent problems much easier.

PERCENT–FRACTION EQUIVALENT TABLE
(in order by fraction)

$50\% = \dfrac{1}{2}$	$33\frac{1}{3}\% = \dfrac{1}{3}$	$16\frac{2}{3}\% = \dfrac{1}{6}$
$25\% = \dfrac{1}{4}$	$66\frac{2}{3}\% = \dfrac{2}{3}$	$83\frac{1}{3}\% = \dfrac{5}{6}$
$75\% = \dfrac{3}{4}$		
$10\% = \dfrac{1}{10}$	$20\% = \dfrac{1}{5}$	$12\frac{1}{2}\% = \dfrac{1}{8}$
$30\% = \dfrac{3}{10}$	$40\% = \dfrac{2}{5}$	$37\frac{1}{2}\% = \dfrac{3}{8}$
$70\% = \dfrac{7}{10}$	$60\% = \dfrac{3}{5}$	$62\frac{1}{2}\% = \dfrac{5}{8}$
$90\% = \dfrac{9}{10}$	$80\% = \dfrac{4}{5}$	$87\frac{1}{2}\% = \dfrac{7}{8}$

Most percentage problems can be solved by using the following proportion:

$$\frac{\%}{100} = \frac{\text{part}}{\text{whole}}$$

Although this method works, it often yields unnecessarily great numbers that are difficult to compute. We will look at the three basic types of percent problems and compare methods for solving them.

To Find a Percent of a Number

 Find 27% of 92.

The correct answer is 24.84.

Proportion Method

$$\frac{27}{100} = \frac{x}{92}$$

$$2{,}484 = 100x$$

$$24.84 = x$$

Short Method

Rewrite the percent as its decimal or fraction equivalent, and multiply. Use fractions only when they are among the familiar ones given in the previous chart.

$$\begin{array}{r} 92 \\ \times\ 0.27 \\ \hline 644 \\ 184 \\ \hline 24.84 \end{array}$$

 Find $12\frac{1}{2}\%$ of 96.

The correct answer is 12.

Proportion Method

$$\frac{12\frac{1}{2}}{100} = \frac{x}{96}$$

$$100x = 1{,}200$$

$$x = 12$$

Decimal Method

$$\begin{array}{r} 96 \\ \times\ 0.125 \\ \hline 480 \\ 192 \\ 96 \\ \hline 12.000 \end{array}$$

Fraction Method

$$\frac{1}{8} \times 96 = 12$$

Which method is easiest? It really pays to memorize those fractional equivalents.

To Find a Number When a Percent of It Is Given

 7 is 5% of what number?

The correct answer is 140.

Proportion Method

$$\frac{5}{100} = \frac{7}{x}$$

$$5x = 700$$

$$x = 140$$

Shorter Method

Translate the problem into an algebraic equation. In doing this, the percent must be written as a fraction or decimal.

$$7 = .05x$$

$$700 = 5x$$

$$140 = x$$

Q 20 is $33\frac{1}{3}\%$ of what number?

The correct answer is 60.

<u>**Proportion Method**</u>

$$\frac{33\frac{1}{3}}{100} = \frac{20}{x}$$

$$33\frac{1}{3}x = 2,000$$

$$\frac{100}{3}x = 2,000$$

$$100x = 6,000$$

$$x = 60$$

<u>**Shorter Method**</u>

$$20 = \frac{1}{3}x$$

$$60 = x$$

Just think of the time you save if you know that $33\frac{1}{3}\% = \frac{1}{3}$.

To Find What Percent One Number Is of Another

Q 90 is what percent of 1,500?

The correct answer is 6%.

<u>**Proportion Method**</u>

$$\frac{x}{100} = \frac{90}{1,500}$$

$$1,500x = 9,000$$

$$15x = 90$$

$$x = 6\%$$

<u>**Shorter Method**</u>

Put the part over the whole. Simplify the fraction and multiply by 100.

$$\frac{90}{1,500} = \frac{9}{150} = \frac{3}{50} \times 100 = 6\%$$

Q 7 is what percent of 35?

The correct answer is 20%.

<u>**Proportion Method**</u>

$$\frac{x}{100} = \frac{7}{35}$$

$$35x = 700$$

$$x - 20\%$$

<u>**Shorter Method**</u>

$$\frac{7}{35} = \frac{1}{5} = 20\%$$

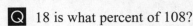 18 is what percent of 108?

The correct answer is $16\dfrac{2}{3}$ **%.**

Proportion Method

$$\frac{x}{100} = \frac{18}{108}$$

$$108x = 1,800$$

Time-consuming long division is necessary to get:

$$x = 16\frac{2}{3}\%$$

Shorter Method

$$\frac{18}{108} = \frac{9}{54} = \frac{1}{6} = 16\frac{2}{3}\%$$

Once again, if you know your fraction equivalent of common percents, you can do computation in a few seconds.

To Find a Percent Greater Than 100

 Find 125% of 64.

The correct answer is 80.

Proportion Method

$$\frac{125}{100} = \frac{x}{64}$$

$$8,000 = 100x$$

$$80 = x$$

Decimal Method

$$\begin{array}{r} 64 \\ \times\ 1.25 \\ \hline 320 \\ 128 \\ 64 \\ \hline 80.00 \end{array}$$

Fraction Method

$$1\frac{1}{4} \cdot 64$$

$$\frac{5}{\cancel{4}} \cdot \overset{16}{\cancel{64}} = 80$$

Q 36 is 150% of what number?

The correct answer is 24.

Proportion Method

$$\frac{150}{100} = \frac{36}{x}$$

$$3,600 = 150x$$

$$360 = 15x$$

$$24 = x$$

Decimal Method

$$36 = 1.50x$$

$$360 = 15x$$

$$24 = x$$

Fraction Method

$$36 = 1\frac{1}{2}x$$

$$36 = \frac{3}{2}x$$

$$72 = 3x$$

$$24 = x$$

60 is what percent of 50?

The correct answer is 120%.

Proportion Method

$$\frac{x}{100} = \frac{60}{50}$$

$$50x = 6,000$$

$$5x = 600$$

$$x = 120\%$$

Shorter Method

$$\frac{60}{50} = \frac{6}{5} = 1\frac{1}{5} = 120\%$$

Exercise: Finding Percents

> *Directions:* Work out each problem in the space provided, then circle your answer.

1. Write 0.2% as a decimal.

   (A) 0.2
   (B) 0.02
   (C) 0.002
   (D) 2

2. Write 3.4% as a fraction.

   (A) $\dfrac{34}{1,000}$

   (B) $\dfrac{34}{10}$

   (C) $\dfrac{34}{100}$

   (D) $\dfrac{340}{100}$

3. Write $\dfrac{3}{4}$% as a decimal.

   (A) 0.75
   (B) 0.075
   (C) 0.0075
   (D) 0.00075

4. Find 60% of 70.

   (A) 420
   (B) 4.2
   (C) $116\frac{2}{3}$
   (D) 42

5. What is 175% of 16?

   (A) $9\frac{1}{7}$
   (B) 28
   (C) 24
   (D) 12

6. What percent of 40 is 16?

   (A) 20
   (B) $2\frac{1}{2}$
   (C) $33\frac{1}{3}$
   (D) 40

7. What percent of 16 is 40?

   (A) 20
   (B) $2\frac{1}{2}$
   (C) 200
   (D) 250

8. $4 is 20% of what?

   (A) $5
   (B) $20
   (C) $200
   (D) $15

9. 12 is 150% of what number?

   (A) 18
   (B) 15
   (C) 6
   (D) 8

10. How many sixteenths are there in $87\frac{1}{2}$%?

    (A) 7
    (B) 14
    (C) 3.5
    (D) 13

Answers and Explanations

1. **The correct answer is (C).** 0.2% = 0.002 (Decimal point moves to the left two places.)

2. **The correct answer is (A).**

$$3.4\% = \frac{3.4}{100} = \frac{34}{1,000}$$

3. **The correct answer is (C).**

$$\frac{3}{4}\% = 0.75\% = 0.0075$$

4. **The correct answer is (D).** $60\% = \frac{3}{5}$

$$\frac{3}{5} \cdot 70 = 42$$

5. **The correct answer is (B).** $175\% = 1\frac{3}{4}$

$$\frac{7}{4} \cdot 16 = 28$$

6. **The correct answer is (D).** $\frac{16}{40} = \frac{2}{5} = 40\%$

7. **The correct answer is (D).**

$$\frac{40}{16} = \frac{5}{2} = 2\frac{1}{2} = 250\%$$

8. **The correct answer is (B).**

$$20\% = \frac{1}{5}, \text{ so } 4 = \frac{1}{5}x$$
$$20 = x$$

9. **The correct answer is (D).**

$$150\% = 1\frac{1}{2} \cdot \frac{3}{2}x = 12 \cdot 3x = 24 \cdot x = 8$$

10. **The correct answer is (B).** $87\frac{1}{2}\% = \frac{7}{8} = \frac{14}{16}$

VERBAL PROBLEMS INVOLVING PERCENT

Certain types of business situations are excellent applications of percent.

Percent of Increase or Decrease

The percent of increase or decrease is found by putting the amount of increase or decrease over the original amount and rewriting this fraction as a percent, as explained previously.

Q Over a five-year period, the enrollment at South High dropped from 1,000 students to 800. Find the percent of decrease.

The correct answer is 20%. $\frac{200}{1,000} = \frac{20}{100} = 20\%$

Q A company normally employs 100 people. During a slow spell, it fired 20% of its employees. By what percent must it now increase its staff to return to full capacity?

The correct answer is 25%. $20\% = \frac{1}{5}$

$$\frac{1}{5} \cdot 100 = 20$$

The company now has 100 − 20 = 80 employees. If it then increases by 20, the percent of increase is

$\frac{20}{80} = \frac{1}{4}$, or 25%.

Discount

A discount is usually expressed as a percent of the marked price, which will be deducted from the marked price to determine the sale price.

Q Bill's Hardware offers a 20% discount on all appliances during a sale week. How much must Mrs. Russell pay for a washing machine marked at $280?

The correct answer is $224.

Long Method	**Shortcut Method**

Long Method

$20\% = \dfrac{1}{5}$

$\dfrac{1}{5} \cdot 280 = \$56$ discount

$\$280 - \$56 = \$224$ sale price

The danger inherent in this method is that $56 is sure to be among the multiple-choice answers.

Shortcut Method

If there is a 20% discount, Mrs. Russell will pay 80% of the marked price.

$80\% = \dfrac{4}{5}$

$\dfrac{4}{5} \cdot 280 = \$224$ sale price

Q A store offers a television set marked at $340, less consecutive discounts of 10% and 5%. Another store offers the same set with a single discount of 15%. How much does the buyer save by buying at the better price?

The correct answer is $1.70. In the first store, the initial discount means the buyer pays 90%, or $\dfrac{9}{10}$ of 340, which is $306. The additional 5% discount means the buyer pays 95% of $306, or $290.70. Note that the second discount must be figured on the first sale price. Taking 5% of $306 is a lesser amount than taking the additional 5% off $340. The second store will therefore have a lower sale price. In the second store, the buyer will pay 85% of $340, or $289, making the price $1.70 less than in the first store.

Commission

Many salespeople earn money on a commission basis. To inspire sales, they are paid a percentage of the value of goods sold. This amount is called a commission.

Q Mr. Saunders works at Brown's Department Store, where he is paid $80 per week in salary plus a 4% commission on all his sales. How much does he earn in a week in which he sells $4,032 worth of merchandise?

The correct answer is $241.28.

Find 4% of $4,032, and add this amount to $80.

$$\begin{array}{r} 4032 \\ \times \quad .04 \\ \hline \end{array}$$

$161.28 + \$80 = \$241.28$

Bill Olson delivers newspapers for a dealer and keeps 8% of all money collected. One month he was able to keep $16. How much did he forward to the dealer?

The correct answer is $184. First we find how much he collected by asking: 16 is 8% of what number?

$$16 = .08x$$

$$1,600 = 8x$$

$$200 = x$$

If Bill collected $200 and kept $16, he gave the dealer $200 – $16, or $184.

Taxes

Taxes are a percent of money spent or money earned.

 Noname County collects a 7% sales tax on automobiles. If the price of a used Ford is $5,832 before taxes, what will it cost when the sales tax is added?

The correct answer is $6,240.24.

Find 7% of $5,832 to find the tax, and then add it to $5,832. This can be done in one step by finding 107% of $5,832.

$$
\begin{array}{r}
5832 \\
\times \quad 1.07 \\
\hline
408.24 \\
5832.0 \\
\hline
\$6240.24
\end{array}
$$

 If income is taxed at the rate of 10% for the first $10,000 of earned income, 15% for the next $10,000, 20% for the next $10,000, and 25% for all earnings over $30,000, how much income tax must be paid on a yearly income of $36,500?

The correct answer is $6,125.

$$
\begin{array}{r}
10\% \text{ of first } \$10,000 = \$1,000 \\
15\% \text{ of next } \$10,000 = \$1,500 \\
20\% \text{ of next } \$10,000 = \$2,000 \\
25\% \text{ of } \$6,500 = \$1,625 \\
\hline
\text{Total tax} = \$6,125
\end{array}
$$

Prepare for the NYSTCE: LAST and ATS-W

Exercise: Verbal Problems Involving Percent

> *Directions:* Work out each problem in the space provided, then circle your answer.

1. A suit is sold for $68 while marked at $80. What is the rate of discount?

   (A) 15%
   (B) 12%
   (C) $17\frac{11}{17}\%$
   (D) 20%

2. A man buys a radio for $70 after receiving a discount of 20%. What was the marked price?

   (A) $84
   (B) $56
   (C) $87.50
   (D) $92

3. Willie receives *r*% commission on a sale of $*s*. How many dollars does he receive?

   (A) rs
   (B) $\dfrac{r}{s}$
   (C) $100rs$
   (D) $\dfrac{rs}{100}$

4. A refrigerator was sold for $273, yielding a 30% profit on the cost. For how much should it be sold to yield only a 10% profit on the cost?

   (A) $210
   (B) $231
   (C) $221
   (D) $235

5. What single discount is equivalent to two successive discounts of 10% and 15%?

   (A) 25%
   (B) 24%
   (C) 24.5%
   (D) 23.5%

6. The net price of a certain article is $306 after successive discounts of 15% and 10% have been allowed on the marked price. What is the marked price?

   (A) $234.09
   (B) $400
   (C) $382.50
   (D) $408

7. If a merchant makes a profit of 20% based on the selling price of an article, what percent does he make on the cost?

   (A) 20%
   (B) 40%
   (C) 25%
   (D) 80%

8. A certain radio costs a merchant $72. At what price must he sell it if he is to make a profit of 20% of the selling price?

   (A) $86.40
   (B) $92
   (C) $90
   (D) $144

9. A baseball team has won 40 games out of 60 played. It has 32 more games to play. How many of these must the team win to make its record 75% for the season?

   (A) 26
   (B) 29
   (C) 28
   (D) 30

10. If prices are reduced 25% and sales increase 20%, what is the net effect on gross receipts?

    (A) They increase by 5%.
    (B) They decrease by 5%.
    (C) They remain the same.
    (D) They decrease by 10%.

11. A salesperson earns a commission of 5% on all sales between $200 and $600, and 8% on all sales over $600. What is the commission earned in a week in which sales total $800?

    (A) $20
    (B) $46
    (C) $88
    (D) $36

12. If the enrollment at State U. grew from 3,000 to 12,000 in the last 10 years, what was the percent of increase in enrollment?

   (A) 125%
   (B) 25%
   (C) 300%
   (D) 400%

13. Six students in a class failed algebra. This represents $16\frac{2}{3}\%$ of the class. How many students passed the course?

   (A) 48
   (B) 36
   (C) 42
   (D) 30

14. A total of 95% of the residents of Coral Estates live in private homes; 40% of these live in air-conditioned homes. What percent of the residents of Coral Estates live in air-conditioned homes?

   (A) 3%
   (B) 30%
   (C) 3.8%
   (D) 38%

15. Mr. Carlson receives a salary of $500 a month and a commission of 5% on all sales. What must be the amount of his sales in July so that his total monthly income is $2,400?

   (A) $48,000
   (B) $38,000
   (C) $7,600
   (D) $3,800

Answers and Explanations

1. **The correct answer is (A).** The amount of discount is $12. Rate of discount is figured on the original price:

   $$\frac{12}{80} = \frac{3}{20} \qquad \frac{3}{20} \cdot 100 = 15\%$$

2. **The correct answer is (C).** $70 represents 80% of the marked price:

   $$70 = 0.80x$$
   $$700 = 8x$$
   $$\$87.50 = x$$

3. **The correct answer is (D).** $r\% = \dfrac{r}{100}$

   Commission is $\dfrac{r}{100} \cdot s = \dfrac{rs}{100}$

4. **The correct answer is (B).** $273 represents 130% of the cost:

   $1.30x = 273$

   $13x = 2,730x$

   $210 = cost$

   New price will add 10% of cost, or $21, for profit:
   New price = $231.

5. **The correct answer is (D).** Work with a simple figure, such as 100. The first sale price is 90% of $100, or $90. The final sale price is 85% of $90, or $76.50. The total discount was $100 – $76.50 = $23.50.

   % of discount $= \dfrac{23.50}{100}$, or 23.5%

6. **The correct answer is (B).** If the marked price $= m$, the first sale price $= .85m$ and the net price $= 0.765m$ ($0.85m - 10\% = 0.765m$)

   $0.765m = 306$

   $m = 400$

   In this case, it would be easy to work from the answers: 15% of $400 is $60, making a first sale price of $340; 10% of this price is $34, making the net price $306. Choices (A), (C), and (D) would not give a final answer in whole dollars.

7. **The correct answer is (C).** Use an easy amount of $100 for the selling price. If profit is 20% of the selling price, or $20, then cost is $80. Profit based on cost is: $\dfrac{20}{80} = \dfrac{1}{4} = 25\%$

8. **The correct answer is (C).** If profit is to be 20% of the selling price, then cost must be 80% of the selling price:

   $72 = 0.80x$

   $720 = 8x$

   $90 = x$

9. **The correct answer is (B).** The team must win 75%, or $\dfrac{3}{4}$, of the games played during the entire season. With 60 games played and 32 more to play, the team must win j of 92 games in all: $j = 92 \cdot \dfrac{3}{4} = 69$. Since 40 games have already been won, the team must win 29 additional games.

10. **The correct answer is (D).** Let original price = p and original sales = s. Therefore, original gross receipts = ps. Let the new price = $.75p$ and new sales = $1.20s$. Therefore, new gross receipts = $.90ps$. Gross receipts are only 90% of what they were.

11. **The correct answer is (B).** 5% of sales between $200 and $600 is $0.05(600) = \$30$. Also, 8% of sales over $600 is $0.08(200) = \$16$. So, the total commission = $30 + $16 = $46.

12. **The correct answer is (C).** The increase is 9,000. The percent of increase is figured on the original:

    $\dfrac{9,000}{3,000} = 3 = 300\%$

13. **The correct answer is (D).** $16\dfrac{2}{3}\% = \dfrac{1}{6}$

    $6 = \dfrac{1}{6}x$

    $36 = x$

    Of 36 students in class, 6 failed and 30 passed.

14. The correct answer is (D).

$$40\% = \frac{2}{5}$$

$$\frac{2}{5} \text{ of } 95\% = 38\%$$

15. The correct answer is (B).

$$\$500 + 0.05s = \$2,400$$

$$0.05s = \$1,900$$

$$5s = \$190,000$$

$$s = \$38,000$$

STATISTICS AND PROBABILITY

Statistics

The *averages* used in statistics include the *arithmetic mean,* the *median,* and the *mode.*

Arithmetic Mean

The most commonly used average of a group of numbers is the *arithmetic mean*. It is found by adding the numbers given and then dividing this sum by the number of items being averaged.

Q Find the arithmetic mean of 2, 8, 5, 9, 6, and 12.

The correct answer is 7.

There are 6 numbers.

$$\text{Arithmetic mean} = \frac{2+8+5+9+6+12}{6}$$

$$= \frac{42}{6}$$

$$= 7$$

The arithmetic mean is 7.

If a problem calls for simply the "average" or the "mean," it is referring to the arithmetic mean.

A more frequently encountered type of average problem will give the average and ask you to find a missing term.

Q The average of three numbers is 43. If two of the numbers are 32 and 50, find the third number.

The correct answer is 47.

Using the definition of average, write the equation

$$\frac{32+50+x}{3} = 43$$

$$32 + 50 + x = 129$$

$$82 + x = 129$$

$$x = 47$$

Another concept to understand is the **weighted average**.

To obtain the average of quantities that are weighted, follow these 5 steps:

- **Set up** a table listing the quantities, their respective weights, and their respective values.
- **Multiply** the value of each quantity by its respective weight.
- **Add** up these products.
- **Add** up the weights.
- **Divide** the sum of the products by the sum of the weights.

Q Andrea has four grades of 90 and two grades of 80 during the spring semester of calculus. What is her average in the course for the semester?

The correct answer is $86\frac{2}{3}$.

$$
\begin{array}{l}
90 \\
90 \\
90 \\
90 \\
80 \quad \text{or} \\
+80 \\
\hline
6)\underline{520} \\
86\frac{2}{3}
\end{array}
\qquad
\begin{array}{l}
90 \cdot 4 = 360 \\
80 \cdot 2 = \underline{160} \\
\hline
6)520 \\
\\
86\frac{2}{3}
\end{array}
$$

Be sure to understand that you cannot simply average 90 and 80, since there are more grades of 90 than 80.

Q Assume that the weights for the following subjects are: English 3, History 2, Mathematics 2, Foreign Languages 2, and Art 1. What would be the average of a student whose marks are: English 80, History 85, Algebra 84, Spanish 82, and Art 90?

The correct answer is 83.2.

Subject	Weight	Mark	
English	3	80	$3 \times 80 = 240$
History	2	85	$2 \times 85 = 170$
Algebra	2	84	$2 \times 84 = 168$
Spanish	2	82	$2 \times 82 = 164$
Art	1	90	$1 \times 90 = \underline{90}$
			832

Sum of the weights: $3 + 2 + 2 + 2 + 1 = 10$.

$$\text{Average} = \frac{832}{10} = 83.2$$

The final concept of average that should be mastered is that of average rate. The average rate for a trip is the total distance covered, divided by the total time used.

Q In driving from New York to Boston, Mr. Portney drove for 3 hours at 40 miles an hour and 1 hour at 48 miles per hour. What was his average rate for this portion of the trip?

The correct answer is 42.

$$\text{Average rate} = \frac{\text{Total distance}}{\text{Total time}}$$

$$\text{Average rate} = \frac{3(40)+1(48)}{3+1}$$

$$\text{Average rate} = \frac{168}{4} = 42 \text{ miles per hour}$$

Since more of the trip was driven at 40 mph, the average should be closer to 40 than to 48, which it is. This will help you to check your answer, or to pick out the correct choice in a multiple-choice question.

Median

If a group of numbers is arranged in order, the middle number is called the **median**. If there is no single middle number (this occurs when there is an even number of items), the median is found by computing the arithmetic mean of the two middle numbers:

The median of 6, 8, 10, 12, and 14 is 10.

The median of 6, 8, 10, 12, 14, and 16 is the arithmetic mean of 10 and 12.

$$\frac{10+12}{2} = \frac{22}{2} = 11$$

Mode

The **mode** of a group of numbers is the number that appears most often:

The mode of 10, 5, 7, 9, 12, 5, 10, 5, and 9 is 5.

SUMMARY CHART OF DATA STATISTICS

Data Statistic	Description
average or arithmetic mean	$= \dfrac{\text{the sum of all the data elements}}{\text{quantity of data elements}}$
median	The "middle" data element when the data is arranged in numerical order. In the case of an even number of elements, it is the mean of the two "middle" numbers.
mode	The data element that appears most often. A set of data can have more than one mode. If all the elements appear with equal frequency there is NO mode.
range	The difference between the greatest data element and the least.

Probability

The study of probability deals with predicting the outcome of chance events; that is, events in which one has no control over the results. For example:

Tossing a coin, rolling dice, and drawing concealed objects from a bag are chance events.

The probability of a particular outcome is equal to the number of ways that outcome can occur, divided by the total number of possible outcomes.

In tossing a coin, there are 2 possible outcomes: heads or tails. The probability that the coin will turn up heads is $1 \div 2$, or $\frac{1}{2}$.

If a bag contains 5 balls of which 3 are red, the probability of drawing a red ball is $\frac{3}{5}$. The probability of drawing a non-red ball is $\frac{2}{5}$.

Note: If an event is certain, its probability is 1.

If a bag contains only red balls, the probability of drawing a red ball is 1.

Note: If an event is impossible, the probability is 0.

If a bag contains only red balls, the probability of drawing a green ball is 0.

Probability is expressed in fractional, decimal, or percent form.

An event having a probability of $\frac{1}{2}$ is said to be 50% probable.

A probability determined by random sampling of a group of items is assumed to apply to other items in that group and in other similar groups.

Q A random sampling of 100 items produced in a factory shows that 7 are defective. How many items of the total production of 50,000 can be expected to be defective?

The correct answer is 3,500.

The probability of an item being defective is $\frac{7}{100}$, or 7%. Of the total production, 7% can be expected to be defective.

$7\% \times 50,000 = 0.07 \times 50,000 = 3,500$ defective items.

Exercise: Statistics and Probability

Directions: Work out each problem in the space provided, then circle your answer.

1. The arithmetic mean of 73.8, 92.2, 64.7, 43.8, 56.5, and 46.4 is:

   (A) 60.6
   (B) 61
   (C) 61.28
   (D) 62.9

2. The median of the numbers 8, 5, 7, 5, 9, 9, 1, 8, 10, 5, and 10 is:

   (A) 5
   (B) 7
   (C) 8
   (D) 9

3. The mode of the numbers 16, 15, 17, 12, 15, 15, 18, 19, and 18 is:

   (A) 15
   (B) 16
   (C) 17
   (D) 18

4. A clerk filed 73 forms on Monday, 85 forms on Tuesday, 54 on Wednesday, 92 on Thursday, and 66 on Friday. What was the average number of forms filed per day?

   (A) 60
   (B) 72
   (C) 74
   (D) 92

5. The grades received on a test by twenty students were: 100, 55, 75, 80, 65, 65, 85, 90, 80, 45, 40, 50, 85, 85, 85, 80, 80, 70, 65, and 60. The average of these grades is:

   (A) 70
   (B) 72
   (C) 77
   (D) 80

6. A buyer purchased 75 six-inch rulers costing 15¢ each, 100 one-foot rulers costing 30¢ each, and 50 one-yard rulers costing 72¢ each. What was the average price per ruler?

   (A) $26\dfrac{1}{8}$¢

   (B) $34\dfrac{1}{3}$¢

   (C) 39¢
   (D) 42¢

7. What is the average of a student who received 90 in English, 84 in algebra, 75 in French, and 76 in music if the subjects have the following weights: English 4, algebra 3, French 3, and music 1?

   (A) 81

   (B) $81\dfrac{1}{2}$

   (C) 82
   (D) 83

Items 8–11 refer to the following information:

A census shows that on a certain block the number of children in each family is 3, 4, 4, 0, 1, 2, 0, 2, and 2 respectively.

8. Find the average number of children per family.

   (A) 2

   (B) $2\dfrac{1}{2}$

   (C) 3

   (D) $3\dfrac{1}{2}$

9. Find the median number of children.
   (A) 6
   (B) 5
   (C) 4
   (D) 2

10. Find the mode of the number of children.

    (A) 0
    (B) 1
    (C) 2
    (D) 4

11. What is the probability that a family chosen at random on this block will have 4 children?

   (A) $\dfrac{4}{9}$

   (B) $\dfrac{2}{9}$

   (C) $\dfrac{4}{7}$

   (D) $\dfrac{5}{7}$

12. What is the probability that an even number will come up when a single die is thrown?

   (A) $\dfrac{1}{6}$

   (B) $\dfrac{1}{5}$

   (C) $\dfrac{1}{4}$

   (D) $\dfrac{1}{2}$

13. A bag contains 3 black balls, 2 yellow balls, and 4 red balls. What is the probability of drawing a black ball?

   (A) $\dfrac{1}{2}$

   (B) $\dfrac{1}{3}$

   (C) $\dfrac{2}{3}$

   (D) $\dfrac{4}{9}$

14. In a group of 1,000 adults, 682 are women. What is the probability that a person chosen at random from this group will be a man?

   (A) .318
   (B) .682
   (C) .5
   (D) 1

15. In a balloon factory, a random sampling on 100 balloons showed that 3 had pinholes in them. In a sampling of 2,500 balloons, how many may be expected to have pinholes?

    (A) 30
    (B) 75
    (C) 100
    (D) 450

16. Find the average of $\sqrt{.64}$, 0.85, and $\dfrac{9}{10}$.

    (A) $\dfrac{21}{25}$
    (B) 3.25
    (C) 2.55
    (D) 85%

17. The average of two numbers is xy. If the first number is y, what is the other number?

    (A) $2xy - y$
    (B) $xy - 2y$
    (C) $2xy - x$
    (D) x

18. 30 students had an average of x, while 20 students had an average of 80. The average for the entire group is:

    (A) $\dfrac{x+80}{50}$

    (B) $\dfrac{x+80}{2}$

    (C) $\dfrac{50}{x+80}$

    (D) $\dfrac{3}{5}x + 32$

19. What is the average of the first 15 positive integers?

    (A) 7
    (B) 7.5
    (C) 8
    (D) 8.5

20. A man travels a distance of 20 miles at 60 miles per hour and then returns over the same route at 40 miles per hour. What is his average rate for the round trip in miles per hour?

    (A) 50
    (B) 48
    (C) 47
    (D) 46

21. A number p equals $\dfrac{3}{2}$ the average of 10, 12, and q. What is q in terms of p?

    (A) $\dfrac{2}{3}p - 22$

    (B) $\dfrac{4}{3}p - 22$

    (C) $2p - 22$

    (D) $\dfrac{1}{2}p + 11$

22. Darren has as average of 86 in 3 examinations. What grade must he receive on his next test if he wants to raise his average to 88?

    (A) 94
    (B) 90
    (C) 92
    (D) 100

23. The heights of the 5 starters on Redwood High's basketball team are 5′11″, 6′3″, 6′, 6′6″, and 6′2″. The average height of these boys is:

    (A) 6′1″
    (B) 6′2″
    (C) 6′3″
    (D) 6′4″

24. Find the average of all numbers from 1 to 100 that end in 2.

    (A) 46
    (B) 47
    (C) 48
    (D) 50

25. Don had an average of 72 on his first 4 math tests. After taking the next test, his average dropped to 70. What was Don's most recent test grade?

    (A) 60
    (B) 62
    (C) 64
    (D) 66

Answers and Explanations

1. **The correct answer is (D).** Find the sum of the values:

   $73.8 + 92.2 + 64.7 + 43.8 + 56.5 + 46.4 = 377.4$

   There are 6 values. Arithmetic mean =

   $\dfrac{377.4}{6} = 62.9$

2. **The correct answer is (C).** Arrange the numbers in order:

   1, 5, 5, 5, 7, 8, 8, 9, 9, 10, 10

   The middle number, or median, is 8.

3. **The correct answer is (A).** The mode is the number appearing most frequently. The number 15 appears three times.

4. **The correct answer is (C).**

   Average $= \dfrac{73 + 85 + 54 + 92 + 66}{5}$

   $= \dfrac{370}{5}$

   $= 74$

5. **The correct answer is (B).** Sum of the grades

   $= 1,440$: $\dfrac{1,440}{20} = 72$

6. **The correct answer is (B).**

75	×	15¢ =	1,125¢
100	×	30¢ =	3,000¢
50	×	72¢ =	3,600¢
225			7,725¢

   $\dfrac{7,725¢}{225} = 34\dfrac{1}{3}¢$

7. **The correct answer is (D).**

Subject	Grade	Weight
English	90	4
Algebra	84	3
French	75	3
Music	76	1

   $(90 \times 4) + (84 \times 3) + (75 \times 3) + (76 \times 1)$

   $360 + 252 + 225 + 76 = 913$

   Weight $= 4 + 3 + 3 + 1 = 11$

   $913 \div 11 = 83$ average

8. **The correct answer is (A).**

   Average $= \dfrac{3 + 4 + 4 + 0 + 1 + 2 + 0 + 2 + 2}{9}$

   $= \dfrac{18}{9} = 2$

9. **The correct answer is (D).** Arrange the numbers in order:

   0, 0, 1, 2, 2, 2, 3, 4, 4

   Of the 9 numbers, the fifth (middle) number is 2.

10. **The correct answer is (C).** The number appearing most often is 2.

11. **The correct answer is (B).** There are 9 families, 2 of which have 4 children. The probability is $\dfrac{2}{9}$.

12. **The correct answer is (D).** Of the possible numbers, three are even (2, 4, and 6). The probability is $\dfrac{3}{6}$ or $\dfrac{1}{2}$.

13. **The correct answer is (B).** There are 9 balls in all. The probability of drawing a black ball is $\dfrac{3}{9}$, or $\dfrac{1}{3}$.

14. **The correct answer is (A).** If 682 people of the 1,000 are women, $1,000 - 682 = 318$ are men. The probability of choosing a man is:

$$\frac{318}{1,000} = .318$$

15. **The correct answer is (B).** There is a probability of $\frac{3}{100} = 3\%$ that a balloon may have a pinhole:

$3\% \times 2,500 = 75$

16. **The correct answer is (D).** In order to average these three numbers, they should all be expressed in the same form. In this case, decimals are easiest to deal with.

$$\sqrt{.64} = .8$$

$$.85 = .85$$

$$\frac{9}{10} = .9$$

$$.8 + .85 + .9 = 2.55$$

$$\frac{2.55}{3} = .85 = 85\%$$

17. **The correct answer is (A).** Let b = the second number.

$$\frac{y+b}{2} = xy$$

$$y + b = 2xy$$

$$b = 2xy - y$$

18. **The correct answer is (D).**

$$\frac{30(x) + 20(80)}{50} = \text{Average}$$

$$\frac{30x + 1,600}{50} = \frac{3x + 160}{5} = \frac{3}{5}x + 32$$

19. **The correct answer is (C).** Positive integers begin with 1.

Sum $= 1 + 2 + 3 + 4 + 5 + 6 + 7 + 8 + 9 + 10 + 11 + 12 + 13 + 14 + 15 = 120$

Number of items $= 15$

$$\text{Average} = \frac{120}{15} = 8$$

Note: Since these numbers are evenly spaced, the average will be the middle number, 8.

20. **The correct answer is (B).**

$$\text{Average rate} = \frac{\text{Total distance}}{\text{Total time}}$$

Total distance $= 20 + 20 = 40$

Since $\text{time} = \frac{\text{distance}}{\text{rate}}$, time for the first part of the trip is $\frac{20}{60}$ or $\frac{1}{3}$ hour, while time for the second part of the trip is $\frac{20}{40}$ or $\frac{1}{2}$ hour.

Total time $= \frac{1}{3} + \frac{1}{2}$, or $\frac{5}{6}$ hour.

$$\text{Average rate} = \frac{40}{\frac{5}{6}} = 40 \cdot \frac{6}{5} = 48$$

21. **The correct answer is (C).**

$$p = \frac{3}{2}\left(\frac{10 + 12 + q}{3}\right)$$

$$p = \frac{10 + 12 + q}{2}$$

$$2p = 22 + q$$

$$2p - 22 = q$$

22. The correct answer is (A).

$$\frac{3(86)+x}{4}=88$$

$$258+x=352$$

$$x=94$$

23. The correct answer is (B).

5'11"

6'3"

6'

6'6"

6'2"

$$29'22''=5\overline{\smash{)}30'10''}\ \ \overset{6'\ 2''}{}$$

24. The correct answer is (B). Sum = 2 + 12 + 22 + 32 + 42 + 52 + 62 + 72 + 82 + 92 = 470

Number of items = 10

Average = $\dfrac{470}{10}=47$

Note: Since these numbers are evenly spaced, the average is the middle number. However, since there is an even number of addends, the average will be halfway between the middle two. Halfway between 42 and 52 is 47.

25. The correct answer is (B).

$$\frac{4(72)+x}{4}=70$$

$$288+x=350$$

$$x=62$$

SIGNED NUMBERS

Basic to successful work in algebra is the ability to compute accurately with signed numbers.

Addition: To add signed numbers with the same sign, add the magnitudes of the numbers and keep the same sign. To add signed numbers with different signs, subtract the magnitudes of the numbers and use the sign of the number with the greater magnitude.

Subtraction: Change the sign of the second number, and follow the rules for addition.

Multiplication: If there are an odd number of negative signs, the product is negative. An even number of negative signs gives a positive product.

Division: If the signs are the same, the quotient is positive. If the signs are different, the quotient is negative.

Exercise: Signed Numbers

Directions: Work out each problem in the space provided, then circle your answer.

1. When +3 is added to –5, the sum is:

   (A) –8
   (B) +8
   (C) –2
   (D) +2

2. When –4 and –5 are added, the sum is:

   (A) –9
   (B) +9
   (C) –1
   (D) +1

3. Subtract: +3 – (–6)

   (A) –3
   (B) +3
   (C) +18
   (D) +9

4. When –5 is subtracted from +10, the result is:

   (A) +5
   (B) +15
   (C) –5
   (D) –15

5. (–6)(–3) equals:

   (A) –18
   (B) +18
   (C) +2
   (D) –9

6. The product of $(-6)\left(+\dfrac{1}{2}\right)(-10)$ is:

   (A) $-15\dfrac{1}{2}$

   (B) $+15\dfrac{1}{2}$

   (C) –30
   (D) +30

7. When the product of (–4) and (+3) is divided by (–2), the quotient is:

   (A) $+\dfrac{1}{2}$

   (B) $+3\dfrac{1}{2}$

   (C) +6

   (D) $-\dfrac{1}{2}$

Answers and Explanations

1. **The correct answer is (C).** In adding numbers with opposite signs, subtract their magnitudes (5 – 3 = 2) and use the sign of the number with the greater magnitude (negative).

2. **The correct answer is (A).** In adding numbers with the same sign, add their magnitudes (4 + 5 = 9) and keep the same sign.

3. **The correct answer is (D).** Change the sign of the second number and follow the rules for addition:

   +3 – (– 6) = +3 + (+6) = +9

4. **The correct answer is (B).** Change the sign of the second number and follow the rules for addition:

   +10 – (–5) = +10 + (+5) = +15

5. **The correct answer is (B).** The product of two negative numbers is a positive number.

6. **The correct answer is (D).** The product of an even number of negative numbers is positive.

7. **The correct answer is (C).** (–4)(+3) = –12. Dividing a negative number by a negative number gives a positive quotient:

   $$\dfrac{-12}{-2} = +6$$

LINEAR EQUATIONS

The next step in gaining confidence in algebra is mastering linear equations. Whether an equation involves numbers or only letters, the four basic steps are the same:

1. If there are fractions or decimals, remove them by multiplication.

2. Collect all terms containing the unknown for which you are solving on the same side of the equation. Remember that whenever a term crosses the equal sign from one side of the equation to the other, it must pay a toll. That is, it must change its sign.

3. Determine the coefficient of the unknown by combining similar terms or factoring when terms cannot be combined.

4. Divide both sides of the equation by this coefficient.

Q Solve $5x - 3 = 3x + 5$.

The correct answer is 4. $2x = 8$
$$x = 4$$

Q Solve for x: $ax - b = cx + d$

The correct answer is $\dfrac{b+d}{a-c}$. $ax - cx = b + d$

$$x(a - c) = b + d$$

$$x = \frac{b+d}{a-c}$$

Q Solve for x: $\dfrac{3}{4}x + 2 = \dfrac{2}{3}x + 3$

The correct answer is 12.

Multiply by 12: $9x + 24 = 8x + 36$
$$x = 12$$

Q Solve for x: $0.7x + 0.04 = 2.49$

The correct answer is 3.5.

Multiply by 100: $70x + 4 = 249$

$$70x = 245$$

$$x = 3.5$$

In solving equations with two unknowns, it is necessary to work with two equations simultaneously. The object is to eliminate one of the two unknowns and solve the resulting single unknown equation.

Q Solve for x: $2x - 4y = 2$

$$3x + 5y = 14$$

The correct answer is 3.

Multiply the first equation by 5: $10x - 20y = 10$

Multiply the second equation by 4: $12x + 20y = 56$

The y terms now have the same numerical coefficients, but with opposite signs, we can eliminate them by adding the two equations. If they had the same signs, we would eliminate them by subtracting the equations. Adding, we have: $22x = 66$

$$x = 3$$

We were only asked to solve for x, so we stop here. If we were asked to solve for both x and y, we would now substitute 3 for x in either equation and solve the resulting equation for y.

$$3(3) + 5y = 14$$

$$9 + 5y = 14$$

$$5y = 5$$

$$y = 1$$

Q Solve for x: $ax + by = c$

$$dx + ey = f$$

The correct answer is $\dfrac{ce - bf}{ae - bd}$.

Multiply the first equation by e: $aex - bey = ce$

Multiply the second equation by b: $bdx - bey = bf$

The y terms now have the same coefficient with the same sign, so we eliminate these terms by subtracting the two equations: $aex - bdx = ce - bf$

Factor to determine the coefficient of x:

$x(ae - bd) = ce - bf$

Divide by the coefficient of x:

$$x = \frac{ce - bf}{ae - bd}$$

Exercise: Linear Equations

Directions: Work out each problem in the space provided, then circle your answer.

1. If $5x + 6 = 10$, then x equals:

   (A) $\dfrac{16}{5}$

   (B) $\dfrac{5}{16}$

   (C) $-\dfrac{5}{4}$

   (D) $\dfrac{4}{5}$

2. Solve for x: $ax = bx + c,\ a \neq b$

   (A) $\dfrac{b+c}{a}$

   (B) $\dfrac{c}{a-b}$

   (C) $\dfrac{c}{b-a}$

   (D) $\dfrac{a-b}{c}$

3. Solve for k: $\dfrac{k}{3} + \dfrac{k}{4} = 1$

   (A) $\dfrac{11}{8}$

   (B) $\dfrac{8}{11}$

   (C) $\dfrac{7}{12}$

   (D) $\dfrac{12}{7}$

4. If $x + y = 8p$ and $x - y = 6q$, then x is:

   (A) $7pq$
   (B) $4p + 3q$
   (C) pq
   (D) $4p - 3q$

5. If $7x = 3x + 12$, then $2x + 5$ is:

   (A) 10
   (B) 11
   (C) 12
   (D) 13

6. In the equation $y = x^2 + rx - 3$, for what value of r will $y = 11$ when $x = 2$?

   (A) 6
   (B) 5
   (C) 4
   (D) $\dfrac{3}{12}$

7. If $1 + \dfrac{1}{t} = \dfrac{t+1}{t}$ what does t equal?

   (A) +1 only
   (B) +1 or −1 only
   (C) +1 or +2 only
   (D) All values except 0

8. If $0.23m = 0.069$, then m is:

   (A) 0.003
   (B) 0.03
   (C) 0.3
   (D) 3

9. If $35rt + 8 = 42rt$, then rt is:

   (A) $\dfrac{8}{7}$

   (B) $\dfrac{8}{87}$

   (C) $\dfrac{7}{8}$

   (D) $\dfrac{87}{8}$

10. For what values of n is $n + 5$ equal to $n - 5$?

    (A) No value
    (B) 0
    (C) All negative values
    (D) All positive values

Answers and Explanations

1. The correct answer is (D).

$$5x = 4$$

$$x = \frac{4}{5}$$

2. The correct answer is (B).

$$ax - bx = c$$

$$x(a - b) = c$$

$$x = \frac{c}{a - b}$$

3. The correct answer is (D). Multiply by 12: $4k + 3k = 12$

$$7k = 12$$

$$k = \frac{12}{7}$$

4. The correct answer is (B). Add equations to eliminate y:

$$2x = 8p + 6q$$

Divide by 2: $x = 4p + 3q$

5. The correct answer is (B). Solve for x:

$$4x = 12$$

$$x = 3$$

$$2x + 5 = 2(3) + 5 = 11$$

6. The correct answer is (B). Substitute given values: $11 = 4 + 2r - 3$

$$10 = 2r$$

$$5 = r$$

7. The correct answer is (D). Multiply by t:
$t + 1 = t + 1$

This is an identity and therefore is true for all values. However, because t was a denominator in the given equation, t may not equal 0, as we can never divide by 0.

8. The correct answer is (C). Multiply by 100 to make the coefficient an integer:

$$23m = 6.9$$

$$m = 3$$

9. The correct answer is (A). Even though this equation has two unknowns, we are asked to solve for rt, which may be treated as a single unknown:

$$8 = 7rt$$

$$\frac{8}{7} = rt$$

10. The correct answer is (A). There is no number such that when 5 is added, we get the same result as when 5 is subtracted. Do not confuse choices (A) and (B). Choice (B) would mean that the number 0 satisfies the equation, which it does not.

LITERAL EXPRESSIONS

Many students who can compute easily with numbers become confused when they work with letters. The computational processes are exactly the same. Just think of how you would do the problem with numbers, and do exactly the same thing with letters.

Q Find the number of inches in 2 feet, 5 inches.

The correct answer is 29. There are 12 inches in a foot, so we multiply 2 feet by 12 to change it to 24 inches and then add 5 more inches, giving an answer of 29 inches.

Q Find the number of inches in f feet and i inches.

The correct answer is $12f + i$. Doing exactly as we did in the previous example, we multiply f by 12, giving $12f$ inches, and add i more inches, giving an answer of $12f + i$ inches.

Q A telephone call from New York to Chicago costs 85 cents for the first 3 minutes and 21 cents for each additional minute. Find the cost of an 8-minute call at this rate.

The correct answer is $1.90. The first 3 minutes cost 85 cents. There are 5 additional minutes above the first 3. These 5 minutes are billed at 21 cents each, for a cost of $1.05. The total cost is $1.90.

Q A telephone call costs c cents for the first 3 minutes and d cents for each additional minute. Find the cost of a call that lasts m minutes if $m > 3$.

The correct answer is $c + dm - 3d$. The first 3 minutes cost c cents. The number of additional minutes is $(m - 3)$. These are billed at d cents each, for a cost of $d(m - 3)$, or $dm - 3d$. Thus the total cost is $c + dm - 3d$. Remember that the first 3 minutes have been paid for in the basic charge. Therefore, you must subtract 3 from the total number of minutes to find the additional minutes.

Exercise: Literal Expressions

Directions: Work out each problem in the space provided, then circle your answer.

1. David had d dollars. After a shopping trip, he returned with c cents. How many cents did he spend?

   (A) $d-c$
   (B) $c-d$
   (C) $100d-c$
   (D) $100c-d$

2. How many ounces are there in p pounds and q ounces?

   (A) $\dfrac{p}{16}+q$
   (B) pq
   (C) $p+16q$
   (D) $16p+q$

3. How many passengers can be seated on a plane with r rows, if each row consists of d double seats and t triple seats?

   (A) rdt
   (B) $rd+rt$
   (C) $2dr+3tr$
   (D) $3dr+2tr$

4. How many dimes are there in $4x-1$ cents?

   (A) $40x-10$
   (B) $\dfrac{2}{5}x-\dfrac{1}{10}$
   (C) $40x-1$
   (D) $4x-1$

5. If u represents the tens' digit of a certain number and t represents the units' digit, then the number with the digits reversed can be represented by:

   (A) $10t+u$
   (B) $10u+t$
   (C) tu
   (D) ut

6. Joe spent k cents of his allowance and has r cents left. Which of the following represents his total allowance in dollars?

   (A) $k + r$

   (B) $k - r$

   (C) $100(k + r)$

   (D) $\dfrac{k + r}{100}$

7. If p pounds of potatoes cost \$$k$, find the cost (in cents) of one pound of potatoes.

   (A) $\dfrac{k}{p}$

   (B) $\dfrac{k}{100p}$

   (C) $\dfrac{p}{k}$

   (D) $\dfrac{100k}{p}$

8. Mr. Unger rents a car for d days. He pays m dollars per day for each of the first 7 days, and he pays half that rate for each additional day. Find the total charge if $d > 7$.

   (A) $m + 2m(d - 7)$

   (B) $m + \dfrac{m}{2}(d - 7)$

   (C) $7m + \dfrac{m}{2}(d - 7)$

   (D) $7m + \dfrac{md}{2}$

9. A salesman earns \$90 per week, plus a 4% commission on all sales over \$1,000. One week he sells \$$r$ worth of merchandise ($r > 1,000$). How much money does he earn that week?

   (A) $50 + .04r$

   (B) $.04r - 50$

   (C) $.04r + 90$

   (D) $r + 3.60$

Prepare for the NYSTCE: LAST and ATS-W

10. Elliot's allowance was just raised to $k per week. He gets a raise of $c per week every two years. How much will his allowance be per week y years from now? (Assume y is an even number.)

(A) $k + cy$

(B) $k + 2cy$

(C) $k + \dfrac{1}{2}cy$

(D) $k - 2c$

Answers and Explanations

1. **The correct answer is (C).** The answer is to be in cents, so we change d dollars to cents by multiplying by 100 and then subtract the c cents he spent.

2. **The correct answer is (D).** There are 16 ounces in a pound. Therefore, we must multiply p pounds by 16 to change to ounces and then add q more ounces.

3. **The correct answer is (C).** Each double seat holds 2 people, so d double seats hold 2d people. Each triple seat holds 3 people, so t triple seats hold 3t people. Therefore, each row holds $2d + 3t$ people. If there are r rows, we must multiply the number of people in each row by r.

4. **The correct answer is (B).** To change cents to dimes, we must divide by 10:

$$\frac{4x-1}{10} = \frac{4}{10}x - \frac{1}{10} = \frac{2}{5}x - \frac{1}{10}$$

5. **The correct answer is (A).** The original number would be $10u + t$. The number with the digits reversed would be $10t + u$.

6. **The correct answer is (D).** Joe's allowance was $k + r$ cents. To change this to dollars, we must divide by 100.

7. **The correct answer is (D).** This can be solved by using a proportion. Remember to change k dollars to 100k cents:

$$\frac{p}{100k} = \frac{1}{x}$$

$$px = 100k$$

$$x = \frac{100k}{p}$$

8. **The correct answer is (C).** He pays m dollars for each of 7 days, for a total of 7m dollars. Then he pays $\dfrac{1}{2}m$ dollars for $(d - 7)$ days, for a cost of $\dfrac{m}{2}(d-7)$. The total charge is $7m + \dfrac{m}{2}(d-7)$.

9. **The correct answer is (A).** He gets a commission of 4% of $(r - 1,000)$, or $.04(r - 1,000)$, which is $.04r - 40$. Adding this to 90, we have $.04r + 50$.

10. **The correct answer is (C).** He gets a raise only every two years, so in y years he will get $\dfrac{1}{2}y$ raises. Each raise is c dollars, so with $\dfrac{1}{2}y$ raises, his present allowance will he increased by $c\left(\dfrac{1}{2}y\right)$.

ROOTS, RADICALS, AND EXPONENTS

Roots and Radicals

Rules for addition and subtraction of radicals are much the same as for addition and subtraction of letters. The radicals must be exactly the same if they are to be added or subtracted and merely serve as a label that does not change:

$$4\sqrt{2} + 3\sqrt{2} = 7\sqrt{2}$$

$\sqrt{2} + 2\sqrt{3}$ cannot be combined

$\sqrt{2} + \sqrt{3}$ cannot be combined

Sometimes, when the radicals are not the same, simplification of one or more radicals will make them the same. Remember that radicals are simplified by factoring out any perfect square factors.

Q Add: $\sqrt{27} + \sqrt{75}$

   The correct answer is $8\sqrt{3}$. $\sqrt{9 \cdot 3} + \sqrt{25 \cdot 3}$

$$3\sqrt{3} + 5\sqrt{3} = 8\sqrt{3}$$

In multiplication and division, the radicals are again treated the same way as letters. They are factors and must be handled as such:

$$\sqrt{2} \cdot \sqrt{3} = \sqrt{6}$$

$$2\sqrt{5} \cdot 3\sqrt{7} = 6\sqrt{35}$$

$$\left(2\sqrt{3}\right)^2 = 2\sqrt{3} \cdot 2\sqrt{3} = 4 \cdot 3 = 12$$

$$\frac{\sqrt{75}}{\sqrt{3}} = \sqrt{25} = 5$$

$$\frac{10\sqrt{3}}{5\sqrt{3}} = 2$$

Exponents

In an expression of the form b^n, b is called the *base* and n is called the *exponent* or *power*. We say "b is raised to the power of n." The following 4 rules exist for operations with exponents:

1. **Multiplying.** When multiplying powers of the same base, keep the base and add the exponents:

$$3^2 \cdot 3^3 = 3^{2+3}$$
$$= 3^5$$
$$= 243$$

2. **Raising a product or quotient to a power.** To raise a product or quotient to a power, raise each to that power, whether that factor is in the numerator or denominator:

$$(2x)^3 = 2^3 x^3$$
$$= 8x^3$$

and

$$\left(\frac{2}{x}\right)^3 = \frac{2^3}{x^3}$$
$$= \frac{8}{x^3}$$

3. **Raising a power to a power.** To raise a power to a power, multiply the exponents:

$$\left(2^3\right)^2 = 2^6$$
$$= 64$$

4. **Dividing.** To divide powers with the same base, retain the base and subtract the exponents:

$$\frac{4^5}{4^2} = 4^3$$
$$= 64$$

Exercise: Exponents

> *Directions:* Work out each problem in the space provided, then circle your answer.

1. If $r = -2$, then $r^4 + 2r^3 + 3r^2 + r = ?$
   - **(A)** 8
   - **(B)** 4
   - **(C)** 0
   - **(D)** 10

2. $[3(a^2b^3)^2]^3 = ?$

    (A) $27a^{12}b^{18}$
    (B) $729a^{12}b^{18}$
    (C) $27a^7b^8$
    (D) $3a^8b^{12}$

3. If $a = -1$ and $b = -2$, what is the value of $(2 - ab^2)^3$?

    (A) 343
    (B) 216
    (C) 125
    (D) 64

4. Which of the following expressions is equivalent in value to $9y - \dfrac{6y^3}{2y^2}$?

    (A) $3 + y$

    (B) $\dfrac{3}{y}$

    (C) $3y$
    (D) $6y$

5. If x and y are positive integers, $x - 2y = 5$, and $x^2 - 4y^2 = 45$, what is the value of $x + 2y$?

    (A) -3
    (B) 0
    (C) 14
    (D) 9

Answers and Explanations

1. **The correct answer is (D).** Substituting: $(-2)^4 + 2(-2)^3 + 3(-2)^2 + (-2) =$ $16 - 16 + 12 - 2 = 10$.

2. **The correct answer is (A).** Working outward from the inner parentheses, $[3(a^2b^3)^2]^3 =$ $[3a^4b^6]^3 = 27a^{12}6^{18}$.

3. **The correct answer is (B).** Substituting: $[2 - (-1)(-2)^2]^3 = [2 - (-4)]^3 = 6^3 = 216$.

4. **The correct answer is (D).** The fraction simplifies to $3y$, and $9y - 3y = 6y$.

5. **The correct answer is (D).** $(x + 2y)(x - 2y) =$ $x^2 - 4y^2$ According to the question, $x^2 - 4y^2 = 45$ and $x - 2y = 5$. Substituting these numbers into the equation: $(x + 2y)(5) = 45$. Therefore, $x + 2y = 9$.

PROBLEM SOLVING IN ALGEBRA

In solving verbal problems, the most important technique is to read accurately. Be sure you understand clearly what you are asked to find. Then represent what you are looking for algebraically. Write an equation that translates the words of the problem to the symbols of mathematics. Then solve that equation by the techniques reviewed previously.

We will review some of the frequently encountered types of algebra problems, although not every problem you may get will fall into one of these categories. However, thoroughly familiarizing yourself with the types of problems that follow will help you to translate and solve all kinds of verbal problems.

Coin Problems

In solving coin problems, it is best to change the value of all monies involved to cents before writing an equation. Thus, the number of nickels must be multiplied by 5 to give their value in cents; likewise, dimes must be multiplied by 10, quarters by 25, half-dollars by 50, and dollars by 100.

 Richard has $3.50 consisting of nickels and dimes. If he has 5 more dimes than nickels, how many dimes does he have?

The correct answer is 25.

$$\text{Let } x = \text{the number of nickels}$$

$$x + 5 = \text{the number of dimes}$$

$$5x = \text{the value of the nickles in cents}$$

$$10x + 50 = \text{the value of the dimes in cents}$$

$$350 = \text{the value of the money he has in cents}$$

$$5x + 10x + 50 = 350$$

$$15x = 300$$

$$x = 20$$

He has 20 nickels and 25 dimes.

In a problem such as this, you can be sure that 20 would be among the multiple-choice answers. You must be sure to read carefully what you are asked to find and then continue until you have found the quantity sought. The correct answer is 25.

Consecutive Integer Problems

Consecutive integers are one apart and are represented by $x, x + 1, x + 2$, etc.

 Three consecutive odd integers have a sum of 33. Find the average of these integers.

The correct answer is 11. Represent the integers as x, $x + 2$, and $x + 4$. Write an equation indicating that the sum is 33:

$$3x + 6 = 33$$

$$3x = 27$$

$$x = 9$$

The integers are 9, 11, and 13. In the case of evenly spaced numbers such as these, the average is the middle number, 11. Because the sum of the three numbers was given originally, all we really had to do was to divide this sum by 3 to find the average, without ever knowing what the numbers were.

Age Problems

Problems of this type usually involve a comparison of ages at the present time, several years from now, or several years ago. A person's age x years from now is found by adding x to his present age. A person's age x years ago is found by subtracting x from his present age.

Q Michelle was 12 years old y years ago. Represent her age b years from now.

The correct answer is $12 + y + b$. Her present age is $12 + y$. In b years, her age will be $12 + y + b$.

Interest Problems

The annual amount of interest paid on an investment is found by multiplying the amount of principal invested by the rate (percent) of interest paid.

Q Mr. Strauss invests $4,000, part at 6% and part at 7%. His income from these investments in one year is $250. Find the amount invested at 7%.

The correct answer is $1,000. Represent each investment:

$$\text{Let } x = \text{ the amount invested at 7\% (always try to let } x \text{ represent}$$

$$\text{what you are looking for)}$$

$$4{,}000 - x = \text{the amount invested at 6\%}$$

$$0.07x = \text{ the income from the 7\% investment}$$

$$0.06(4{,}000 - x) = \text{ the income from the 6\% investment}$$

$$0.07x + 0.06(4{,}000 - x) = 250$$

$$7x + 6(4{,}000 - x) = 25{,}000$$

$$7x + 24{,}000 - 6x = 25{,}000$$

$$x = 1{,}000$$

He invested $1,000 at 7%.

Prepare for the NYSTCE: LAST and ATS-W

Fraction Problems

A fraction is a ratio between two numbers. If the value of a fraction is $\frac{2}{3}$, it does not mean that the numerator must be 2 and the denominator 3. The numerator and denominator could be 4 and 6, respectively, or 1 and 1.5, or 30 and 45, or any of infinitely many other combinations. All we know is that the ratio of numerator to denominator will be 2:3. Therefore, the numerator may be represented by $2x$, the denominator by $3x$, and the fraction by $\frac{2x}{3x}$.

Q The value of a fraction is $\frac{3}{4}$. If 3 is subtracted from the numerator and added to the denominator, the value of the fraction is $\frac{2}{5}$. Find the original fraction.

The correct answer is $\frac{9}{12}$. Let the original fraction be represented by $\frac{3x}{4x}$. If 3 is subtracted from the numerator and added to the denominator, the new fraction becomes $\frac{3x-3}{4x+3}$.

The value of the new fraction is $\frac{2}{5}$: $\dfrac{3x-3}{4x+3} = \dfrac{2}{5}$

Cross-multiply to eliminate fractions: $15x - 15 = 8x + 6$

$$7x = 21$$

$$x = 3$$

Therefore, the original fraction is: $\dfrac{3x}{4x} = \dfrac{9}{12}$

Mixture Problems

You should be familiar with two kinds of mixture problems. The first kind refers to problems in which we mix dry ingredients of different values, such as nuts or coffee. The second kind of mixture problems are those that mix chemical ingredients, such as water and alcohol. Also solved by the same method are problems such as those dealing with tickets at different prices. In solving these types of problems, it is best to organize the data in a chart of three rows and three columns, labeled as illustrated in the following problem.

Q A dealer wishes to mix 20 pounds of nuts selling for 45 cents per pound with some more expensive nuts selling for 60 cents per pound, to make a mixture that will sell for 50 cents per pound. How many pounds of the more expensive nuts should he use?

The correct answer is 10.

	No. of lbs.	×	Price/lb.	=	Total Value
Original	20		0.45		0.45(20)
Added	x		0.60		0.60(x)
Mixture	20 + x		0.50		0.50(20 + x)

The value of the original nuts plus the value of the added nuts must equal the value of the mixture. Almost all mixture problems require an equation that comes from adding the final column:

$0.45(20) + 0.60(x) = 0.50(20 + x)$

Multiply by 100 to remove decimals.

$$45(20) + 60(x) = 50(20 + x)$$

$$900 + 60x = 1,000 + 50x$$

$$10x = 100$$

$$x = 10$$

He should use 10 lbs. of 60-cent nuts.

In solving the second type, or chemical, mixture problem, we are dealing with percents rather than prices, and amounts instead of value.

Q How much water must be added to 20 gallons of a solution that is 30% alcohol to dilute it to a solution that is only 25% alcohol?

The correct answer is 4.

	No. of gals.	×	% alcohol	=	Amt. Alcohol
Original	20		0.30		0.30(20)
Added	x		0		0
Mixture	20 + x		0.25		0.25(20 + x)

Note: The percent of alcohol in water is 0. Had we added pure alcohol to strengthen the solution, the percent would have been 100. The equation again comes from the last column. The amount of alcohol added (none, in this case) plus the amount we had to start with must equal the amount of alcohol in the new solution.

$$0.30(20) = 0.25(20 + x)$$

$$30(20) = 25(20 + x)$$

$$600 = 500 + 25x$$

$$100 = 25x$$

$$4 = x$$

Motion Problems

The fundamental relationship in all motion problems is that Rate × Time = Distance. The problems at the level of this examination usually derive their equation from a relationship concerning distance. Most problems fall into one of 3 types:

1. **Motion in opposite directions.** When two objects start at the same time and move in opposite directions, or when two objects start at points at a given distance apart and move toward each other until they meet, then

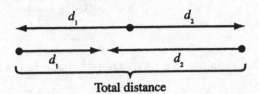

In either of the above cases, $d_1 + d_2$ = total distance

2. **Motion in the same direction.** This type of problem is sometimes called the "catch-up" problem. Two objects leave the same place at different times and different rates, but one "catches up" to the other. In such a case, the two distances must be equal.

3. **Round trip.** In this type of problem, the rate going is usually different from the rate returning. The times are also different. But if we go somewhere and then return to the starting point, the distances must be the same.

To solve any motion problem, it is helpful to organize the data in a box with columns for rate, time, and distance. A separate line should be used for each moving object. Remember that if the rate is given in miles per hour, the time must be in hours and the distance in miles.

Q Two cars leave a restaurant at 1 p.m., with one car traveling east at 60 miles per hour and the other west at 40 miles per hour along a straight highway. At what time will they be 350 miles apart?

The correct answer is 4:30 p.m.

	Rate	×	Time	=	Distance
Eastbound	60		x		$60x$
Westbound	40		x		$40x$

Note: The time is unknown because we must discover the number of hours traveled. However, the cars start at the same time and stop when they are 350 miles apart, so their times are the same.

$$60x + 40x = 350$$

$$100x = 350$$

$$x = 3\frac{1}{2}$$

In $3\frac{1}{2}$ hours, it will be 4:30 p.m.

Q Gloria leaves home for school, riding her bicycle at a rate of 12 miles per hour. Twenty minutes after she leaves, her mother sees Gloria's English paper on her bed and leaves to bring it to her. If her mother drives at 36 miles per hour, how far must she drive before she reaches Gloria?

The correct answer is 6 miles.

	Rate	×	Time	=	Distance
Gloria	12		x		$12x$
Mother	36		$x - \dfrac{1}{3}$		$36\left(x - \dfrac{1}{3}\right)$

Note: 20 minutes has been changed to $\dfrac{1}{3}$ of an hour. In this problem, the times are not equal, but the distances are:

$$12x = 36\left(x - \frac{1}{3}\right)$$

$$12x = 36x - 12$$

$$12 = 24x$$

$$x = \frac{1}{2}$$

If Gloria rode for $\dfrac{1}{2}$ hour at 12 miles per hour, the distance covered was 6 miles.

Q Judy leaves home at 11 a.m. and rides to Mary's house to return her bicycle. Judy travels at 12 miles per hour and arrives at 11:30 a.m. She turns right around and walks home. How fast does Judy walk if she returns home at 1 p.m.?

The correct answer is 4 miles per hour.

	Rate	×	Time	=	Distance
Going	12		$\dfrac{1}{2}$		6
Returning	x		$1\dfrac{1}{2}$		$\dfrac{3}{2}x$

Note: The distances are equal.

$$6 = \frac{3}{2}x$$

$$12 = 3x$$

$$4 = x$$

She walked at 4 miles per hour.

Work Problems

In most work problems, a complete job is broken into several parts, each representing a fractional part of the entire job. For each fractional part (which represents the portion completed by one person, one machine, one pipe, etc.), the numerator should represent the time actually spent working, and the denominator should represent the total time needed to do the entire job alone. The sum of all the individual fractions should be 1.

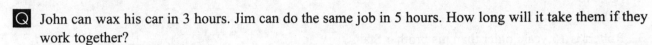 John can wax his car in 3 hours. Jim can do the same job in 5 hours. How long will it take them if they work together?

The correct answer is $1\dfrac{7}{8}$ hours. If multiple-choice answers are given, you should realize that the correct answer will be less than the shortest time given: No matter how slow a helper may be, he does do part of the job, and therefore it will be completed in less time.

Let $x =$ the amount of time each spent working together:

$$\frac{\text{Time spent}}{\text{Total time needed to do job alone}} \rightarrow \begin{matrix} \textbf{John} & \textbf{Jim} \\ \dfrac{x}{3} & + & \dfrac{x}{5} = 1 \end{matrix}$$

Multiply by 15 to eliminate fractions:

$$5x + 3x = 15$$
$$8x = 15$$
$$x = 1\frac{7}{8} \text{ hours}$$

Exercise: Problem Solving in Algebra

Directions: Work out the problem in the space provided, then circle your answer.

1. Sue and Nancy wish to buy a gift for a friend. They combine their money and find they have $4, consisting of quarters, dimes, and nickels. If they have 35 coins and the number of quarters is half the number of nickels, how many quarters do they have?

(A) 5
(B) 10
(C) 20
(D) 3

2. Three times the first of three consecutive odd integers is three more than twice the third. Find the third integer.

   (A) 9
   (B) 11
   (C) 13
   (D) 15

3. Robert is 15 years older than his brother Stan. However, y years ago Robert was twice as old as Stan. If Stan is now b years old and $b > y$, find the value of $b - y$.

   (A) 13
   (B) 14
   (C) 15
   (D) 16

4. How many ounces of pure acid must be added to 20 ounces of a solution that is 5% acid to strengthen it to a solution that is 24% acid?

   (A) $2\frac{1}{2}$
   (B) 5
   (C) 6
   (D) $7\frac{1}{2}$

5. A dealer mixes a lbs. of nuts worth b cents per pound with c lbs. of nuts worth d cents per pound. At what price should he sell a pound of the mixture if he wishes to make a profit of 10 cents per pound?

   (A) $\dfrac{ab+cd}{a+c}+10$
   (B) $\dfrac{ab+cd}{a+c}+0.10$
   (C) $\dfrac{b+d}{a+c}+10$
   (D) $\dfrac{b+d}{a+c}+0.10$

6. Barbara invests $2,400 at 5%. How much additional money must she invest at 8% so that the total annual income will be equal to 6% of her entire investment?

   (A) $2,400
   (B) $3,600
   (C) $1,000
   (D) $1,200

7. Frank left Austin to drive to Boxville at 6:15 p.m. and arrived at 11:45 p.m. If he averaged 30 miles per hour and stopped 1 hour for dinner, how many miles is Boxville from Austin?

   (A) 120
   (B) 135
   (C) 180
   (D) 165

8. A plane traveling 600 miles per hour is 30 miles from Kennedy Airport at 4:58 p.m. At what time will it arrive at the airport?

   (A) 5 p.m.
   (B) 5:01 p.m.
   (C) 5:02 p.m.
   (D) 5:20 p.m.

9. Mr. Bridges can wash his car in 15 minutes, but his son Dave takes twice as long to do the same job. If they work together, how many minutes will the job take them?

   (A) 5

   (B) $7\frac{1}{2}$

   (C) 10

   (D) $22\frac{1}{2}$

10. The value of a fraction is $\frac{2}{5}$. If the numerator is decreased by 2 and the denominator is increased by 1, the resulting fraction is equivalent to $\frac{1}{4}$. Find the numerator of the original fraction.

    (A) 3
    (B) 4
    (C) 6
    (D) 10

Answers and Explanations

1. **The correct answer is (B).** Let x = number of quarters, $2x$ = number of nickels, and $35 - 3x$ = number of dimes. Write all money values in cents.

$$25(x) + 5(2x) + 10(35 - 3x) = 400$$

$$25x + 10x + 350 - 30x = 400$$

$$5x = 50$$

$$x = 10$$

2. **The correct answer is (D).**

$$\text{Let } x = \text{first integer}$$

$$x + 2 = \text{second integer}$$

$$x + 4 = \text{third integer}$$

$$3(x) = 3 + 2(x + 4)$$

$$3x = 3 + 2x + 8$$

$$x = 11$$

The third integer is 15.

3. **The correct answer is (C).**

$$b = \text{Stan's age now}$$

$$b + 15 = \text{Robert's age now}$$

$$b - y = \text{Stan's age } y \text{ years ago}$$

$$b + 15 - y = \text{Robert's age } y \text{ years ago}$$

$$b + 15 - y = 2(b - y)$$

$$b + 15 - y = 2b - 2y$$

$$15 = b - y$$

4. **The correct answer is (B).**

	No. of oz.	×	% acid	=	Amt. acid
Original	20		0.05		1
Added	x		1.00		x
Mixture	$20 + x$		0.24		$0.24(20 + x)$

$$1 + x = 0.24(20 + x)$$

Multiply by 100 to eliminate decimal.

$$100 + 100x = 480 + 24x$$

$$76x = 380$$

$$x = 5$$

5. **The correct answer is (A).** The *a* lbs. of nuts are worth a total of *ab* cents. The *c* lbs. of nuts are worth a total of *cd* cents. The value of the mixture is *ab* + *cd* cents. Because there are *a* + *c* pounds, each

   pound is worth $\dfrac{ab+cd}{a+c}$ cents.

   The dealer wants to add 10 cents to each pound for profit, and the value of each pound is in cents, so we add 10 to the value of each pound.

6. **The correct answer is (D).** If Barbara invests *x* additional dollars at 8%, her total investment will amount to 2,400 + *x* dollars.

$$0.05(2,400)+0.08(x)=0.06(2,400+x)$$
$$5(2,400)+8(x)=6(2,400-x)$$
$$12,000+8x=14,400+6x$$
$$2x=2,400$$
$$x=1,200$$

7. **The correct answer is (B).** The total time elapsed is $5\frac{1}{2}$ hours. However, one hour was used for dinner. Therefore, Frank drove at 30 miles per hour for $4\frac{1}{2}$ hours, covering 135 miles.

8. **The correct answer is (B).** Time $= \dfrac{\text{Distance}}{\text{Rate}} = \dfrac{30}{600} = \dfrac{1}{20}$ hour, or 3 minutes.

   4:58 + 3 minutes = 5:01.

9. **The correct answer is (C).** Dave takes 30 minutes to wash the car alone.

$$\frac{x}{15}+\frac{x}{30}=1$$
$$2x+x=30$$
$$3x=30$$
$$x=10$$

10. **The correct answer is (C).** Let 2*x* = original numerator and 5*x* = original denominator

$$\frac{2x-2}{5x+1}=\frac{1}{4}$$

   Cross-multiply: $8x-8=5x+1$
$$3x=9$$
$$x=3$$

   The original numerator is 2(3), or 6.

GEOMETRY

Numerical relationships from geometry should be reviewed thoroughly. A list of the most important formulas with illustrations follows:

Area

1. **Rectangle:** bh
   Area $= (6)(3) = 18$

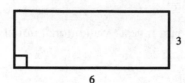

b = base
h = height

2. **Parallelogram:** bh
   Area $= 8 \times 4 = 32$

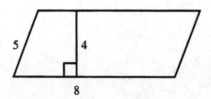

b = base
h = height

3. **Rhombus:** $\frac{1}{2} d_1 d_2$
   If $AC = 10$ and $BD = 8$,
   then area is $\frac{1}{2}(10)(8) = 40$

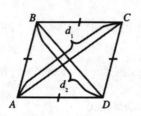

d_1 = diagonal 1
d_2 = diagonal 2

4. **Square:** s^2 or $\frac{1}{2} d^2$
   Area $= 6^2 = 36$

s = side
d = diagonal

   Area $= \frac{1}{2}(10)^2 = 50$

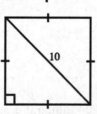

5. **Triangle:** $\frac{1}{2} bh$
   Area $= \frac{1}{2}(12)(4) = 24$

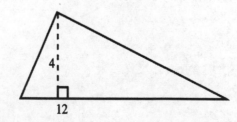

b = base
h = height

6. **Equilateral triangle:** $\dfrac{s^2}{4}\sqrt{3}$

   Area $= \dfrac{36}{4}\sqrt{3} = 9\sqrt{3}$

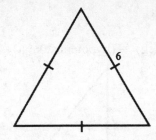

s = side

7. **Trapezoid:** $\dfrac{1}{2}h(b_1 + b_2)$

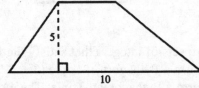

h = height
b_2 = base 2 (bottom)
b_1 = base 1 (top)

   Area $= \dfrac{1}{2}(5)(6 + 10) = \dfrac{1}{2}(5)(16) = 40$

8. **Circle:** πr^2

   Area $= \pi(6)^2 = 36\pi$

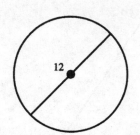

r = radius
d = diameter

$r = \dfrac{1}{2}d$

Perimeter/Circumference

1. **Any polygon:** simply add all sides

   $P = 5 + 8 + 11 = 24$

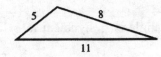

2. **Circle:** πd or $2\pi r$ (called circumference)

   $C = \pi(12) = 12\pi$

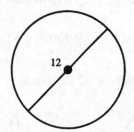

r = radius
d = diameter
C = circumference

3. The distance covered by a wheel in one revolution is equal to the circumference of the wheel.

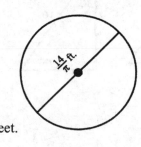

   In one revolution, this wheel covers $\pi \times \dfrac{14}{\pi}$, or 14 feet.

Right Triangles

1. **Pythagorean Theorem:** $(\text{leg})^2 + (\text{leg})^2 = (\text{hypotenuse})^2$

$$4^2 + 5^2 = x^2$$

$$16 + 25 = x^2$$

$$41 = x^2$$

$$\sqrt{41} = x$$

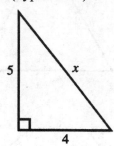

2. **Pythagorean Triples:** These are sets of integers that satisfy the Pythagorean Theorem. When a given set of numbers such as 3, 4, 5 form a Pythagorean Triple ($3^2 + 4^2 = 5^2$), any multiples of this set (such as 6, 8, 10 or 15, 20, 25) also form a Pythagorean Triple. The most common Pythagorean Triples, which should be memorized, are listed here:

3, 4, 5

5, 12, 13

8, 15, 17

7, 24, 25

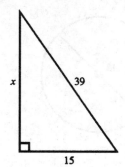

Squaring these numbers to apply the Pythagorean Theorem would take too much time. Instead, recognize the hypotenuse as 3(13). Suspect a 5, 12, 13 triangle. Because the given leg is 3(5), the missing leg must be 3(12), or 36. With this method, no computation is necessary and you save a great deal of time.

3. **The 30°-60°-90° Triangle:**

A. The leg opposite the 30° angle is $\frac{1}{2}$ hypotenuse.

B. The leg opposite the 60° angle is $\frac{1}{2}$ hypotenuse $\cdot \sqrt{3}$.

C. An altitude in an equilateral triangle forms a 30°-60°-90° triangle and is therefore equal to $\frac{1}{2}$ the side of the equilateral triangle $\cdot \sqrt{3}$. Altitude = $\frac{1}{2}s\sqrt{3}$.

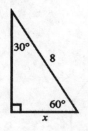 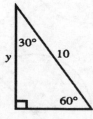 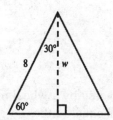 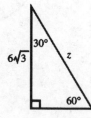

$x = 4$ $y = 5\sqrt{3}$ $z = 12$

$$w = \frac{1}{2}(8)\sqrt{3}$$

$$= 4\sqrt{3}$$

4. **The 45°-45°-90° Triangle (isosceles right triangle)**

A. Each leg is $\frac{1}{2}$ hypotenuse × $\sqrt{2}$.

B. Hypotenuse is leg × $\sqrt{2}$.

C. The diagonal in a square forms a 45°-45°-90° triangle and is therefore equal to a side of the square times $\sqrt{2}$. Diagonal = $s\sqrt{2}$.

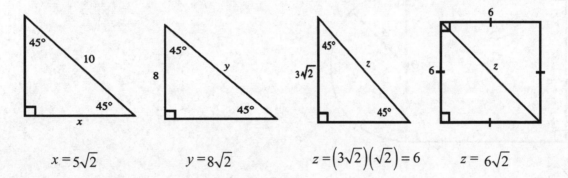

$$x = 5\sqrt{2} \qquad y = 8\sqrt{2} \qquad z = \left(3\sqrt{2}\right)\left(\sqrt{2}\right) = 6 \qquad z = 6\sqrt{2}$$

Exercise: Geometry

> *Directions:* Work out each problem in the space provided, then circle your answer.

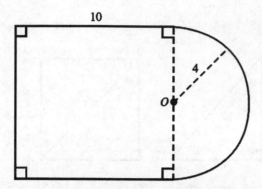

1. Find the area of the region shown in the figure above. **Note:** The curved side is a semicircle.

    (A) $20 + 4\pi$
    (B) $20 + 6\pi$
    (C) $40 + 6\pi$
    (D) $80 + 8\pi$

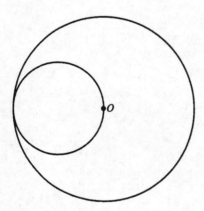

2. In the figure above, the larger circle shown has an area of 36π. What is the circumference of the smaller circle?

    (A) 2π
    (B) 4π
    (C) 6π
    (D) 8π

3. What is the perimeter of a rectangle that is twice as long as it is wide, and has the same area as a circle of diameter 8?

(A) $8\sqrt{\pi}$

(B) $8\sqrt{2\pi}$

(C) 8π

(D) $12\sqrt{2\pi}$

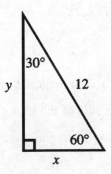

4. Solve for x above.

(A) 6

(B) $\sqrt{12}$

(C) $12\sqrt{y}$

(D) 4

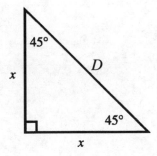

5. Solve for D in terms of x.

(A) $x\sqrt{4}$

(B) $2x\sqrt{D}$

(C) $x\sqrt{2}$

(D) x^2

Answers and Explanations

1. **The correct answer is (D).** The dotted line divides the region into a rectangle and a semicircle. Since the radius of the circular arc is 4, the diameter is 8, and that is the width of the rectangle. The length is 10. Hence, its area is 80. The area of the whole circle would be $\pi r^2 = \pi(4^2) = 16\pi$. Hence, the area of the semicircle is half of that, or 8π. Therefore, the total area is choice (D), $80 + 8\pi$.

2. **The correct answer is (C).** The larger circle has area $A_L = \pi(r)^2 = 36\pi$. That means that $r^2 = 36$, and $r = 6$. The diameter of the smaller circle equals the radius of the larger one, so its radius is $\frac{1}{2}(6) = 3$. Its circumference must be $C_s = 2\pi(3) = 6\pi$, choice (C).

3. **The correct answer is (D).** The area of a circle of diameter 8 is $\pi 4^2 = 16\pi$, since its radius is 4. Let the width of the rectangle be w. Its length is $2w$ and its area is $2w^2$, which must equal 16π. Thus,

   $$2w^2 = 16\pi$$

   $$w^2 = 8\pi \text{ and } w = \sqrt{8\pi} = 2\sqrt{2\pi}$$

   Thus, $L = 4\sqrt{2\pi}$

   The perimeter is $2w + 2L =$

   $$8\sqrt{2\pi} + 4\sqrt{2\pi} = 12\sqrt{2\pi}$$

4. **The correct answer is (A).** The leg opposite the 30° is $\frac{1}{2}$ the hypotenuse. The hypotenuse is 12.

   Hence:

   $$x = \frac{1}{2}(12)$$

   $$x = 6$$

5. **The correct answer is (C).** The diagonal of a 45°-45°-90° triangle is the side of the triangle times $\sqrt{2}$. The side $= x$, so the diagonal is $x\sqrt{2}$.

Chapter 4
SCIENCE REVIEW

SCIENTIFIC REASONING

Scientific reasoning is a process that involves several steps. These steps are: formulating a hypothesis, designing the experiment, collecting and organizing data, and drawing conclusions.

Let us look at each step in turn.

Step 1: Form a Hypothesis

A scientist conducts an experiment to try to prove or disprove an idea. This idea is an attempt to explain how something works and is called a *hypothesis*. The hypothesis is what helps the scientist to decide what experiments to do and what things to measure. For example, a scientist might formulate the hypothesis that drivers are more likely to break the traffic laws when they are not being watched. Her next step would be to design experiments to prove whether her hypothesis is reasonable.

Step 2: Design an Experiment

In this case, the scientist might decide to test how likely it is for drivers to break one particular rule, such as running a red light, and to see whether a driver is more likely to break the rule at night or during the day. In doing this, the scientist assumes there is a correlation between the time of day and a driver's perception of being watched. In limiting herself to very specific things to test, our scientist has shown an understanding of good experimental design.

Good experimental design has two requirements. First, you must look for the effect of only one variable at a time. Our scientist would not want to compare how often people run red lights at night in a blizzard to how often they run them on a spring afternoon. If she did, how would she know how much of the red-light running was due to the dark and how much was because of the weather? She may record the results for all kinds of weather, but she will keep in mind that she can compare directly only those experiments that differ in just one variable. When she designs the experiment, she will try to make the only difference between the day and night drivers the fact that one set drove during the day and the other at night. So she will probably make all her observations at one intersection, on the same day of the week (could it make a difference if she compared Monday afternoon to Saturday night?), under the same weather conditions.

The second requirement for good experimental design is that there must be a control group. A control group tells you whether there is any real change in results when you change the factor. If our scientist told you that 2 percent of the night drivers run red lights, you might be tempted to think that drivers pretty much always obey the law no matter what. But when she tells you that only one-tenth of 1 percent of the daytime drivers break that law, you realize that a driver is 20 times more likely to run the light at night. A control group gives you a context in which to judge your results.

Step 3: Observe and Record Information

After the experiment has been designed, the scientist must collect the information. But just getting the facts together isn't enough. The facts must be organized so that others can make sense of what has been done. One way to do this is to describe how the experiment was done, what a given observation would mean, and what the result of the experiment actually was. This is called a *research summary*. Research summaries are often prepared for experiments that test for color changes or some other data that is not easy to put into numbers.

In some experiments, just having numbers is not good enough. For example, if our scientist reported that 10 cars ran a red light on a warm, clear night, that information would not mean much to you. Even if she added that only 5 cars ran that same light during the day, you still have not learned much. The information means very little because it does not answer the original question of how likely a driver is to break the law. To answer this question, you also need to know how many cars went through the intersection during the day and during the night. If 50 cars went through the intersection during the day and 100 went through during the night, the fact that twice as many cars ran red lights at night does not prove the hypothesis. However, if 50 cars went through the intersection during the day and only 20 went through at night, the facts about running red lights take on a very different look. In this study, the scientist would obviously have to calculate percentages before beginning to analyze the data, and she would have to arrange the data in such a way that trends are easy to spot. There are three common ways to organize data: tables, graphs, and charts. All three help a scientist to relate a change in one factor to a change in another.

Tables are almost always the first step in organizing data. (In fact, most scientists set up empty tables to fill in while they are doing the experiments.) Tables are arranged into columns and rows. Every cell (where a column and row intersect) describes the results for one condition.

Another common way to organize data is to use graphs. Once again, we will be comparing only one factor in relation to another. The value of one factor becomes the abscissa (the x-coordinate or independent variable) and the value of the other becomes the ordinate (the y-coordinate or dependent variable). The two together make a point on the graph. We can use tables to read the points for our graph. We would use the value in a row for one axis, and the value in the column for that row for the other axis.

Let's look at a graph for the effect temperature in dry weather has on the likelihood that a daytime driver will run a red light. (Notice that we won't mix the "wet" and "dry" values.)

If we claim that temperature influences driving, we make temperature the x or independent variable. One point on this graph will have an x value of 20–39. To know what the y value is, we look to the correct column and read the number in the row marked 20–39. A y value of 2 is present at the intersection of the row marked "20–39" and the column labeled "day." Graphs can give a lot of information at a glance about the relation of one variable to another. If the line connecting the points slants upwards (a positive slope), that implies that the variable on the y-axis increases as the variable on the x-axis increases. If there is no relation, we won't get a line at all—just a random scattering of points on the graph. We will look at examples of different kinds of graphs in the data representation portion of this section.

Another way to show relationships between variables is to make a map, chart, or diagram. You have probably seen maps showing air pressure or temperature curves in earth science and diagrams of the ear or the digestive system in biology. These are other ways of organizing information to show relationships.

Step 4: Draw a Conclusion

From the collected and organized information, the scientist will draw a conclusion as to whether her hypothesis is correct. Based on that conclusion, she will design other experiments to test how general the rule is or to make the relationship even clearer. Our scientist, for example, might try to see if law-breaking trends are the same for speeding as well as red-light running. You can probably think of several other experiments that could help answer questions about the hypothesis. As you think of those experiments, you will be getting involved in experimental design—and you will start to reason like a scientist. With that in mind, let's go on to look at the type of questions you'll be asked on the LAST.

Science Reasoning on Your Test

Science Reasoning questions are all multiple choice. They ask you to demonstrate your mastery of increasingly difficult levels of scientific reasoning. To answer the questions correctly, you will have to do all of the following:

- Show that you understand information provided in the readings

- Analyze relationships between the information provided and conclusions drawn from that information

- Generalize from the given information and predict what may happen under different circumstances

Here is a simple, 6-step plan to help you answer Science Reasoning questions:

- **Step 1:** Read the passage and examine any accompanying graphs, charts, or diagrams.

- **Step 2:** Read the accompanying questions one by one. Phrase each one in your own words to make sure you understand it.

- **Step 3:** Determine what you need to know to solve each problem. A question may refer to only a selection of the given data, such as a step in an experiment or a portion of the results. Focus on the information required to answer the question.

- **Step 4:** Analyze the data and draw your conclusion. Use the scientific method to organize the information you have selected, and then reason your way to a logical answer to each question.

- **Step 5:** Look for your answer among the answer choices. If it's there, mark your answer sheet and go on. If it's not, review the data again and rethink the logic of your conclusion.

- **Step 6:** Answer every question in a set, even if you have to guess. Coming back to a question set involves doing a lot of rereading and rethinking, which takes precious time. So, answer every question before moving on. If you don't know an answer, guess.

TABLE 1

Experiment	Temperature (°C)	Average food intake (g)	Age when first gave birth (mo.)
1	25	15	7
2	25	30	6
3	25	45	4
4	35	15	5
5	35	30	3
6	35	45	3

What Does the Table Show?

One of the first things you should notice is that you are looking at the effect of two variables—temperature and food—on the sexual maturity of the animal. If you are interested in the effect of food, look down the age column and compare experiments 1, 2, and 3, or compare experiments 4, 5, and 6. In each of those groupings, temperature remains constant so that a change in age can be related (as far as we know) only to a change in the amount of food. If you want to look at the effect of temperature, you must compare rows in which the only factor that changes is the temperature. Can you pick out rows that will allow you to look for the effect of temperature? The second question in the Sample Question Set will give you the correct answer.

If you haven't already done so, figure out what the trends are for the effects of increasing food and increasing temperature on the age of sexual maturity. When you have done that, take a moment to picture in your mind how the experiments might have been performed. Once you have completed all the steps outlined, you are ready to handle typical questions about the table.

TESTSMARTS

What is the difference between an independent variable and a dependent variable?

An independent variable is what can be changed by the experimenter. Examples of independent variables are amount of sunlight, amount of liquid added, and so on. A dependent variable cannot be directly manipulated by the experimenter.

Sample Question Set

Q Which of the following would be good animals to use for the experiment?

(A) Adult females
(B) Newborn females
(C) Newborn males
(D) Adult males

The correct answer is (B). You should be able to eliminate choices (C) and (D) right away. You cannot use a male at any age to determine the age at which a female gives birth. You can rule out choice (A) with a little thought. If you start the experiment with adults, then you have no way of knowing how big a role the current control of their environment has on them compared to their past.

Q Which of the pairs of experiments listed here would be useful for studying the effect of temperature on age of first birth?

(A) 1 and 2
(B) 1 and 5
(C) 1 and 4
(D) 2 and 6

The correct answer is (C). The correct answer is the one in which the only factor that varies is the one you are interested in. Only choice (C) includes two experiments in which food intake is the same (15g) and temperature varies.

The first two questions illustrate one type of data interpretation question. They ask something about the nature of the experiment, about how it should be set up or studied. The next three questions represent another type of data interpretation question. These questions ask you to predict what will happen if you change a variable in the experiment to compare the results of two or more trials. Answering these questions requires knowledge of the trends.

Prepare for the NYSTCE: LAST and ATS-W

Q If all other variables are kept constant, which of the following will result in an increase in the age at which the animals give birth?

(A) Increase in temperature from 25°C to 35°C
(B) Increase in food from 15g to 45g
(C) Decrease in food from 30g to 15g
(D) Increase in temperature from 25°C to 30°C

The correct answer is (C). Both an increase in food and an increase in temperature will cause a decrease in the age at first birth. You are asked for the factor that will cause an increase in the age, and a decrease in temperature or food will cause a rise in the birth age.

The previous question is a reminder that you must answer the question that was actually asked, not the one you assumed was asked. If you are not careful, you can lose points on questions that you really can answer.

Q Which experiment was the control for temperature for Experiment 5?

(A) Experiment 1
(B) Experiment 2
(C) Experiment 3
(D) Experiment 6

The correct answer is (D). Again, you must look for two experiments that can be compared, which means two experiments that have only one variable that differs. You should compare choice (B), if you are looking for the effect of temperature (food is kept constant; food is the control), or choice (D), the correct answer, since you are looking for the effect of food with temperature controlled.

Q If an experiment was set up with the temperature set at 30°C and the food intake at 30g, which of the following would be a reasonable prediction of the age in months of the animals when they first gave birth?

(A) 7.5
(B) 6.0
(C) 4.5
(D) 2.5

The correct answer is (C). To solve this problem, you must compare this experiment to Experiments 2 and 5. (Remember, you can estimate the effect of the change in temperature only if you hold the food variable constant.) The table shows that an increase in temperature from 25°C to 35°C results in a decrease in age from six months to three months. Therefore, it is not unreasonable to conclude that the age at first birth at 30°C will be between three and six months.

The next question illustrates the third type of data interpretation question. It requires you to draw conclusions based on data presented. The major difficulty with this type of question is drawing conclusions that are not valid because you make assumptions that are not justified by the data.

Q Which of the following conclusions is consistent with the data presented in Table 1?

(A) The weight of the firstborn is proportional to the food intake.
(B) The weight of the firstborn is related to the temperature.
(C) The age of the mother at the time of the first offspring's birth increases with decreasing food intake.
(D) The age of the mother at the time of the first offspring's birth decreases with decreasing food intake.

The correct answer is (C). In answering this question, keep in mind that all you know about is the effect of temperature and food on the mother. You know nothing about the offspring at all. So, even though it might not be unreasonable to suppose that some of the extra food goes to the infant, you have no information to back up that idea. Therefore, neither choices (A) nor (B) can be correct. To decide between choices (C) and (D), look at the table and note the trend. The age of the mother decreases with increasing food intake, so food and age go in opposite directions; as one goes up, the other goes down. Choice (D) has both age and food going down simultaneously. Choice (C) has one going up while the other goes down.

TESTSMARTS

Make sure you answer the question that is being asked.

This advice may sound silly, but it is not. Be sure you know which point of view, which experiment, or which table is being questioned.

GRAPHS

Graphs show the relationship between two variables, one measured along the x-axis and the other measured along the y-axis.

A straight line means that there is a simple (linear) relationship between the variables that can be described by the equation, $y = mx + b$. Just multiplying the x value by some number (which is the slope) and adding a constant gives you the value for the other variable. To make life even simpler, in many cases, b, the y-intercept, equals zero, so we not only start at the origin of the coordinate system, but we can focus our attention on the slope. The slope can be positive, negative, or zero. If the slope is positive, then the value of the y variable increases as the value of the x variable increases. An example of this is Case A:

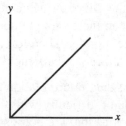

A special case of a positive slope is when the x variable and the y variable being plotted are the same. For example, if you plot force on the x-axis and mass times acceleration on the y-axis, the x and y values for any point will be the same (because $F = ma$). The straight line that results will be at a 45° angle.

A second possibility is that the y variable decreases as the x variable increases. The result is a curve with a negative slope.

RESEARCH SUMMARIES

Research summaries are used when the data that is collected is not suitable for a table or graph. This can be because the data involves changes that cannot easily be put into numbers, such as a change in color or a change in pitch of a sound, or because the experiment is done on a model. Models are used to get a simplified picture of what processes are occurring in real life. So, while the actual measurements are meaningless, the general trends (if the model is valid) are useful. For example, a model of an eardrum can be made by stretching a thin rubber sheet across a round metal hoop. A set of experiments could be run on this model to see how charting the frequency or loudness of a sound affects how the sheet vibrates. Even though a measure of the response of the sheet tells us little in and of itself, the pattern of responses might suggest why we seem to hear shriller noises better than lower-pitched ones, and why we can't hear dog whistles.

TESTSMARTS

Look for design flaws in the experiment.

Poorly designed experiments give flawed results.

Research summaries of experiments are just descriptions of how particular experiments were carried out and the results of those experiments. If any special information is needed, such as the meaning of a chemical test result, it will be spelled out in the description of the experiment. Research summaries may also explain the hypothesis that the experiments were designed to test before discussing the experiments.

1. **Questions about the design of the experiments.** These can be questions asking you to identify what a given part of the experiment represents. Going back to the ear model for a moment, you might be asked what the metal hoop represents (the supporting bone for the eardrum). Another question might focus on the controlled variables in the experiment (the rubber sheet and the metal hoop).

2. **Questions involving predicting results,** taking into account the trends you observed in the experiments. These questions are very similar to the questions on tables discussed earlier, but the answers are not in numerical form. Because of this, it is important to be sure that you understand not only the experiment itself, but also any special results (such as the meaning of a certain color or the forming of a solid).

3. **Questions involving relating experiments to hypotheses.** You may be asked how the experiments can be altered to test a new hypothesis or which of a group of hypotheses a particular experiment supports. In redesigning the experiments to test a new hypothesis, the first step is to determine what the new factor to be varied will be. Then decide what variables will now have to be fixed. The correct answer will have the correct variable as the only factor that can change.

To pick the hypothesis that is supported by an experiment, a good rule of thumb is to choose the most specific hypothesis that is in line with the data. Going back to the ear model again, a hypothesis that stated something about flexible membranes on round frames would be better than one that made claims about flexible membranes on frames in general. The reason for this is that the first hypothesis does not generalize to cases (we have no information about non-round frames), but the second hypothesis does.

Sample Question Set

To investigate the hypothesis that the quality of the detail of a fossil depends on the size of the particles that make up the rock surrounding the fossil, three experiments were performed using a particular type of leaf with many fine veins.

Experiment 1

A leaf was placed on a flat bed made of a paste of extra-fine plaster. The leaf was then completely covered with more of the same plaster paste. A glass cover with a 5-pound weight was placed on top of the paste for one hour until the plaster set. The plaster was then baked for 30 minutes at 250°C. When the cast was opened, the imprint of the leaf showed all the veins, including the finest ones.

Experiment 2

A leaf was placed on a flat bed made of a paste of fine-grade plaster. The leaf was then completely covered with more of the same plaster paste. A glass cover with a 5-pound weight was placed on top of the plaster for one hour. The plaster was then baked for 30 minutes at 250°C. When the cast was opened, all the main veins were visible, but only isolated traces of the finer veins were found.

Experiment 3

A leaf was placed on a flat bed made of a paste of coarse-grain plaster. The leaf was then completely covered with more of the same plaster paste. A glass cover with a 5-pound weight was placed on top of the plaster for one hour. The plaster was then baked for 30 minutes at 250°C. When the cast was opened, only the thickest veins were visible, and some of the edge of the leaf was difficult to discern.

Q Should the investigator have used a different type of leaf in each experiment?

(A) Yes, because different types of structure could be studied
(B) Yes, because in real life many different types of fossils are found
(C) No, because the fossil served as a controlled variable
(D) No, because the nature of the fossil is not important

The correct answer is (C). In this question, you are asked to think about how the experiment was set up. You know from the hypothesis that the only factor you want to change is the coarseness of the plaster. To compare the casts, you should be looking at the same imprints so that you can easily see the differences.

Q When a fossil is formed, the sediment that surrounds it is normally compressed by the tons of earth deposited over it. What part of the model simulates this sediment?

(A) The 5-pound weight
(B) The veins
(C) The leaf
(D) The baking oven

The correct answer is (A). To answer this question, you must ask yourself what the sediment does to the fossil. From the question itself, it is obvious that the sediment applies pressure to the fossil. According to Newton's Third Law, since the plastic is directly over the leaf, it must apply pressure. The 5-pound weight serves this function.

TESTSMARTS

Watch for *assumptions*

Make sure that you understand which statements in a Science Reasoning passage are assumptions and which are facts.

The first two questions tested your ability to understand the model being used. This next question tests your ability to predict results based on experiments.

Q A fourth experiment was set up the same way as the previous three, except that the paste was made by mixing equal amounts of very coarse sand with the extra-fine plaster. The investigator is likely to discover

(A) no change from Experiment 1 because only the plaster counts.

(B) no change because the same kind of leaf is used.

(C) the imprint is better than in Experiment 1 because the sand provides air pockets.

(D) the imprint is worse than in Experiment 1 because the average particle size is bigger.

The correct answer is (D). The three experiments show that the larger the particles in the plaster, the fewer details are visible in the imprint. You could then conclude that mixing the plaster with a coarser grain would make the image worse.

It often helps to work out the answer to the question before looking at the choices—on occasion, some of the reasons given are so bizarre that you might be led to wonder about whether you had forgotten to take something into account.

The next two questions relate the experiments to hypotheses.

Q Which of the following hypotheses are supported by the results of Experiment 1 alone?

(A) The finer the sediment, the greater the detail of the resulting fossil.

(B) Hardened sediment can preserve the *imprint* of a specimen.

(C) All fossils must have been baked at high temperatures.

(D) Only organic material can leave imprints in sediment.

The correct answer is (B). Choices (C) and (D) can be ruled out because they claim knowledge that is not provided by Experiment 1. No experiment was done that attempted to make the imprint without baking, so we don't know that baking is a requirement. Also, there was no attempt to make an imprint of anything besides the leaf, so there is no support for the claim that only organic material can leave an imprint. Experiment 1 shows that a very fine plaster produces imprints with detail. There is no way of knowing that it produced an imprint superior to coarser grades of plaster until you examine the results of Experiments 2 and 3. So, choice (A) cannot be supported by Experiment 1 alone. Remember, to read the question carefully!

Q Which of the following changes in the experiment would have permitted a test of the hypothesis that the quality of a fossil imprint depends on the pressure applied?

(A) Repeat the experiments, but use a 10-pound weight in Experiment 2 and a 20-pound weight in Experiment 3.

(B) Choose one of the plasters, and run experiments using the same plaster in all trials while varying the weights.

(C) Rerun all the experiments without the glass.

(D) Vary the depth of the leaf in each new trial, because in nature increased pressure means the fossil is in a greater depth.

The correct answer is (B). Choice (B) is best because it limits the number of changeable variables to one. In this case, different pressures are applied using different weights while all other variables stay the same.

Exercise: Data Representation

Directions: Read each passage and answer the questions that follow it, then circle your answer.

Passage I

Table 1 shows the percentages of certain materials in the blood entering the kidney and the percentages of the same materials in the urine leaving the body.

TABLE 1

Substance	Percent in blood	Percent in urine
Protein	7.0	0.0
Water	91.5	96.0
Glucose	0.1	0.0
Sodium	0.33	0.29
Potassium	0.02	0.24
Urea	0.03	2.70

1. According to Table 1, which substance is more highly concentrated in the urine than the blood?

   (A) Water
   (B) Sodium
   (C) Protein
   (D) Glucose

2. According to Table 1, which substance is more highly concentrated in the blood than the urine?

   (A) Protein
   (B) Water
   (C) Potassium
   (D) Urea

3. What is the likeliest explanation for the increase of water going from blood to urine?

   (A) The kidney manufactures water.
   (B) Blood is naturally dehydrated.
   (C) The percentage of water increased because other substances were removed.
   (D) The water becomes hydrogen bonded to the potassium and sodium salts.

4. Which of the following is NOT a valid conclusion based on the data?

   (A) The composition of urine is different from that of blood.
   (B) The volume of water leaving the body is greater than the volume of water entering the kidneys.
   (C) The protein in the blood is not passed into the urine.
   (D) The glucose in the blood is not passed into the urine.

5. A scientist wishes to investigate the effect of age on urine content. Which of the following sets of experiments might give him the clearest answer?

   (A) Analyze urine samples of people at the age of 65.
   (B) Analyze urine samples of people with varying disease states.
   (C) Analyze urine samples of people who differ only in age.
   (D) Analyze people who do not differ in age.

6. What hypothesis is supposed by the previous data?

   (A) All bodily fluids should have equal concentrations of substances to maintain homeostasis.
   (B) All salts are harmful to the body.
   (C) The body manufactures glucose.
   (D) The healthy body will not excrete useful materials.

7. A similar study was done on another individual of the same species. The results were not identical. A reasonable hypothesis explaining this is

   (A) there will be some variation among individuals in a species.
   (B) the second experiment was run improperly.
   (C) the first experiment did not measure the concentration of glycerol.
   (D) the second experiment must have been performed on a female instead of a male.

8. To investigate the effect of time of day on the blood and urine chemistry, a scientist might reasonably

   (A) test five individuals once a day at the same time.
   (B) test one individual five different times during a day.
   (C) alternate between male and female subjects for each blood test.
   (D) test subjects who have different work schedules.

Passage II

Q is a substance believed to inhibit molting in grasshoppers. A scientist investigated the relationship between consumption of Q and age in days at time of first molting. The data is presented here:

TABLE 2

Experiment	Amount of Q per feeding (in mg)	Age at first molt (days)
1	0	4
2	1	3
3	2	5
4	4	6
5	6	10
6	8	Does not molt

9. What is the effect of Q on molting?

   (A) A small amount triggers early molting; larger amounts slow first molting.
   (B) First molting occurs later if Q is fed to grasshoppers.
   (C) All molting occurs later in grasshoppers fed Q.
   (D) Only the first molting is affected by the presence of Q in the diet.

10. What effect does Q have on crickets?

   (A) The same because crickets belong to the same genus as grasshoppers
   (B) The same because crickets have the same life cycle
   (C) Different because crickets are a different species than grasshoppers
   (D) Not enough data

11. Which experiment was the control?

   (A) Experiment 1
   (B) Experiment 2
   (C) Experiment 3
   (D) There was no control.

12. When would a grasshopper eating 5mg of Q be likely to molt for the first time?

   (A) 5 days
   (B) 8 hours
   (C) 8 days
   (D) Never

13. If a scientist were interested in how long the second molting was delayed he would do best to

   (A) continue observing the current experiments.
   (B) repeat the experiment with older grasshoppers.
   (C) increase the dosage of Q.
   (D) decrease the dosage of Q.

14. Which of the following factors would not influence the outcome of the experiment?

   (A) Species of grasshopper
   (B) Temperature
   (C) Type of clock
   (D) How the dose of Q was given

Answers and Explanations

1. **The correct answer is (A).** Water has a higher percentage in the urine column.

2. **The correct answer is (A).** Protein has a higher percentage in the blood column than in the urine column.

3. **The correct answer is (C).** As materials are removed, the *percentage* of what remains increases because the sum of all the percents must be 100.

4. **The correct answer is (B).** Percentages give *no* information on absolute amounts.

5. **The correct answer is (C).** This set will provide only one new variable: age.

6. **The correct answer is (D).** Protein and glucose, useful materials, were not passed into urine.

7. **The correct answer is (A).** Not every individual is identical. Consider height and hair color, for example.

8. **The correct answer is (B).** This way the only variable is time, which is what is being tested.

9. **The correct answer is (A).** Compare Experiments 1, 2, and 3.

10. **The correct answer is (D).** The experiments provide no information about the effect of Q on crickets. Choice (C) assumes a difference without data to back up the assumption.

11. **The correct answer is (A).** Q is not normally in the grasshopper's diet, so the normal condition to which everything else is compared is Experiment 1.

12. **The correct answer is (C).** Expect a value between Experiments 4 and 5. Note the units.

13. **The correct answer is (A).** In the current experiments, all the proper variables are controlled.

14. **The correct answer is (C).** Measurement is in days, so clocks really don't matter.

Exercise: Research Summaries

> *Directions:* Read each passage and answer the questions that *follow* it, then circle your answer.

Passage I

To study the response of a spider to being repeatedly "tricked," three experiments were performed.

Experiment 1
A small blade of grass was used to vibrate a magnum spider's web at 15-minute intervals. On the first two trials, the spider responded within 35 seconds. On the third trial, the spider responded in 41 seconds. On the fourth trial, the spider responded in 50 seconds. The spider did not respond to any further trials.

Experiment 2
One small, live fly was placed in the web of a magnum spider every quarter-hour. The struggles of the fly caused the web to vibrate. On every trial, the spider moved to the fly in 30 to 35 seconds.

Experiment 3
A small blade of grass was used to vibrate a magnum spider's web at 15-minute intervals. On the first two trials, the spider responded within 35 seconds. On the third trial, the spider responded in 42 seconds. On the fourth trial, a live fly was used to vibrate the web instead of the blade of grass. The response time was 49 seconds. On the fifth and sixth trials, a blade of grass was used and the spider responded within 35 seconds.

1. Which experiment served as a control?

    (A) Experiment 1
    (B) Experiment 2
    (C) Experiment 3
    (D) There was no control.

2. What conclusion can be drawn from Experiment 2 alone?

    (A) Spiders can distinguish between a fly and a blade of grass by the vibration.
    (B) Spiders can smell their prey.
    (C) Spiders respond to vibrations in their webs.
    (D) Spiders can tell the size of their prey from the amount of vibration in the web.

3. What conclusion can be drawn from Experiment 1?

   (A) Spiders will not continue to respond unless rewarded.
   (B) Spiders will increase response time and eventually stop responding if there is no reward.
   (C) Spiders will decrease response time and eventually stop responding if there is no reward.
   (D) Spiders lose their ability to respond to vibrations as they age.

4. What conclusion can be drawn from Experiments 1 and 3?

   (A) Spiders will not continue to respond unless rewarded.
   (B) Spiders will increase response time and eventually stop responding.
   (C) Spiders will decrease response and eventually stop responding.
   (D) Spiders lose their ability to respond to vibrations as they age.

5. What conclusion can be drawn from all experiments?

   (A) The response time will increase if the spider is not rewarded, but will return to normal if the spider is given a reward.
   (B) The response time will decrease if the spider is not rewarded, but will return to normal if the spider is given a reward.
   (C) The response time will increase until the spider no longer responds at all, unless it is rewarded with a fly. If rewarded, the spider will react with normal response times on future trials.
   (D) The response of the spider is unpredictable.

6. Which of the following is necessarily a controlled variable in the experiments?

   (A) The flies
   (B) The blade of grass
   (C) The response of the spider
   (D) The species of spider

7. What would be the likely result if the spider in Experiment 2 were tricked once on the sixth trial?

   (A) The response time on the seventh trial would increase compared to that in the sixth trial.
   (B) The response time on the seventh trial would decrease compared to that in the sixth trial.
   (C) The resume time on the seventh trial would be identical to that in the sixth trial.
   (D) The result cannot be predicted.

Passage II

A scientist wished to investigate factors affecting inheritance of eye color of the Australian kiwi flea. All Australian kiwi fleas have either red or blue eyes. For the experiments, the scientist used fleas from lines of pure red- and pure blue-eyed fleas. The results of the investigator's breeding experiments are given here.

Experiment 1

A tank was set up with conditions conducive to the growth of the Australian kiwi flea. One hundred red-eyed fleas and 100 blue-eyed fleas were placed in the tank. Three out of 4 fleas in the first generation were red-eyed, and the rest were blue-eyed. This proportion did not change, even after 12 generations.

Experiment 2

A tank was set up with conditions conducive to the growth of the Australian kiwi flea. Red-eyed males and blue-eyed females were placed in the tank. The first generation of fleas were all red-eyed. After 10 generations, about one-quarter of the fleas were blue-eyed. A single white-eyed flea was observed in the seventh generation.

Prepare for the NYSTCE: LAST and ATS-W

Experiment 3

A tank was set up with conditions conducive to the growth of the Australian kiwi flea. Only red-eyed fleas were placed in this tank. After 10 generations of fleas, only red-eyed fleas were observed.

8. Which experiment served as a control for the purity of strain of flea?

   (A) Experiment 1
   (B) Experiment 2
   (C) Experiment 3
   (D) There was no control.

9. What is the likeliest explanation for the appearance of the white-eyed flea in Experiment 2?

   (A) A red-eyed male and a blue-eyed female give rise to white-eyed offspring.
   (B) A blue-eyed male and a red-eyed female give rise to white-eyed offspring.
   (C) The white-eyed flea was blinded.
   (D) The white-eyed flea was a mutation.

10. Which of the following is a reasonable control for purity of strain?

   (A) Experiment 2
   (B) Experiment 1
   (C) A tank with only blue-eyed fleas
   (D) A tank with only red-eyed male fleas

11. Which of the following conclusions can be supported by Experiment 3 alone?

   (A) Red-eyed fleas are infertile.
   (B) Red-eyed fleas give rise to large numbers of mutants.
   (C) Red eyes are a dominant trait.
   (D) Red-eyed fleas in this batch give rise to red-eyed fleas.

12. Why should there have been a difference in the outcomes of Experiments 1 and 2?

   (A) There was no difference. By the tenth generation, the results were the same.
   (B) The fleas were different in each experiment.
   (C) In one experiment, a red-eyed flea had to mate with a blue-eyed flea.
   (D) There must have been extra ultraviolet light in the tank with the mutated flea.

13. Which of the following is a valid conclusion based on the experiments?

   (A) Red eyes are a dominant trait among Australian kiwi fleas.
   (B) All red-eyed Australian kiwi fleas are female.
   (C) Blue eyes are a dominant trait among Australian kiwi fleas.
   (D) All blue-eyed Australian kiwi fleas are heterozygous.

14. If a fourth experiment used red-eyed males and blue-eyed female, how would the results differ from those of Experiment 2?

   (A) The proportions of red and blue eyes would be reversed.
   (B) There would be fewer mutations.
   (C) There would be more mutations.
   (D) There would be no difference.

Passage III

An investigation was done to determine the relationship between the color of light to which a Diffnia plant is exposed and the number of flowers it develops. A summary of the investigation is presented here.

Experiment 1

Ten Diffnia were grown under green lights at constant temperature with controlled amounts of moisture and food. The plants had, on average, two flowers each.

Experiment 2

Ten Diffnia were grown under normal sunlight at constant temperature with controlled amounts of moisture and food. The plants produced, on average, four flowers each.

Experiment 3

Ten Diffnia were grown under blue lights at constant temperature with controlled amounts of moisture and food. The plants produced, on average, six flowers each.

Experiment 4

Ten Diffnia were grown under red lights at constant temperature with controlled amounts of moisture and food. The plants did not produce flowers.

15. Which experiment served as a control?

   (A) Experiment 1
   (B) Experiment 2
   (C) Experiment 3
   (D) Experiment 4

16. Which is a valid conclusion based on Experiment 3 alone?

   (A) Blue lights make Diffnia produce more flowers than normal.
   (B) Blue lights make Diffnia produce fewer flowers than normal.
   (C) The Diffnia produces flowers if exposed to blue light.
   (D) The Diffnia produces flowers only if exposed to blue light.

17. Which of the following is a method for checking whether red light stops the growth of flowers?

   (A) That was checked in Experiment 4.
   (B) Grow 10 Diffnia under both red and blue lights shown simultaneously.
   (C) Mix green and blue light to produce red light, and grow 10 Diffnia under this light.
   (D) This cannot be done.

18. If the investigator wished to study the effect of light intensity on flower production, which of the following would be most helpful?

   (A) Intensity depends on color, so the investigator should repeat the experiments with more colors.
   (B) All the experiments should be repeated with a different wattage bulb for each color.
   (C) One of the first three experiments should be repeated several times, with a different wattage bulb each time.
   (D) The fourth experiment should be repeated several times, using a different wattage bulb each time.

19. Which of the following was a variable in this series of experiments?

    (A) Temperature
    (B) Color
    (C) Food
    (D) Species studied

20. Which of the following is a valid conclusion based on Experiments 2 and 4?

    (A) Light slows flower production.
    (B) A decrease in light causes a decrease in the number of flowers produced.
    (C) An increase in light causes a decrease in the number of flowers produced.
    (D) A change in the color of light affects the number of flowers produced by Diffnia.

Passage IV

An investigation was conducted to determine the relationship between electric currents and magnetism. The results are presented here.

Experiment 1

A compass pointing north was placed over a copper wire pointing north. The needle continued to point north.

Experiment 2

A compass pointing north was placed over a copper wire pointing north. As soon as a current of 2 amps was passed south to north through the wire, the compass needle pointed west.

Experiment 3

A compass pointing north was placed under a copper wire pointing north. As soon as a current of 2 amps was passed south to north through the wire, the compass needle pointed east.

21. Which of the following is the best reason for performing Experiment 1?

    (A) To make sure that the compass was working
    (B) To act as a control for gravitational fluctuations
    (C) To act as a control for the influence of the wire on the compass
    (D) To see whether the magnetic field of the compass would induce a current in the wire

22. Which of the following conclusions is valid based on Experiment 2 alone?

    (A) There is a magnetic field above the wire, directed west.
    (B) There is a magnetic field above the wire, directed east.
    (C) There is a magnetic field above the wire, directed south.
    (D) Compasses are unreliable indicators of magnetic field direction.

23. Which of the following conclusions is valid based on all three experiments?

    (A) A wire carrying a south-to-north current creates magnetic fields of opposite directions above and below the wire.
    (B) The needle of a compass is deflected to the west by a wire carrying current.
    (C) The needle of a compass is deflected to the east by a wire carrying current.
    (D) Compasses are unreliable indicators of magnetic field direction.

24. Which of the following will most likely cause a compass above a wire pointed north and carrying a current to point east?

    (A) Pass a current north to south
    (B) Pass a current south to north
    (C) Pass a current east to west
    (D) Pass a current west to east

25. Which of the following is the most likely result of bringing a compass pointing north above a wire pointing east, with no current?

    (A) The needle of the compass must be deflected, so it will point south.
    (B) The needle of the compass will be deflected west.
    (C) The needle of the compass will be deflected east.
    (D) The needle of the compass will continue to point north.

26. Which of the following is the best method for testing the relationship between current and the effect on the compass?

    (A) Repeat Experiment 2 or 3, using different wires measured against the amount of deflection.
    (B) Repeat Experiment 2 or 3, measuring the distance between the wire and the compass against the amount of deflection.
    (C) Repeat Experiment 2 or 3 with different currents measured against the amount of deflection.
    (D) Repeat Experiment 2 or 3, measuring the amount of deflection based on varying the current and the compass-to-wire distance.

Answers and Explanations

1. **The correct answer is (B).** This is the normal situation from which changes will be noted.

2. **The correct answer is (C).** Remember to answer on the basis of Experiment 2 only. Do not draw upon information provided by Experiments 1 and 3.

3. **The correct answer is (B).** This answer is more specific than choice (A).

4. **The correct answer is (A).** Experiment 1 shows that the spider will stop responding, while Experiment 3 shows that a reward will keep the spider coming on more trials.

5. **The correct answer is (C).** Choice (C) is more specific than choice (A) (it mentions that the spider will stop responding under certain conditions).

6. **The correct answer is (D).** There might be a major difference in the results if the species were to differ.

7. **The correct answer is (C).** Use the results of Experiment 1 or 3. Only repeated trickery causes increase in response time.

8. **The correct answer is (C).** Only "reds" were used to see whether reds could produce blues.

9. **The correct answer is (D).** If the genetic code normally allows only red or blue, another color must be a mutation.

10. **The correct answer is (C).** If a check for purity is desired, mixing different types introduces a new variable.

11. **The correct answer is (D).** Choice (C) is invalid because in considering only Experiment 3, we have no counter-gene for red to be dominant over.

12. **The correct answer is (C).** In the other experiment, all combinations were possible: blue–blue, red–blue, and red-red, because there were males and females of both strains present.

13. **The correct answer is (A).** More red eyes appear.

14. **The correct answer is (D).** There would still be only red-blue matings possible in the first generation. Dominance is a trait of the gene, not the carrier of the gene.

15. **The correct answer is (B).** This is the experiment that is set up under natural conditions.

16. **The correct answer is (C).** Only Experiment 3 is to be considered, so no comparisons are possible; thus choices (A) and (B) are invalid. There is no information provided in Experiment 3 about the effect of any other light on the production of flowers.

17. **The correct answer is (B).** If red stops flower production, then fewer flowers will be produced under a combination of red and blue light than would be produced under all blue light.

18. **The correct answer is (C).** This way the intensity will be the only variable.

19. **The correct answer is (B).** This variable was changed in each experiment.

20. **The correct answer is (D).** We can make a comparison between a normal condition and one color only.

21. **The correct answer is (C).** Experiment 1 is a control.

22. **The correct answer is (A).** The compass will deflect in the direction of the magnetic field.

23. **The correct answer is (A).** When there is a current in the wire, there is a magnetic field that circles the wire and deflects the compass. A south-to-north current causes the compass to deflect to the west above the wire and east below the wire.

24. **The correct answer is (A).** Based on Experiments 2 and 3, a south-to-north current causes a compass deflection to the west above the wire and to the east below. A reversal of the current (north-to-south current) causes a reversal of the effect.

25. **The correct answer is (D).** There is no magnetic field if there is no current in the wire. The compass will not be deflected and will continue to point north.

26. **The correct answer is (D).** The amount of deflection depends on both the distance from the wire and the amount of current. Both should be tested independently.

Answer Sheet for Chapter 5

PRACTICE QUESTIONS—LAST

1. Ⓐ Ⓑ Ⓒ Ⓓ
2. Ⓐ Ⓑ Ⓒ Ⓓ
3. Ⓐ Ⓑ Ⓒ Ⓓ
4. Ⓐ Ⓑ Ⓒ Ⓓ
5. Ⓐ Ⓑ Ⓒ Ⓓ
6. Ⓐ Ⓑ Ⓒ Ⓓ
7. Ⓐ Ⓑ Ⓒ Ⓓ
8. Ⓐ Ⓑ Ⓒ Ⓓ
9. Ⓐ Ⓑ Ⓒ Ⓓ
10. Ⓐ Ⓑ Ⓒ Ⓓ
11. Ⓐ Ⓑ Ⓒ Ⓓ
12. Ⓐ Ⓑ Ⓒ Ⓓ
13. Ⓐ Ⓑ Ⓒ Ⓓ
14. Ⓐ Ⓑ Ⓒ Ⓓ
15. Ⓐ Ⓑ Ⓒ Ⓓ
16. Ⓐ Ⓑ Ⓒ Ⓓ
17. Ⓐ Ⓑ Ⓒ Ⓓ

18. Ⓐ Ⓑ Ⓒ Ⓓ
19. Ⓐ Ⓑ Ⓒ Ⓓ
20. Ⓐ Ⓑ Ⓒ Ⓓ
21. Ⓐ Ⓑ Ⓒ Ⓓ
22. Ⓐ Ⓑ Ⓒ Ⓓ
23. Ⓐ Ⓑ Ⓒ Ⓓ
24. Ⓐ Ⓑ Ⓒ Ⓓ
25. Ⓐ Ⓑ Ⓒ Ⓓ
26. Ⓐ Ⓑ Ⓒ Ⓓ
27. Ⓐ Ⓑ Ⓒ Ⓓ
28. Ⓐ Ⓑ Ⓒ Ⓓ
29. Ⓐ Ⓑ Ⓒ Ⓓ
30. Ⓐ Ⓑ Ⓒ Ⓓ
31. Ⓐ Ⓑ Ⓒ Ⓓ
32. Ⓐ Ⓑ Ⓒ Ⓓ
33. Ⓐ Ⓑ Ⓒ Ⓓ
34. Ⓐ Ⓑ Ⓒ Ⓓ

35. Ⓐ Ⓑ Ⓒ Ⓓ
36. Ⓐ Ⓑ Ⓒ Ⓓ
37. Ⓐ Ⓑ Ⓒ Ⓓ
38. Ⓐ Ⓑ Ⓒ Ⓓ
39. Ⓐ Ⓑ Ⓒ Ⓓ
40. Ⓐ Ⓑ Ⓒ Ⓓ
41. Ⓐ Ⓑ Ⓒ Ⓓ
42. Ⓐ Ⓑ Ⓒ Ⓓ
43. Ⓐ Ⓑ Ⓒ Ⓓ
44. Ⓐ Ⓑ Ⓒ Ⓓ
45. Ⓐ Ⓑ Ⓒ Ⓓ
46. Ⓐ Ⓑ Ⓒ Ⓓ
47. Ⓐ Ⓑ Ⓒ Ⓓ
48. Ⓐ Ⓑ Ⓒ Ⓓ
49. Ⓐ Ⓑ Ⓒ Ⓓ
50. Ⓐ Ⓑ Ⓒ Ⓓ
51. Ⓐ Ⓑ Ⓒ Ⓓ

52. Ⓐ Ⓑ Ⓒ Ⓓ
53. Ⓐ Ⓑ Ⓒ Ⓓ
54. Ⓐ Ⓑ Ⓒ Ⓓ
55. Ⓐ Ⓑ Ⓒ Ⓓ
56. Ⓐ Ⓑ Ⓒ Ⓓ
57. Ⓐ Ⓑ Ⓒ Ⓓ
58. Ⓐ Ⓑ Ⓒ Ⓓ
59. Ⓐ Ⓑ Ⓒ Ⓓ
60. Ⓐ Ⓑ Ⓒ Ⓓ
61. Ⓐ Ⓑ Ⓒ Ⓓ
62. Ⓐ Ⓑ Ⓒ Ⓓ
63. Ⓐ Ⓑ Ⓒ Ⓓ
64. Ⓐ Ⓑ Ⓒ Ⓓ
65. Ⓐ Ⓑ Ⓒ Ⓓ
66. Ⓐ Ⓑ Ⓒ Ⓓ
67. Ⓐ Ⓑ Ⓒ Ⓓ

Chapter 5

PRACTICE QUESTIONS— LAST

> *Directions:* Each question or incomplete statement is followed by four answer choices. For each question, decide which answer or completion is best and blacken the letter of your choice on the answer sheet.

1. Which of the following is NOT a myth?

   (A) Vitamins give you "pep" and "energy."
   (B) Timing of vitamin intake is crucial.
   (C) Vitamin C protects against the common cold.
   (D) Synthetic vitamins, manufactured in the laboratory, are identical to natural vitamins in their effect on the body.

2. The unit of electrical energy most commonly associated with the use of electrical appliances is the

   (A) horsepower.
   (B) watt.
   (C) kilowatt-hour.
   (D) amp.

3. Which of the following is a high-fiber food?

   (A) Ice cream
   (B) White rice
   (C) Pizza
   (D) Brown rice

4. The introduction of solid food to a baby's diet is normally recommended at the age of

   (A) 1–3 months.
   (B) 2–4 months.
   (C) 4–6 months.
   (D) 6–8 months.

5. Which of the following has the greatest number of calories?

   (A) Four celery sticks
   (B) A small apple
   (C) A large green pepper
   (D) Ten mushrooms

6. If 3 teaspoons = 1 tablespoon

   16 tablespoons = 1 cup

   2 cups = 1 pint

   then $\frac{1}{2}$ pint is equivalent to how many teaspoons?

   (A) $10\frac{1}{2}$
   (B) 12
   (C) 21
   (D) 48

7. All the following are faucet components EXCEPT

   (A) stem.
   (B) O-ring.
   (C) escutcheon.
   (D) float ball.

Questions 8 and 9 are based on the following bill:

Valley Water Company INCORPORATED
SW 360 West End Road ● Redwood, New York 10994

BILLING DATE		SERVICE ADDRESS		
JUN 03		15 JONES AVE		

METER NUMBER	FOR THE PERIOD FROM	TO	NO OF DAYS IN PERIOD	RATE CODE	METER READINGS PREVIOUS	PRESENT	CONSUMPTION IN 100 CU. FT.	BILLING CODE	AMOUNT
05445074	0221	0331	38		1355	1364	9		
30669921	0331	0522	52		0000	0022	22		
					SUMMER RATE				31.19
					WINTER RATE				62.71

BUDGET PAYMENT PLAN	
COST FOR WATER	BALANCE IN PLAN
CONSUMED THIS PERIOD	AFTER PAYMENT OF AMOUNT DUE

ONE HUNDRED CUBIC FEET EQUALS 748 GALLONS. YOUR CONSUMPTION FOR THE CURRENT BILLING PERIOD WAS 23,188 GALLONS.

AMOUNT DUE **$93.90**

PAYABLE ON OR BEFORE JUN 20 86

8. Based on this bill, how many gallons of water were used from February 21 to March 31?

(A) 1364 gallons
(B) 6732 gallons
(C) 16456 gallons
(D) 28424 gallons

9. How much does 100 cubic feet of water cost in the winter, given the fact that the winter rate ends on March 31?

(A) $1.42
(B) $1.46
(C) $3.02
(D) $6.97

10. Do not use lightweight plastic containers such as margarine tubs in a microwave because they

(A) reflect the microwaves, causing sparks.
(B) inhibit the cooking process.
(C) melt.
(D) burn the corners of the heated item.

11. Local authorities are most likely to receive the greatest part of their revenues from

(A) sales taxes.
(B) property taxes.
(C) payroll taxes.
(D) personal income taxes.

12. How many square yards of carpet are required to completely cover the floor of a 9-by-12-foot room?

(A) 6 sq. yards
(B) 12 sq. yards
(C) 27 sq. yards
(D) 54 sq. yards

13. It is recommended that each of the following not be frozen EXCEPT

(A) margarine.
(B) hard-cooked eggs.
(C) mayonnaise.
(D) mashed potatoes.

14. The sentence that is NOT true with respect to preventing or retarding mildew growth is:

(A) Avoid putting away any clothing or material items that are wet.
(B) Poorly lighted areas help prevent growth and can even kill the mildew.
(C) Disinfectant can slow or stop growth.
(D) Silica gel is effective against mildew growth.

15. The tool used to locate a point directly below a ceiling hook is a

(A) plumb bob.
(B) line level.
(C) transit.
(D) drop gauge.

16. A recession may be best described as

    (A) a limited period when unemployment rises and business activity slows down.
    (B) a limited period of rising prices, increased industrial output, and failing wages.
    (C) the extended aftermath of a long depression.
    (D) a sudden and acute rise in unemployment, business activity, and industrial output.

17. In a sample survey, questions are asked of a group of people who

    (A) volunteer to participate in the sample.
    (B) are able to understand the goals of the researcher.
    (C) are carefully selected to be representative of a larger group.
    (D) are familiar with statistical techniques.

18. The short form of the 1980 census asked questions on all of the following EXCEPT

    (A) whether a person was of Spanish/ Hispanic origin or descent.
    (B) whether a person was married.
    (C) whether a home had complete indoor plumbing.
    (D) whether a person was heterosexual.

19. In a well-known experiment, psychologists frustrated young children by placing a wire fence between the children and a pile of toys. When finally allowed to play with the toys, the children smashed and destroyed them. This reaction is an example of

    (A) displaced aggression.
    (B) absence of aggression.
    (C) dormant aggression.
    (D) rational aggression.

20. A convertible mortgage is which of the following?

    (A) An adjustable-rate mortgage that, at the buyer's option, can be converted to a fixed-rate loan
    (B) A fixed-rate mortgage that, at the buyer's option, can be converted to an adjustable-rate loan

    (C) A fixed-rate mortgage that, at the lender's option, can be converted to an adjustable-rate loan
    (D) An adjustable-rate mortgage that, at the lender's option, can be converted to a fixed-rate loan

21. The federal agency that insures deposits in savings and loan associations and savings banks is

    (A) FNMA.
    (B) FHA.
    (C) FSB.
    (D) FSLIC.

22. Which instrument is specially designed for fixed-income and retiree homeowners who have little or no mortgage debt, offering them the ability to receive monthly payments to supplement income while still retaining their homes?

    (A) Reverse-annuity mortgage
    (B) Conventional mortgage
    (C) Balloon mortgage
    (D) Variable-rate mortgage

23. All of the following draw funds from a deposit account EXCEPT

    (A) ATM card.
    (B) asset card.
    (C) credit card.
    (D) debit card.

24. Insurance that extends the liability coverage beyond the underlying limits for auto and home, usually up to $1 million, is called

    (A) whole-life coverage.
    (B) umbrella coverage.
    (C) over-insured coverage.
    (D) accidental coverage.

25. This type of insurance has no savings or investment component, is relatively inexpensive pure insurance for young people, and gives coverage for a defined number of years before it must be renewed. Its premiums increase with age.

    (A) Whole life
    (B) Straight life
    (C) Limited-payment life
    (D) Term

Questions 26 and 27 refer to the following map:

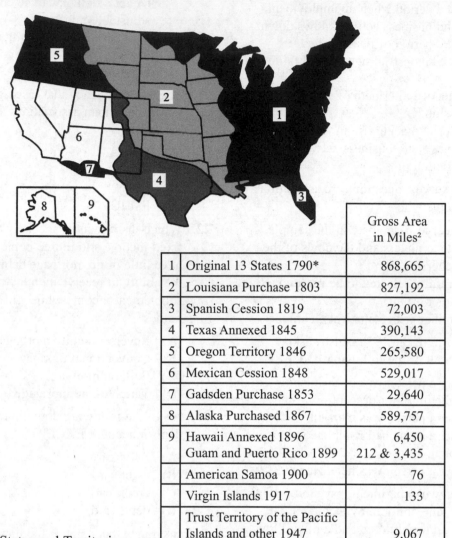

		Gross Area in Miles²
1	Original 13 States 1790*	868,665
2	Louisiana Purchase 1803	827,192
3	Spanish Cession 1819	72,003
4	Texas Annexed 1845	390,143
5	Oregon Territory 1846	265,580
6	Mexican Cession 1848	529,017
7	Gadsden Purchase 1853	29,640
8	Alaska Purchased 1867	589,757
9	Hawaii Annexed 1896 Guam and Puerto Rico 1899	6,450 212 & 3,435
	American Samoa 1900	76
	Virgin Islands 1917	133
	Trust Territory of the Pacific Islands and other 1947	9,067

*Original 13 States and Territories

26. Which of the following represents the largest acquisition of land?

(A) Texas Annexation
(B) Spanish Cession
(C) Oregon Territory
(D) Louisiana Purchase

27. Which of the following represents the last addition to the contiguous United States?

(A) Alaska Purchase
(B) Gadsden Purchase
(C) Hawaii Annexation
(D) Texas Annexation

28. What aspect of constitutional law did Hamilton and Jefferson interpret differently when arguing over the constitutionality of the First National Bank?

(A) The extent of executive powers in Article II
(B) The elastic clause in Article I
(C) The system of checks and balances
(D) The guarantee of rights in the First Amendment

29. "We maintain that no compensation should be given to the planters emancipating their slaves because it would be a surrender of the great fundamental principle that man cannot hold property in man; because slavery is a crime, and therefore it is not an article to be sold . . . freeing the slaves is not depriving [the owner] of property, but restoring it to the right owner; it is not wronging the master, but righting the slave—restoring him to himself."

This statement expresses the views on emancipation held by

(A) colonization societies in the 1820s.
(B) the Democratic Party in 1860.
(C) an antislavery society in the 1830s.
(D) Jefferson in 1800.

30. The term *helot* refers to a(n)

(A) Spartan slave.
(B) Athenian ruler.
(C) Roman legislator.
(D) Phoenician workman.

31. The sex ratio of a given population is the

(A) number of men per 100 women.
(B) number of women per 100 men.
(C) number of children born per every 100 women.
(D) biological maximum number of births.

32. The theory that "bad money drives out good money" is known as

(A) Say's law.
(B) Gresham's law.
(C) Pareto's law.
(D) Parkinson's law.

U.S. FAMILIES BY INCOME LEVEL (FICTITIOUS)

Income Level	Millions of Families	% of Families
Under $5,000	7.0	14.3
Between $5,000 and $10,000	6.8	13.9
Between $10,000 and $15,000	8.7	17.8
Between $15,000 and $20,000	11.9	24.4
Between $20,000 and $25,000	10.0	20.4
$25,000 or over	4.5	9.2
	48.9	100%

33. The previous table illustrates

(A) disposable personal income.
(B) real income.
(C) functional distribution of wages.
(D) personal income distribution.

34. Put the following events in Chinese history into chronological order:

I.   The Opium War
II. The Boxer Rebellion
III. The Long March
IV. The Kuomintang

(A) I, II, III, IV
(B) II, I, III, IV
(C) II, I, IV, III
(D) I, II, IV, III

35. Which of the following statements about Congress is incorrect?

(A) Members of the House of Representatives are elected every two years.
(B) The Speaker of the House is elected by a vote of his or her peers.
(C) No congressional officers are mentioned in the Constitution.
(D) Congress has authority to declare war.

36. Which of the following purposes would be best served by a confiscatory tax?

    (A) Making home mortgages more difficult to obtain
    (B) Increasing consumption of a particular product
    (C) Discouraging the exports of raw materials
    (D) Implicitly cutting off consumption of a particular product

37. The function of a Congressional conference committee is to

    (A) judge the moral conduct of members of Congress.
    (B) determine the rules for congressional procedures.
    (C) iron out differences between House and Senate versions of bills.
    (D) present to the President bills that have been passed by both houses of Congress.

PERCENTAGE OF THE U.S. POPULATION IN URBAN AREAS 1790–1970

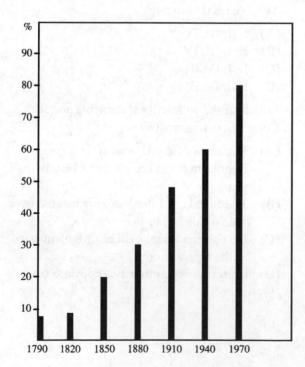

38. Using the information presented on the graph, it is possible to conclude all of the following EXCEPT

    (A) during the decade of the 1920s, the U.S. population was approximately half urban and half nonurban.
    (B) the population of urban areas tripled between 1790 and 1850.
    (C) the proportion of the population in nonurban areas has been decreasing ever since 1790.
    (D) the proportion of the population in urban areas approximately doubled between 1880 and 1940.

39. Which of the following statements most accurately describes the impact of the National Origins Act of 1924 on American immigration policy?

    (A) It ended immigration to the United States.
    (B) It provided immigration quotas favoring northern and western Europeans.
    (C) It introduced immigration quotas favoring southern and eastern Europeans.
    (D) It limited immigration to the United States by introducing literacy testing.

40. In the 1984 presidential primaries, all of the following were candidates on the Democratic ticket EXCEPT

    (A) Alan Cranston.
    (B) Jesse Jackson.
    (C) Claiborne Pell.
    (D) George McGovern.

41. Which is the correct chronological order of the following events?

    I. Franklin D. Roosevelt's second inauguration as President
    II. Congress rejects the "Court packing" bill
    III. Passage of the National Industrial Recovery Act
    IV. Establishment of the Reconstruction Finance Corporation

    (A) IV, III, I, II
    (B) I, III, IV, II
    (C) I, IV, III, II
    (D) III, IV, I, II

42. The *Liberator* was a periodical published and edited by

   (A) Tom Paine.
   (B) Frederick Douglass.
   (C) W. E. B. DuBois.
   (D) William Lloyd Garrison.

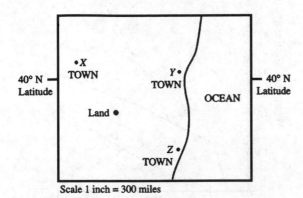

Scale 1 inch = 300 miles

43. The information shown above could most accurately support which of the following statements about climate?

   (A) *Z*-town will have a wetter climate than *Y*-town.
   (B) *Y*-town most likely will have a drier climate than *X*-town.
   (C) All three towns will have similar climates.
   (D) *X*-town is likely to have cooler winters than *Y*-town.

44. "Although these eighteenth-century monarchs enjoyed great reputations as 'enlightened' or 'benevolent' rulers, they modified only certain aspects of absolute monarchy and suffered little real loss of power."

   This statement best describes

   (A) Catherine the Great and Frederick the Great.
   (B) George II and George III.
   (C) Queen Anne and Nicholas I.
   (D) Philip II and Louis XV.

45. An economic conservative would be likely to advocate

   (A) increased government protection of the elderly.
   (B) the abolition of private property.
   (C) government control over natural resources.
   (D) decreased government intervention in the economy.

46. The Federal Reserve System was

   (A) a direct result of the Greenback movement.
   (B) a reform measure enacted by Congress in 1913.
   (C) the result of a Constitutional amendment in 1933.
   (D) an executive branch reform measure of 1935.

47. In which of the following presidential elections did the victor win the electoral college vote without winning the popular vote?

   I.   When Lincoln defeated Douglas
   II. When Hayes defeated Tilden
   III. When Harrison defeated Cleveland
   IV. When Nixon defeated Humphrey

   (A) I, II, III, and IV
   (B) II, III, and IV only
   (C) II and IV only
   (D) II and III only

Questions 48 and 49 refer to the following graph:

A family has a monthly income of $3,600. Its monthly expenditures are as shown in the following graph:

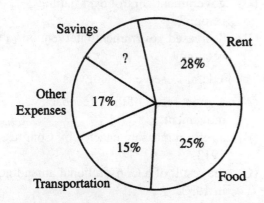

48. How much money does the family save in a year?

  (A) $6,000
  (B) $6,320
  (C) $6,480
  (D) $6,900

49. What is the cost of rent each month?

  (A) $612
  (B) $750
  (C) $1,000
  (D) $1,008

50. A part-time worker at a fast-food restaurant is paid $4.50 per hour. If he works 4 hours on Monday, 3 hours on Tuesday, 5 hours on Wednesday, 4 hours on Thursday, and 4 hours on Saturday, his income could be expressed algebraically as $x = $?

  (A) $(4 + 3 + 5 + 4 + 4) + 4.50$
  (B) $(4.50)(4 \times 3 \times 5 \times 4 \times 6)$
  (C) $(4.50)(24)$
  (D) $(4 + 3 + 5 + 4 + 4)(4.50)$

Questions 51–53 are based on the following graph:

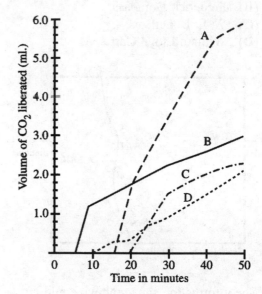

51. From which solution was CO_2 liberated first?

  (A) A
  (B) B
  (C) C
  (D) D

52. In how many minutes was the same volume of CO_2 liberated from solution A and solution B?

  (A) 1.1
  (B) 1.6
  (C) 6
  (D) 20

53. From which solution was the most CO_2 liberated at the end of 30 minutes?

  (A) A
  (B) B
  (C) C
  (D) D

54. A statement that is always true whether its premises are true or false is called a(n)

  (A) syllogism.
  (B) tautology.
  (C) equivalence.
  (D) paradox.

55. Two numbers are relatively prime if their greatest common divisor is 1. Which pair of numbers is relatively prime?

(A) 3 and 12
(B) 15 and 28
(C) 25 and 30
(D) 18 and 36

56. The sum of two coins of value x and three coins of value y is 50 cents. Which of the following equations can be used to express this relationship?

(A) $x + y = 5$
(B) $x + 3y = 50$
(C) $2x = 50 - 3y$
(D) $x = 50 - y$

57. 11 to the fourth power may be expressed correctly as:

(A) $11 + 11 + 11 + 11$
(B) $4(11)$
(C) $4 + 11$
(D) $(11)(11)(11)(11)$

58. $\dfrac{6,464}{32} = ?$

(A) 0.2
(B) 2
(C) 20
(D) 202

59. Express the integer 30 as a percent.

(A) 3,000%
(B) 300%
(C) 30%
(D) 3%

60. How many 25-passenger buses are required to transport 105 people?

(A) 3 buses
(B) 4 buses
(C) 5 buses
(D) 6 buses

61. At 30 miles per hour, a trip from Town A to Town B takes 6 hours. If the speed were doubled, how many hours would the trip take?

(A) 18 hours
(B) 12 hours
(C) 6 hours
(D) 3 hours

62. $21 (73 \times 26)$ is equivalent to all the following EXCEPT

(A) $21(73) \times 26$
(B) $21 \times (73)(26)$
(C) $(21)(73)(26)$
(D) $21(73) + 21(26)$

63. Simplify the equation: $5x + 5y + 5z = 5$

(A) $x + y + z = 1$
(B) $21x = 5$
(C) $5x + 11y + 5z = 1$
(D) $11x + 5y + 5z = 5$

64. What is the product of all the consecutive integers from -5 to $+5$?

(A) -120
(B) -15
(C) 0
(D) $+15$

65. What is the mode of the following numbers?

1, 2, 2, 3, 3, 3, 4, 4, 4, 4, 5, 5, 5, 5, 5

(A) 1
(B) 2
(C) 3
(D) 5

66. 10% of 13 is equivalent to all of the following EXCEPT

(A) $\left(\dfrac{10}{100}\right) \times 13$
(B) 2% of 5% of 13
(C) $10 \times \left(\dfrac{13}{100}\right)$
(D) 13% of 10

67. The scale of a map represents 12 miles as 1 inch. If the distance between two cities on the map is 30 inches, what is the actual distance, in miles, between the cities?

(A) 2.5
(B) 40
(C) 360
(D) 400

ANSWER KEY

1. D	24. D	46. B
2. C	25. D	47. D
3. D	26. D	48. C
4. C	27. B	49. D
5. B	28. B	50. D
6. D	29. D	51. B
7. D	30. A	52. D
8. B	31. A	53. A
9. D	32. B	54. B
10. C	33. D	55. B
11. B	34. D	56. C
12. B	35. C	57. D
13. D	36. D	58. D
14. B	37. C	59. A
15. A	38. B	60. C
16. A	39. B	61. D
17. C	40. C	62. D
18. D	41. A	63. A
19. A	42. D	64. C
20. A	43. D	65. D
21. D	44. A	66. B
22. A	45. D	67. C
23. B		

Part II
LAST PRACTICE TESTS

Answer Sheet for Chapter 6

LAST—PRACTICE TEST 1

1. Ⓐ Ⓑ Ⓒ Ⓓ   21. Ⓐ Ⓑ Ⓒ Ⓓ   41. Ⓐ Ⓑ Ⓒ Ⓓ   61. Ⓐ Ⓑ Ⓒ Ⓓ

2. Ⓐ Ⓑ Ⓒ Ⓓ   22. Ⓐ Ⓑ Ⓒ Ⓓ   42. Ⓐ Ⓑ Ⓒ Ⓓ   62. Ⓐ Ⓑ Ⓒ Ⓓ

3. Ⓐ Ⓑ Ⓒ Ⓓ   23. Ⓐ Ⓑ Ⓒ Ⓓ   43. Ⓐ Ⓑ Ⓒ Ⓓ   63. Ⓐ Ⓑ Ⓒ Ⓓ

4. Ⓐ Ⓑ Ⓒ Ⓓ   24. Ⓐ Ⓑ Ⓒ Ⓓ   44. Ⓐ Ⓑ Ⓒ Ⓓ   64. Ⓐ Ⓑ Ⓒ Ⓓ

5. Ⓐ Ⓑ Ⓒ Ⓓ   25. Ⓐ Ⓑ Ⓒ Ⓓ   45. Ⓐ Ⓑ Ⓒ Ⓓ   65. Ⓐ Ⓑ Ⓒ Ⓓ

6. Ⓐ Ⓑ Ⓒ Ⓓ   26. Ⓐ Ⓑ Ⓒ Ⓓ   46. Ⓐ Ⓑ Ⓒ Ⓓ   66. Ⓐ Ⓑ Ⓒ Ⓓ

7. Ⓐ Ⓑ Ⓒ Ⓓ   27. Ⓐ Ⓑ Ⓒ Ⓓ   47. Ⓐ Ⓑ Ⓒ Ⓓ   67. Ⓐ Ⓑ Ⓒ Ⓓ

8. Ⓐ Ⓑ Ⓒ Ⓓ   28. Ⓐ Ⓑ Ⓒ Ⓓ   48. Ⓐ Ⓑ Ⓒ Ⓓ   68. Ⓐ Ⓑ Ⓒ Ⓓ

9. Ⓐ Ⓑ Ⓒ Ⓓ   29. Ⓐ Ⓑ Ⓒ Ⓓ   49. Ⓐ Ⓑ Ⓒ Ⓓ   69. Ⓐ Ⓑ Ⓒ Ⓓ

10. Ⓐ Ⓑ Ⓒ Ⓓ   30. Ⓐ Ⓑ Ⓒ Ⓓ   50. Ⓐ Ⓑ Ⓒ Ⓓ   70. Ⓐ Ⓑ Ⓒ Ⓓ

11. Ⓐ Ⓑ Ⓒ Ⓓ   31. Ⓐ Ⓑ Ⓒ Ⓓ   51. Ⓐ Ⓑ Ⓒ Ⓓ   71. Ⓐ Ⓑ Ⓒ Ⓓ

12. Ⓐ Ⓑ Ⓒ Ⓓ   32. Ⓐ Ⓑ Ⓒ Ⓓ   52. Ⓐ Ⓑ Ⓒ Ⓓ   72. Ⓐ Ⓑ Ⓒ Ⓓ

13. Ⓐ Ⓑ Ⓒ Ⓓ   33. Ⓐ Ⓑ Ⓒ Ⓓ   53. Ⓐ Ⓑ Ⓒ Ⓓ   73. Ⓐ Ⓑ Ⓒ Ⓓ

14. Ⓐ Ⓑ Ⓒ Ⓓ   34. Ⓐ Ⓑ Ⓒ Ⓓ   54. Ⓐ Ⓑ Ⓒ Ⓓ   74. Ⓐ Ⓑ Ⓒ Ⓓ

15. Ⓐ Ⓑ Ⓒ Ⓓ   35. Ⓐ Ⓑ Ⓒ Ⓓ   55. Ⓐ Ⓑ Ⓒ Ⓓ   75. Ⓐ Ⓑ Ⓒ Ⓓ

16. Ⓐ Ⓑ Ⓒ Ⓓ   36. Ⓐ Ⓑ Ⓒ Ⓓ   56. Ⓐ Ⓑ Ⓒ Ⓓ   76. Ⓐ Ⓑ Ⓒ Ⓓ

17. Ⓐ Ⓑ Ⓒ Ⓓ   37. Ⓐ Ⓑ Ⓒ Ⓓ   57. Ⓐ Ⓑ Ⓒ Ⓓ   77. Ⓐ Ⓑ Ⓒ Ⓓ

18. Ⓐ Ⓑ Ⓒ Ⓓ   38. Ⓐ Ⓑ Ⓒ Ⓓ   58. Ⓐ Ⓑ Ⓒ Ⓓ   78. Ⓐ Ⓑ Ⓒ Ⓓ

19. Ⓐ Ⓑ Ⓒ Ⓓ   39. Ⓐ Ⓑ Ⓒ Ⓓ   59. Ⓐ Ⓑ Ⓒ Ⓓ   79. Ⓐ Ⓑ Ⓒ Ⓓ

20. Ⓐ Ⓑ Ⓒ Ⓓ   40. Ⓐ Ⓑ Ⓒ Ⓓ   60. Ⓐ Ⓑ Ⓒ Ⓓ   80. Ⓐ Ⓑ Ⓒ Ⓓ

Chapter 6

LAST—PRACTICE TEST 1

The Liberal Arts and Sciences Test (LAST) tests knowledge and skills in the following areas:

    I. Scientific and mathematical processes

   II. History and social sciences

  III. Humanities and artistic expression

  IV. Communication skills

   V. Written expression and analysis

The test is divided into 80 multiple-choice questions on topics I through IV. Each test question has four choices. Scoring is based upon the number of correct answers only.

Topic V, Written Expression and Analysis, requires you to write a cogent essay following the rules of proper grammar, diction, and punctuation on an assigned topic. The essay should be between 300 and 600 words. The grade is based on your ability to express and support an opinion on the topic that is given in correct American English.

Two educators score each essay according to specific scoring procedures. The essay is graded holistically; that is, the reader forms a judgment about the essay and assigns a score from 0 (the lowest score) to 3 (the highest score).

TIME: 4 Hours—80 Questions

> *Directions:* Each statement or passage in this test is followed by one or more questions. Read each statement or passage, and then answer the accompanying questions, basing your answer on what is stated or implied in the passage. Each item on this test has four choices following the question. Choose the best response, and blacken the letter of your answer choice on the answer sheet.

1. "Resolved that whoever shall be aiding, or assisting, in the landing or carting of such tea, from any ship, or vessel, or shall hire any house . . . whatsoever, to deposit the tea, subject to a duty as aforesaid, he shall be deemed an enemy to the liberties of America. . . . Whoever shall transgress any of these resolutions, we will not deal with, or employ, or have any connection with him."

This statement is most likely to have been made by

(A) Parliament in the Tea Act of 1773.
(B) Joseph Galloway in the "Plan of Union."
(C) The Sons of Liberty in a resolution.
(D) Lord North in the "Intolerable Acts."

2. CIVIL WAR CASUALTIES

	Union	Confederacy
Total serving in armed forces	1,556,678	1,082,119
Killed in battle or died from wounds	110,070	94,000
Died from illness	249,458	164,000
Wounded	275,175	100,000

Based on the chart of Civil War casualties, all the statements about Civil War soldiers are true EXCEPT

(A) the number who died from illness, in both the Union and Confederate armies, exceeded the number who were killed in battle or died from wounds.

(B) the number of deaths in both the Union and Confederate armies exceeded the number of wounded.

(C) the total number of deaths in the Union Army exceeded the total number of deaths in the Confederate Army.

(D) the total number of dead and wounded in the Union Army was more than double the total number of dead and wounded in the Confederate Army.

Questions 3 and 4 refer to the following graph:

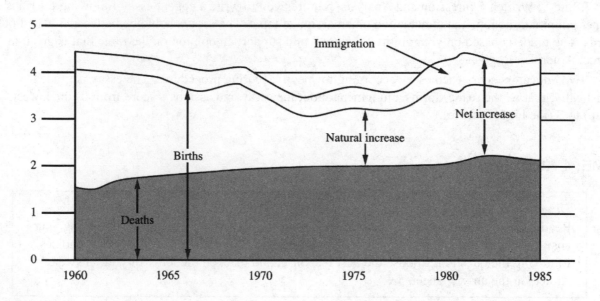

3. According to this graph, which of the following outcomes could be supported in describing the U.S. population between 1960 and 1985?

(A) The birth rate declined sharply in the 1970s.

(B) Immigration decreased considerably in the 1980s.

(C) The rate of population growth will continue to decline.

(D) The birth rate became the highest ever recorded.

4. Based on the information recorded in the graph, what portion of the net population increase in the 1980s was due to immigration?

(A) 4 percent
(B) 12 percent
(C) 16 percent
(D) 25 percent

　　　　　　　　Prepare for the NYSTCE: LAST and ATS-W

5. "It's official! Chattering Teddy Bears sold by competitive companies are now outselling virtually every other toy in America. Demand is so great that even models introduced one year ago still sell for higher prices in the stores! But we are able to offer these adorable toys at far, far less, through this special introductory mail offer."

This type of advertising is called
(A) meaningless claim.
(B) misrepresentation.
(C) bait and switch.
(D) referral sales scheme.

6. Lyndon B. Johnson followed which president's precedent when he created "The Great Society," in which government took a more active role in the affairs of the country?

(A) Woodrow Wilson
(B) John F. Kennedy
(C) Herbert Hoover
(D) Franklin D. Roosevelt

7. Which of the following is NOT a weapon of a labor union?

(A) The union shop
(B) The strike
(C) The lockout
(D) The boycott

8. Which medium most regularly presents opinions and interpretations of the news?

(A) National television news programs
(B) Local television news program
(C) Newspaper editorial pages
(D) Teletype news agency reports

9. Which of the following best defines *internal migration*?

(A) The movement of any large group of people, as in the Mongol invasion of Europe
(B) Migration necessitated by natural disaster, such as the movement of residents of a flooded area to a safe area
(C) The movement of persons within a specific country, such as the move of a family from Chicago to New York
(D) The involuntary movement of a large group of people, such as the movement of captured slaves from Africa to the Americas

10. The Manhattan Project was a

(A) secret committee investigating security clearances during the early 1950s.
(B) pressure group seeking support for urban renewal projects.
(C) group of physicists working at Los Alamos under J. Robert Oppenheimer.
(D) presidential advisory commission concerned with rehabilitation of the victims of Hiroshima and Nagasaki.

Questions 11 and 12 are based on the following chart:

Year	Total	Urban Population United States Population	% of Total Population	Rural Population Total	% of Total Population
1790	3,929,000	202,000	5%	3,728,000	95%
1820	9,618,000	693,000	7%	8,945,000	93%
1850	23,261,000	3,544,000	15%	19,648,000	85%
1880	50,262,000	14,130,000	28%	36,026,000	72%
1910	92,407,000	41,999,000	45%	49,973,000	55%
1940	132,122,000	74,424,000	56%	57,245,000	44%
1970	203,810,000	149,325,000	73%	54,054,000	27%

11. A net loss in rural population is evident in which of the following periods?

    (A) 1790–1820
    (B) 1820–1850
    (C) 1880–1910
    (D) 1940–1970

12. Which of the following statements is best supported by the data in the chart on the previous page?

    (A) The number of people living in rural areas in 1970 was less than the number living in rural areas in 1880.
    (B) The percentage of the total population living in rural areas increased during the 1990s.
    (C) The number of people living in urban areas declined during the nineteenth century.
    (D) A majority of the people were living in urban areas by 1940.

13. Which explanation best accounts for the change in urban population during the late 1800s and early 1900s?

    (A) Decrease in farm production
    (B) Increase in industrial jobs
    (C) Expansion of immigration quotas
    (D) Improvements in transportation

14. Which of the following is incorrectly paired with the political cause or principle he espoused?

    (A) Douglas—popular sovereignty
    (B) Calhoun—state sovereignty
    (C) Lincoln—the nation undivided
    (D) Jackson—the establishment of the Second U.S. Bank

15. "This system will provide pensions as well as widows' and orphans' benefits. It will help the states provide public health services and care for the crippled and blind. It will relieve economic distress, boost the economy, and give old-age insurance to most employees."

    The system described in the statement is the
    (A) Medicare system.
    (B) Social Security system.
    (C) Fire Enterprise system.
    (D) negative income tax.

16. When Fidel Castro gained control of Cuba in 1959, what kind of government did he overthrow?

    (A) Monarchy
    (B) Democracy
    (C) Dictatorship
    (D) Communism

LIFE EXPECTANCY IN THE UNITED STATES IN 2000

Classification	Life Expectancy in Years
Total population	75.4
Total White	74.0
White Male	72.6
White Female	75.3
Total Nonwhite	72.4
Nonwhite Male	68.4
Nonwhite Female	76.3

17. On the basis of the above table, it is possible to conclude all of the following EXCEPT

    (A) in 2000, the average life expectancy of white people was about two years longer than that of nonwhite people.
    (B) in 2000, female life expectancies exceeded male life expectancies in both white and nonwhite groups.
    (C) in 2000, white males could expect to live longer than nonwhite males.
    (D) in 2000, socioeconomic factors had an impact on life expectancy.

Questions 18 and 19 refer to the following paragraph:

Today there are more than 200 reservations in the United States established for various tribes of Native Americans through special treaties with the federal government. The largest is the Navajo reservation in Arizona, New Mexico, and Utah. Its 15 million acres make it about the size of New England. Many of the 1.4 million Native Americans have moved to cities, where they have sought to maintain at least a semblance of tribal customs and organization in their new surroundings. Other groups, particularly in the Southwest, still maintain many elements of their ancient heritage.

Prepare for the NYSTCE: LAST and ATS-W

18. According to this passage, which of the following is true about reservations?

    (A) Only the Navajos live on reservations.
    (B) All Native Americans live on reservations.
    (C) The Navajo reservation is in New England.
    (D) The largest reservation is in Arizona, New Mexico, and Utah.

19. The reservations were established

    (A) through treaties between the federal government and various tribes.
    (B) to keep all Native Americans in one place.
    (C) to make Native Americans conform to the "ways of white people".
    (D) through grants by the various state governments.

Slave Population as Percentage of Total Black Population, 1790–1860

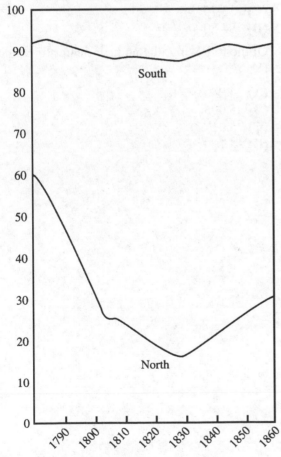

20. The graph supports all of the following conclusions EXCEPT

    (A) from 1790 to 1860, free blacks remained a small percentage of the total black population in the South.
    (B) from 1790 to 1860, the number of slaves in the South remained the same.
    (C) the percentage of slaves in the Northern black population decreased until 1830 and then began to rise.
    (D) the slave population of the North, from 1790 to 1860, never diminished to fewer than ten percent of the total Northern black population.

Questions 21–23 refer to the following maps:

North America in 1689

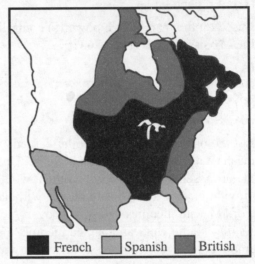

North America in 1763

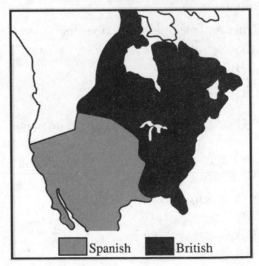

21. Which of the following choices best explains the changes between the two maps?

   (A) The French defeated the British in the French and Indian Wars, 1754–1763.

   (B) The Spanish diverted their forces to do battle in Mexico.

   (C) The British made the colonies bear their part in the cost of maintaining the British Empire.

   (D) The Treaty of France eliminated France as a colonial power in North America.

22. According to the map, which power controlled Louisiana in 1689?

   (A) France

   (B) England and France

   (C) Spain

   (D) England

23. Based on the map, which power(s) controlled the Mississippi River in 1763?

   (A) Spain

   (B) England

   (C) Spain and England

   (D) Spain and France

24. "At the present time, every dollar earned means a dollar lost in welfare benefits. Under the proposed system, the government would provide income subsidies to people without work or with incomes below the poverty level. As they found work and gained income, the amounts received from the government would be gradually reduced. This would provide an incentive for the subsidized poor to find employment."

This statement best describes the

   (A) profit motive.

   (B) welfare system.

   (C) socialist system.

   (D) negative income tax.

25. "Their legislative system would be much better if it were more like ours," commented an English diplomat in an African nation. This statement could be best described as

   (A) comparative.

   (B) ethnological.

   (C) ethnocentric.

   (D) competitive.

26. The coordinates of point P on the graph are:

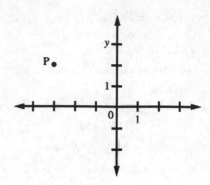

   (A) $(2, -3)$

   (B) $(-3, 2)$

   (C) $(-2, 3)$

   (D) $(3, -2)$

27. The cost of 30 sandwich rolls at $1.50 per dozen is:

   (A) $3

   (B) $3.45

   (C) $3.75

   (D) $4.50

28. Of the following, the number nearest in value to 5 is:

   (A) 4.985

   (B) 5.005

   (C) 5.01

   (D) 5.1

Questions 29 and 30 refer to the following picture graph:

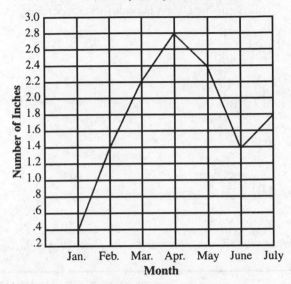

RAINFALL IN DAMP CITY
January–July, 1998

The picture graph represents how many men (male figures), women (female figures), boys (circles), and girls (triangles) visited a museum one particular week. Each figure represents 100.

29. Over the five-day period, the ratio of men visitors to women visitors was:

(A) 3:4
(B) 4:3
(C) 3:7
(D) 4:7

30. The total number of visitors to the museum during the week was:

(A) 3,000
(B) 2,200
(C) 1,400
(D) 300

31. If a 5-pound mixture of nuts contains 2 pounds of cashews and the rest peanuts, what percent of the mixture is peanuts?

(A) 20 percent
(B) 30 percent
(C) 40 percent
(D) 60 percent

32. The product of .010 and .001 is:

(A) .01100
(B) .10100
(C) .00001
(D) .01000

33. The information given in the graph supports all of the following statements EXCEPT

(A) the rainfall in April was twice the rainfall in February.
(B) June had greater rainfall than February.
(C) the month with the least rainfall was January.
(D) March had .4 inches greater rainfall than July.

34. If 1 ounce is approximately equal to 28 grams, then the number of grams in a 1-pound box of candy is most nearly

(A) 250 grams.
(B) 350 grams.
(C) 450 grams.
(D) 550 grams.

35. In 2 hours, the minute hand of a clock rotates through an angle of

(A) 90 degrees.
(B) 180 degrees.
(C) 360 degrees.
(D) 720 degrees.

36. A recent survey shows that .25 percent of smokers find it easy to stop. Which of the following fractions is equal to .25 percent?

(A) $\dfrac{1}{400}$

(B) $\dfrac{1}{40}$

(C) $\dfrac{1}{4}$

(D) $\dfrac{5}{2}$

Questions 37 and 38 refer to the following data:

ATTENDANCE AT SPORTS EVENTS (IN MILLIONS)								
Activity	**1980**	**1985**	**1990**	**1994**	**1995**	**1996**	**1997**	**1998**
Baseball, major leagues:								
Regular season	19.9	22.4	28.7	30.0	29.8	31.3	38.7	40.6
American League	9.2	8.9	12.1	13.0	13.2	14.7	19.6	20.5
National League	10.7	13.6	16.7	17.0	16.6	16.7	19.1	20.1
Basketball, professional, NBA	2.0	2.8	5.1	6.9	7.9	8.5	11.0	10.9
Football, collegiate	20.4	24.7	29.5	31.2	31.7	32.0	32.9	34.3
Football, professional, NFL	3.2	4.7	10.0	10.7	10.7	11.6	11.6	13.4
Horseracing	46.9	62.9	69.7	74.9	78.7	79.3	76.0	76.0
Greyhound racing	7.9	10.9	2.7	16.3	17.5	19.0	20.0	20.1
Hockey, NHL	2.4	2.8	6.0	8.6	9.5	9.1	8.6	8.5

37. In which year did attendance at American League baseball games first exceed attendance at National League games?

(A) 1980
(B) 1990
(C) 1995
(D) 1997

38. Which sporting event was the most popular during 1985?

(A) Baseball
(B) Horseracing
(C) Football
(D) Hockey

39. The term *demographic transition* refers to the

(A) migration of a large number of people from a rural area to an urban area.
(B) migration of a large number of people from an urban area to a suburban area.
(C) movement of a large number of people into or out of a given area.
(D) model that describes population change over time.

40. The Napoleonic Code was a

(A) military strategy.
(B) style of politics.
(C) style of etiquette.
(D) legal system.

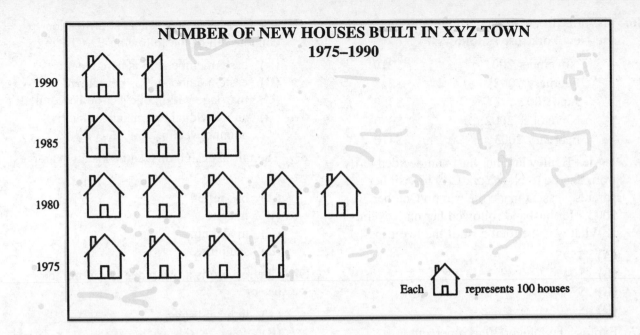

NUMBER OF NEW HOUSES BUILT IN XYZ TOWN
1975–1990

1990

1985

1980

1975

Each [house] represents 100 houses

41. According to the graph above, how many more new houses were built in 1980 than in 1985?

(A) 100
(B) 150
(C) 200
(D) 250

42. If $2x + y = 7$, what is the value of y when $x = 3$?

(A) 1
(B) 3
(C) 5
(D) 7

43. A shopper bought apples at 30 cents each and grapefruit at 50 cents each. If the shopper spent exactly $10, which of the following could NOT be the number of grapefruit purchased?

(A) 2
(B) 4
(C) 8
(D) 14

44. Which of the following shows the greatest to the least?

(A) $\dfrac{9}{16}, \dfrac{7}{10}, \dfrac{5}{8}, \dfrac{4}{5}$

(B) $\dfrac{9}{16}, \dfrac{5}{8}, \dfrac{7}{10}, \dfrac{4}{5}$

(C) $\dfrac{4}{5}, \dfrac{9}{16}, \dfrac{7}{10}, \dfrac{5}{8}$

(D) $\dfrac{4}{5}, \dfrac{7}{10}, \dfrac{5}{8}, \dfrac{9}{16}$

45. If a recipe for a cake calls for $2\dfrac{1}{2}$ cups of flour and Mary wishes to make three such cakes, the number of cups of flour she must use is:

(A) 5

(B) $6\dfrac{1}{2}$

(C) $7\dfrac{1}{2}$

(D) 9

46. The price of an airplane flight between Seattle and New York rose as follows:

November 2001	$210
February 2002	$245
June 2002	$350
November 2002	$390
February 2003	$410

Jessica Henley and her husband decided to fly from Seattle to New York City to visit her parents. Jessica made the trip on October 30, 2002. Her husband followed her on November 2. What was the total cost of the two trips?

(A) $595
(B) $645
(C) $700
(D) $740

47. Express the integer 30 as a percent.

(A) 3,000%
(B) 300%
(C) 30%
(D) 3%

48. How many 25-passenger buses are required to transport 105 people?

(A) 3 buses
(B) 4 buses
(C) 5 buses
(D) 6 buses

49. What is 75,389 rounded to the nearest hundred?

(A) 75,400
(B) 75,390
(C) 75,380
(D) 75,000

50. "The apparition of these faces in the crowd: Petals on a wet, black bough."

These lines may be described as
(A) blank verse.
(B) onomatopoeia.
(C) a triolet.
(D) a quatrain.

51. If a doctor describes a patient as dehydrated, the patient

(A) has a contagious disease.
(B) needs insulin.
(C) has just been inoculated.
(D) has lost a great deal of water.

52. The caste system of social stratification connotes all of the following EXCEPT

(A) caste membership is hereditary.
(B) caste membership is permanent.
(C) marriage within one's caste is required.
(D) an individual can change caste by gaining wealth.

53. The raised design on a cameo is an example of

(A) bas-relief.
(B) intaglio.
(C) modeling.
(D) sculpture.

54. Chiaroscuro is a technique involving the use of

(A) light and shade.
(B) color.
(C) pictorial illusion.
(D) geometric forms.

55. Ground water and surface water become polluted by

(A) runoff from pesticides used on gardens and farms.
(B) improper disposal of chemical wastes.
(C) deposit of untreated sewage into rivers and lakes.
(D) All of the above

56. What principle protects citizens from being punished twice for the same crime?

(A) Trial by jury
(B) Presentment
(C) Double jeopardy
(D) Self-incrimination

57. LED is an abbreviation for Light-Emitting Diode. LEDs are most frequently used in

(A) hand-held calculators.
(B) manual typewriters.
(C) diesel engines.
(D) cancer medication.

Questions 58 and 59 refer to the following line of poetry:

"Full fathom five thy father lies; Of his bones are coral made; Those are pearls that were his eyes: Nothing of him that doth fade. . . ."

58. The opening line employs the technique of

   (A) symbolism.
   (B) anthropomorphism.
   (C) metaphor.
   (D) alliteration.

59. The lines relate to which setting?

   (A) Desert
   (B) Mountain
   (C) Sea
   (D) Tropics

60. 6 is what percent of 3?

   (A) 50%
   (B) 100%
   (C) 150%
   (D) 200%

61. During which Western European cultural era was the painting to the right completed?

   (A) Baroque
   (B) Romantic
   (C) Classical
   (D) Renaissance

Questions 62–64 refer to the following poem:

(A) Between the dark and the daylight,
   When the night is beginning to lower,
   Comes a pause in the day's occupations,
   That is known as the Children's Hour.
(B) All are architects of Fate,
   Working in these walls of Time:
   Some with massive deeds and great.
   Some with ornaments of rhyme.
(C) 'Tis an old maxim in the schools,
   That flattery's the food of fools;
   Yet now and then your men of wit
   Will condescend to take a bit.
(D) He drew a circle that shut me out—Heretic,
   rebel, a thing to flout.
   But Love and I had the wit to win.
   We drew a circle that took him in.

62. Which stanza uses a metaphor?

63. Which stanza deals with the theme of belonging?

64. Which stanza utilizes irony to make a point?

65. The painting above embodies all of the following EXCEPT

(A) softly blended colors.
(B) large, simplified shapes and form.
(C) sharp, angular lines.
(D) fluid planes.

66. A short period of somewhat decreased business activity is known as a

(A) boom.
(B) depression.
(C) recession.
(D) crash.

Questions 67 and 68 refer to the following poem:

> When, in disgrace with fortune and men's eyes,
> I all alone beweep my outcast state,
> And trouble deaf heaven with my bootless cries,
> And look upon myself, and curse my fate . . .
> Yet in these thoughts myself almost despising,
> Haply I think on thee—and then my state,
> Like to the lark at break of day arising
> From sullen earth, sings hymns at heaven's gate;
> For thy sweet love remembered such wealth brings
> That then I scorn to change my state with kings.

67. The poet's mood changes when he

(A) thinks about his love.
(B) weeps about his state.
(C) curses his fate.
(D) changes his state with kings.

68. The poet states ". . . I scorn to change my state with kings" because he

(A) is afraid of the power.
(B) does not have the wealth of kings.
(C) looks down upon the monarchy.
(D) considers himself happier than kings.

Prepare for the NYSTCE: LAST and ATS-W

Questions 69 and 70 refer to the following lines of poetry:

> Where, like a pillow on a bed,
> A pregnant bank swelled up to rest
> The violet's reclining head,
> Sat we two, one another's best.

69. These lines employ the technique of

   (A) blank verse.

   (B) simile.

   (C) apostrophe.

   (D) onomatopoeia.

70. The rhyme scheme employed in these lines follows a pattern of

   (A) ABAB.

   (B) ABBA.

   (C) AABB.

   (D) ABCD.

71. Which of the following provides the best description of the painting by Claude Monet shown above?

   (A) Our position appears to be below the subject.

   (B) Colors are painted using flat, broad shapes.

   (C) The mood is dismal and dark.

   (D) The figure of the woman has refined details.

72. Which of the following is NOT an accurate description of the painting on the next page?

   (A) Obvious exaggeration of ornamentation on furnishings compared to time period

   (B) Typical form of art of its period: the portraiture of royalty and rulers

   (C) The subject for the painting is Napoleon

   (D) Correct detail rendering of period costume

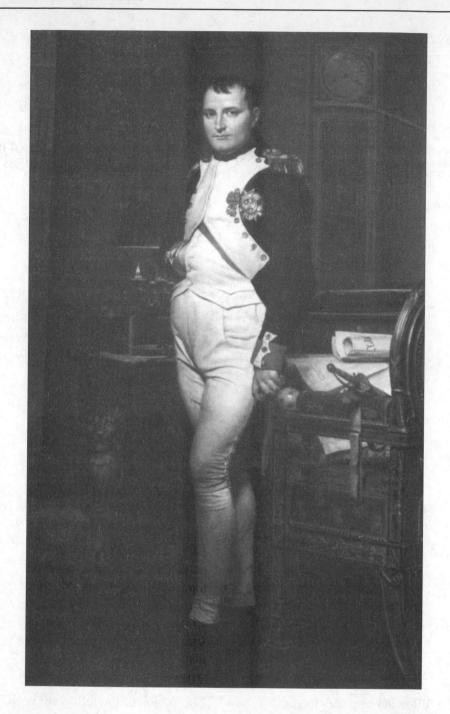

Prepare for the NYSTCE: LAST and ATS-W

Questions 73–75 refer to the following figures:

(A)

(B)

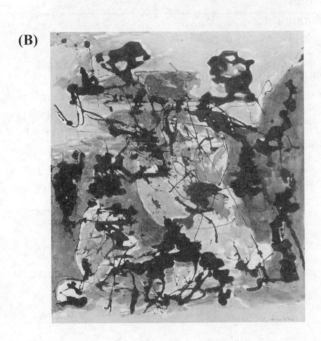

(C)

(D)

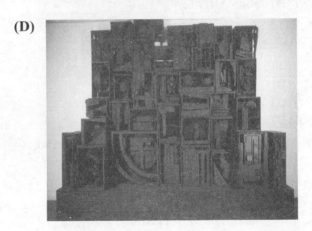

73. Which painting was painted in the impressionist style?

74. Which is an abstract expressionist painting?

75. Which is by Louise Nevelson?

76. "O where ha' you been, Lord Randal, my son?
    And where ha' you been, my handsome young man?"
    "I ha' been at the greenwood; mother, mak my bed soon.
    For I'm wearied wi' huntin', and fain wad lie down."

    The form of these lines is a(n)

    (A) ballad.
    (B) sonnet.
    (C) limerick.
    (D) epic.

Questions 77 and 78 refer to the following lines of poetry:

> so much depends
> upon a red wheel
> barrow glazed with rainwater
> beside the white chickens.

77. These lines were composed by

    (A) William Shakespeare.
    (B) Edgar A. Poe.
    (C) William Carlos Williams.
    (D) John Milton.

78. The main figure of speech employed in the poem is

    (A) an allusion.
    (B) a simile.
    (C) personification.
    (D) imagery.

79. Taking an examination is like baking bread. First you gather the ingredients, mix them, and let them rise. Then you bake the loaves and wait to see how they turn out.

    This paragraph suffers from

    (A) oversimplification.
    (B) a faulty comparison.
    (C) alliteration.
    (D) an omitted conclusion.

80. "The female child of 5 years reacts to her parents and other contacts from the framework of the oral stage, in which sexual feelings express themselves before going into the latency period," said the psychiatrist.

    "Oh, brother. If I wanted to hear that stuff, I would have read a book," the patient said.

    The patient criticizes the psychiatrist because his remarks are

    (A) detailed and circumstantial.
    (B) impolite and disrespectful.
    (C) general and illogical.
    (D) unfeeling and academic.

ESSAY

Now is the time when many older "senior" teachers will soon be retiring. A whole generation of well-educated teachers with many years of educational experience will eventually be part of our historical past. Some critics of the schools say that it's about time to let younger teachers with new ideas take the reins of our academic institutions. Other observers claim that the solid, leavening influence of the more experienced teachers is both necessary and helpful for our schools to meet the many needs of our students.

With which point of view do you agree? Do you think that schools would be better served with older teachers, or do they need the younger teachers' points of view? Write a clear, well-presented essay giving your opinion and the reasons for your opinion. You can continue on a separate piece of paper.

_____

_____

_____

_____

_____

_____

_____

_____

_____

_____

_____

_____

_____

_____

_____

_____

ANSWER KEY

1. C	15. B	29. A	42. A	55. D	68. D
2. D	16. C	30. A	43. B	56. C	69. B
3. A	17. D	31. D	44. D	57. A	70. A
4. D	18. D	32. C	45. C	58. D	71. A
5. A	19. A	33. B	46. D	59. C	72. A
6. D	20. B	34. C	47. A	60. D	73. A
7. C	21. D	35. D	48. C	61. D	74. B
8. C	22. A	36. A	49. A	62. B	75. D
9. C	23. C	37. D	50. A	63. B	76. A
10. C	24. D	38. B	51. D	64. D	77. C
11. D	25. C	39. D	52. D	65. C	78. D
12. D	26. B	40. D	53. A	66. C	79. B
13. B	27. C	41. C	54. A	67. A	80. D
14. D	28. B				

ANSWERS AND EXPLANATIONS

1. **The correct answer is (C).** The statement is an excerpt from a colonial resolution of opposition to the Tea Act of 1773. It was more likely to have been made by the Sons of Liberty than by Parliament, a British official, Galloway, or Paine.

2. **The correct answer is (D).** The total number of dead and wounded in the Union Army was not more than double the total number of dead and wounded in the Confederate Army. It was somewhat less than double.

3. **The correct answer is (A).** The line representing births takes a dip in the 1970s, with only a slight rise at the end of the decade. Therefore, choices (B), (C), and (D) are unsupported.

4. **The correct answer is (D).** About 75 percent of the net increase is represented as a natural increase on the chart. The remaining 25 percent is represented as net immigration.

5. **The correct answer is (A).** This is a meaningless claim. While the ad may seem to be an example of misrepresentation, there are no real facts here to be exaggerated. No prices are given in the advertisement, so no comparison is possible.

6. **The correct answer is (D).** Lyndon B. Johnson followed Franklin Delano Roosevelt's politics and expanded the role of the federal government.

7. **The correct answer is (C).** A lockout is an employer's weapon rather than a union's weapon. It occurs when an employer closes the door of his place of business to his employees and refuses to let them enter.

8. **The correct answer is (C).** News programs and reports are generally intended to present facts. The editorial pages of a newspaper regularly present opinions and interpretations.

9. **The correct answer is (C).** Internal migration is population movement within the confines of a country.

10. **The correct answer is (C).** The Manhattan Project, a secret effort to develop a transportable atomic bomb, was initiated in 1942. The bomb was constructed at Los Alamos.

11. **The correct answer is (D).** The next-to-last column shows the actual number of people in rural communities for each census year. The number continued to grow until 1940, and then decreased in the period 1940–1970.

12. **The correct answer is (D).** The fourth column shows the total percentage of the U.S. population living in urban areas for each census year.

13. **The correct answer is (B).** The availability of factory and other industrial jobs in urban areas attracted farm workers as well as immigrants.

14. **The correct answer is (D).** President Jackson was vigorously opposed to the Second Bank of the United States, campaigned against it, and brought it to an end by vetoing the congressional bill for rechartering it.

15. **The correct answer is (B).** The Social Security Act, passed in 1935, created a national system of old-age insurance, in which most employees were compelled to participate. It also created a federal-state system of unemployment insurance and helped states provide public health services and care for the disabled.

16. **The correct answer is (C).** Castro overthrew the regime of Fulgencia Batista, who had headed a military dictatorship in Cuba since 1952.

17. **The correct answer is (D).** According to the table, sex differences (biological factors) affect life expectancy, as does race.

18. **The correct answer is (D).** The second sentence gives this information.

19. **The correct answer is (A).** The first sentence states that the reservations were established "through special treaties with the federal government."

20. **The correct answer is (B).** The graph does *not* indicate that the number of slaves in the South remained approximately the same from 1790 to 1860. The graph gives only percentages. It shows that the free black population remained about the same percentage of the total black population in the South during this period.

21. **The correct answer is (D).** France was eliminated as a power, thus vanishing from the map.

22. **The correct answer is (A).** Louisiana is in the southern part of the area controlled by France.

23. **The correct answer is (C).** According to the map, the Mississippi River divides the land controlled by Spain from the land controlled by England. We can assume, therefore, that they share control of the river.

24. **The correct answer is (D).** The negative income tax principle was part of a proposal for a family assistance program made by the Nixon administration in 1969 and rejected by Congress. The "negative tax" refers to the subsidy received by someone with no income, a subsidy that would be gradually reduced after he/she starts to earn income.

25. **The correct answer is (C).** Ethnocentrism is a belief that one's own society is superior to others. The ethnocentric individual tends to evaluate the cultural traits of others in terms of his/her own culture.

26. **The correct answer is (B).** Point P has coordinates $x = -3$, $y = 2$.

27. **The correct answer is (C).** If 1 dozen rolls cost \$1.50, each roll costs \$1.50 divided by 12, or \$.125. Then 30 rolls will cost:

    30 (\$.125) = \$3.75

28. **The correct answer is (B).** Find the difference between each choice and 5. The smallest difference is .005; therefore, 5.005 is closer than the other choices to 5.

29. **The correct answer is (A).** There are 6 symbols representing men and 8 symbols representing women. The ratio is 6:8, or 3:4.

30. **The correct answer is (A).** There are 30 symbols in all. Each symbol represents 100 people.

    30(100) = 3,000

31. **The correct answer is (D).** There are 3 lbs. of peanuts. Three-fifths equals .60 = 60%.

32. **The correct answer is (C).** Multiply .010 by .001. The product is .000010. The final 0 may be dropped, yielding .00001.

33. **The correct answer is (B).** The rainfall in June was 1.4 inches, the same as the rainfall in February.

34. **The correct answer is (C).** 1 pound = 16 ounces, therefore:

    (16)(28) = 448 (approximately 450 grams)

35. **The correct answer is (D).** In 1 hour, the minute hand rotates through 360°. In 2 hours, it rotates through twice that, or 720°.

36. **The correct answer is (A).** .25% = .0025. Therefore, the correct answer is choice (A) in fractional form.

37. **The correct answer is (D).** The first time that the American League overtook the attendance figures was in 1997, when the American League attendance was 19.6 million and National League attendance was 19.1 million.

38. **The correct answer is (B).** The most popular sporting event in 1985 is in the column for 1985. The largest attendance was 62.9 million, for horseracing.

39. **The correct answer is (D).** Demographic transition is the shift from great population growth to a leveling-off period. This occurred from pre-modern to modern times.

40. **The correct answer is (D).** The Napoleonic Code covered all areas of civil law.

41. **The correct answer is (C).** There are two more symbols for 1980 than for 1985. Each symbol represents 100 houses. Therefore, 200 more houses were built in 1980.

42. **The correct answer is (A).**

    $$2x + y = 7$$
    $$2(3) + y = 7$$
    $$6 + y = 7$$
    $$y = 1$$

43. **The correct answer is (B).** Four grapefruit cost $2, leaving $8 for apples. Eight dollars does not buy an integral number of apples; therefore, the correct answer is choice (B).

44. **The correct answer is (D).** Write all the fractions the same denominator. The Lowest Common Denominator (LCD) is 80. Choice (D) goes from greatest to least.

45. **The correct answer is (C).** Multiply the number of cups of flour needed for one cake by the number of cakes. The correct answer is $7\frac{1}{2}$.

46. **The correct answer is (D).** Jessica Henley's trip cost $350; her husband's flight cost $390. Together the two trips cost $740.

47. **The correct answer is (A).** Multiplying a number by 100 yields percent. Therefore:

    $$30 \times 100 = 3,000\%$$

48. **The correct answer is (C).** If you divide 105 by 25, you get 4, with a remainder of 5. However, these 5 people need seats, so you would need 5 buses to transport 105 people.

49. **The correct answer is (A).** The hundreds place is denoted by 389. The closest hundred is 400; therefore, the correct answer is 75,400.

50. **The correct answer is (A).** Blank verse is unrhymed verse.

51. **The correct answer is (D).** *Dehydrated* means "lacking water."

52. **The correct answer is (D).** The caste system is permanent and unchangeable; therefore, one cannot change castes by gaining wealth. It is a totally stratified social system.

53. **The correct answer is (A).** A bas-relief denotes a three-dimensional design.

54. **The correct answer is (A).** *Chiaroscuro* means "light and dark"; thus, it is an artistic technique of using shading to obtain desired results.

55. **The correct answer is (D).** All the reasons given contribute to pollution of ground water and surface water.

56. **The correct answer is (C).** Double jeopardy is covered in the Fifth Amendment: "No person shall be subject for the same offense to be twice put in jeopardy of life or limb."

57. **The correct answer is (A).** LEDs are most often found in hand-held calculators.

58. **The correct answer is (D).** Alliteration is the literary technique of repeating the first sound of a word.

59. **The correct answer is (C).** The author is referring to the sea. Seawater is measured in fathoms of depth. Coral and pearls also come from the sea.

60. **The correct answer is (D).** 6 is twice 3; therefore, the answer is 200%.

61. **The correct answer is (D).** Leonardo da Vinci painted the famous *Mona Lisa* between 1503 and 1506, the Renaissance period in Europe.

62. **The correct answer is (B).** The poet calls human beings "architects of Fate" bound by "walls of Time."

63. **The correct answer is (B).** The theme of the poem is the ability of people to include or exclude others. The author includes, whereas his fellow man excludes.

64. **The correct answer is (D).** The poet Jonathan Swift often uses irony in his works. He is saying that although flattery is considered "the food of fools" by men of learning, they often "condescend to take a bit"; that is, they are happy to be flattered.

65. **The correct answer is (C).** In Pierre Auguste Renoir's *Strawberries and Almonds*, all the answers apply to the painting except for choice (C), the use of sharp, angular lines.

66. **The correct answer is (C).** A *recession* is a period in which business declines, but not so greatly as in a depression or a crash.

67. **The correct answer is (A).** Lines 6 and 7 show a distinct change in mood from sullen and depressed to happy.

68. **The correct answer is (D).** The poet describes himself as so happy when he thinks of his love that he would not want to exchange his status for that of a king.

69. **The correct answer is (B).** *Simile* is a figure of speech that makes a comparison between unlike things by using "like" or "as." In this poem, "a pregnant bank" is compared to "a pillow on a bed."

70. **The correct answer is (A).** *Rhyme scheme* is determined by the final sounds in lines of poetry. In this poem, *bed* and *head* rhyme, as do *rest* and *best*, so the scheme is said to be ABAB.

71. **The correct answer is (A).** Claude Monet painted *La Promenade* in 1875 from the viewpoint of the observer, who is looking up toward the woman and boy on the grassy hill.

72. **The correct answer is (A).** This portrait of Napoleon completed by Jacques Louis David does not exaggerate the ornamentation on furnishings. They are pictured as realistic and correct.

73. **The correct answer is (A).** *Impressionist* work is fuzzy and indistinct. Details are purposely omitted.

74. **The correct answer is (B).** Jackson Pollock painted *Number 12* in 1952.

75. **The correct answer is (D).** Louise Nevelson created *Sky Cathedral* between 1958 and 1959.

76. **The correct answer is (A).** Ballads are stories told in song and passed down by word of mouth from singer to singer. "Lord Randal" is a ballad from the fifteenth century.

77. **The correct answer is (C).** William Carlos Williams was a physician who became one of the United States' leading contemporary poets.

78. **The correct answer is (D).** Williams wanted to show the inseparability of vivid imagery and thought. He created a picture in words, trying also to write as Americans spoke.

79. **The correct answer is (B).** The comparison of taking an examination with baking bread is a weak comparison.

80. **The correct answer is (D).** The patient criticizes the psychiatrist for a textbook explanation of feelings and reactions rather than a personal explanation.

ESSAY RESPONSE

We now stand at the crossroads of education. Many older teachers have reached retirement age and will be leaving the school system and new, younger teachers will take their place. While arguments can be made for the benefits of exchanging the old for the young, I believe that the influence of older teachers is crucial in guiding our students and our schools.

Although it may be true that younger teachers bring new ideas to a school system, the solid, leavening influence of the more experienced teachers is both essential and advantageous. Older teachers have the benefit of twenty, or thirty, or more years of teaching, and they have already dealt with a wide variety of students with varying abilities and interests. Older teachers know their subject matter well; they know what works and what does not, how best to approach new topics, and how to involve all of the students in the subject discussion. Having taught a subject for a long time, they have developed "tricks of the trade" both in approaching the topic and in helping their students understand and retain the material.

Younger teachers likely won't have mastered all of the necessary skills at the start of their career and will need time and experience to develop their expertise. Consequently, senior teachers are an invaluable resource to their younger colleagues. Experienced teachers can teach their new coworkers, both by observation and by direct coaching, some of the important tools needed to be an expert pedagogue.

Experienced teachers can provide valuable information to younger teachers about getting students involved in classroom activities and subject discussions. Also, by sharing their "tricks of the trade," they help younger teachers develop their own techniques. I firmly believe that schools and their students would be best served if the experience and knowledge of older teachers were utilized.

Answer Sheet for Chapter 7

LAST—PRACTICE TEST 2

1. Ⓐ Ⓑ Ⓒ Ⓓ   21. Ⓐ Ⓑ Ⓒ Ⓓ   41. Ⓐ Ⓑ Ⓒ Ⓓ   61. Ⓐ Ⓑ Ⓒ Ⓓ

2. Ⓐ Ⓑ Ⓒ Ⓓ   22. Ⓐ Ⓑ Ⓒ Ⓓ   42. Ⓐ Ⓑ Ⓒ Ⓓ   62. Ⓐ Ⓑ Ⓒ Ⓓ

3. Ⓐ Ⓑ Ⓒ Ⓓ   23. Ⓐ Ⓑ Ⓒ Ⓓ   43. Ⓐ Ⓑ Ⓒ Ⓓ   63. Ⓐ Ⓑ Ⓒ Ⓓ

4. Ⓐ Ⓑ Ⓒ Ⓓ   24. Ⓐ Ⓑ Ⓒ Ⓓ   44. Ⓐ Ⓑ Ⓒ Ⓓ   64. Ⓐ Ⓑ Ⓒ Ⓓ

5. Ⓐ Ⓑ Ⓒ Ⓓ   25. Ⓐ Ⓑ Ⓒ Ⓓ   45. Ⓐ Ⓑ Ⓒ Ⓓ   65. Ⓐ Ⓑ Ⓒ Ⓓ

6. Ⓐ Ⓑ Ⓒ Ⓓ   26. Ⓐ Ⓑ Ⓒ Ⓓ   46. Ⓐ Ⓑ Ⓒ Ⓓ   66. Ⓐ Ⓑ Ⓒ Ⓓ

7. Ⓐ Ⓑ Ⓒ Ⓓ   27. Ⓐ Ⓑ Ⓒ Ⓓ   47. Ⓐ Ⓑ Ⓒ Ⓓ   67. Ⓐ Ⓑ Ⓒ Ⓓ

8. Ⓐ Ⓑ Ⓒ Ⓓ   28. Ⓐ Ⓑ Ⓒ Ⓓ   48. Ⓐ Ⓑ Ⓒ Ⓓ   68. Ⓐ Ⓑ Ⓒ Ⓓ

9. Ⓐ Ⓑ Ⓒ Ⓓ   29. Ⓐ Ⓑ Ⓒ Ⓓ   49. Ⓐ Ⓑ Ⓒ Ⓓ   69. Ⓐ Ⓑ Ⓒ Ⓓ

10. Ⓐ Ⓑ Ⓒ Ⓓ   30. Ⓐ Ⓑ Ⓒ Ⓓ   50. Ⓐ Ⓑ Ⓒ Ⓓ   70. Ⓐ Ⓑ Ⓒ Ⓓ

11. Ⓐ Ⓑ Ⓒ Ⓓ   31. Ⓐ Ⓑ Ⓒ Ⓓ   51. Ⓐ Ⓑ Ⓒ Ⓓ   71. Ⓐ Ⓑ Ⓒ Ⓓ

12. Ⓐ Ⓑ Ⓒ Ⓓ   32. Ⓐ Ⓑ Ⓒ Ⓓ   52. Ⓐ Ⓑ Ⓒ Ⓓ   72. Ⓐ Ⓑ Ⓒ Ⓓ

13. Ⓐ Ⓑ Ⓒ Ⓓ   33. Ⓐ Ⓑ Ⓒ Ⓓ   53. Ⓐ Ⓑ Ⓒ Ⓓ   73. Ⓐ Ⓑ Ⓒ Ⓓ

14. Ⓐ Ⓑ Ⓒ Ⓓ   34. Ⓐ Ⓑ Ⓒ Ⓓ   54. Ⓐ Ⓑ Ⓒ Ⓓ   74. Ⓐ Ⓑ Ⓒ Ⓓ

15. Ⓐ Ⓑ Ⓒ Ⓓ   35. Ⓐ Ⓑ Ⓒ Ⓓ   55. Ⓐ Ⓑ Ⓒ Ⓓ   75. Ⓐ Ⓑ Ⓒ Ⓓ

16. Ⓐ Ⓑ Ⓒ Ⓓ   36. Ⓐ Ⓑ Ⓒ Ⓓ   56. Ⓐ Ⓑ Ⓒ Ⓓ   76. Ⓐ Ⓑ Ⓒ Ⓓ

17. Ⓐ Ⓑ Ⓒ Ⓓ   37. Ⓐ Ⓑ Ⓒ Ⓓ   57. Ⓐ Ⓑ Ⓒ Ⓓ   77. Ⓐ Ⓑ Ⓒ Ⓓ

18. Ⓐ Ⓑ Ⓒ Ⓓ   38. Ⓐ Ⓑ Ⓒ Ⓓ   58. Ⓐ Ⓑ Ⓒ Ⓓ   78. Ⓐ Ⓑ Ⓒ Ⓓ

19. Ⓐ Ⓑ Ⓒ Ⓓ   39. Ⓐ Ⓑ Ⓒ Ⓓ   59. Ⓐ Ⓑ Ⓒ Ⓓ   79. Ⓐ Ⓑ Ⓒ Ⓓ

20. Ⓐ Ⓑ Ⓒ Ⓓ   40. Ⓐ Ⓑ Ⓒ Ⓓ   60. Ⓐ Ⓑ Ⓒ Ⓓ   80. Ⓐ Ⓑ Ⓒ Ⓓ

Chapter 7

LAST—PRACTICE TEST 2

TIME: 4 Hours—80 Questions

> *Directions:* Each statement or passage in this test is followed by one or more questions. Read each statement or passage, and then answer the accompanying questions, basing your answer on what is stated or implied in the passage. Blacken the letter of your answer choice on the answer sheet.

Questions 1–4 refer to the following passage:

Monseigneur, one of the great lords in power at the court, held his fortnightly reception in his grand hotel in Paris. Monseigneur was in his inner room, his sanctuary of sanctuaries, the Holiest of Holiests to the crowd of worshippers in the suite of rooms without. Monseigneur took his royal chocolate at this time. Monseigneur could swallow a great many things with ease, and was by some few sullen minds supposed to be rather rapidly swallowing France.

1. The locale of this passage is

   (A) the opera.
   (B) a sweet shop.
   (C) the field of battle.
   (D) an apartment.

2. The tone of the selection is

   (A) sarcastic.
   (B) inquiring.
   (C) objective.
   (D) informative.

3. Monseigneur represents a

   (A) person who elicits sympathy.
   (B) simpleton who cannot provide for himself.
   (C) profligate who cares little about others.
   (D) miser who has moments of extravagance.

Questions 4 and 5 are based on the following information:

Farmers and scientists are able to make use of the fact that many plants and animals are able to reproduce asexually, that is, without the need for two parents. Some of the methods used by plants and animals are described here as follows:

I. Budding—a plant pinches off a little piece of itself. This little piece will develop into an entire organism that is exactly like the parent.

II. Sporing—a plant produces thousands of little seeds called spores. Each spore is capable of growing into an entire plant.

III. Grafting—farmers take a twig from one plant and attach it to the stem of another plant. In this way, it exhibits features from both plants.

IV. Tubers—the plant produces thick, fleshy underground stems with many "eyes" or buds. Each bud is able to grow into a new organism.

V. Regeneration—some plants and animals are able to regrow lost parts.

For each question, choose the one method of reproduction described by the situation.

4. One of the enemies of the clam fisherman is the starfish. A particular fisherman had the habit of cutting up the starfish that he caught and throwing the pieces back into the water. However, he noticed that each year he found fewer and fewer clams. This was probably due to the fact that the starfish were reproducing by

(A) budding.
(B) sporting.
(C) grafting.
(D) regeneration.

5. A recent ad in a magazine advertised a special tree that produces Bosc, Anjou, and Bartlett pears. This tree was made possible by

(A) budding.
(B) sporing.
(C) grafting.
(D) tubers.

6. Radio astronomers can make their observations

(A) only at night, when most radio stations are silent.
(B) in a pattern similar to optical astronomers.
(C) day or night.
(D) only on clear, cloudless days.

7. Gulls can identify their own species by the distinguishing ring pattern around the eye. This is an example of

(A) geographic isolation.
(B) ecological isolation.
(C) natural selection.
(D) behavioral isolation.

8. The results of some of the early experiments on plant hormones can be easily reproduced by the following experiment. The tips of four oat seedlings were cut off. One tip was placed on a small block of agar for 2 hours and then was discarded. The four plants then were treated in the following manner: 1) The first plant was left without a tip. 2) The tip was replaced on the second plant. 3) The agar cube that was in contact with a cut tip was placed on the third plant. 4) An agar cube that was not in contact with a tip was placed on the fourth plant. The plants were then observed for one or two days.

PLANT	GROWTH
#1	No
#2	Yes
#3	Yes
#4	No

From the data obtained from all four plants, it is apparent that

(A) there is a chemical substance present in agar that causes oat seedlings to grow.
(B) negative geotropism causes oat seedlings to grow.
(C) it is possible to stop growth in oat seedlings because the tissues are not differentiated.
(D) the growth-inducing element in oat seedlings is probably a chemical that can diffuse into agar from the tip of the seedling.

Questions 9 and 10 refer to the following passage:
The spring wind is raw and the mud is still frosted with ice, yet the husky young engineer takes pride in this barren, rocky landscape and points out a mineral that glitters invitingly throughout the black earth.

All that glitters is not gold. But in this case, it is something better—iron ore, in billion-ton quantities.

"When you wash the kiddies in the bath tub," the engineer brags, "the water leaves an iron scum."

9. The purpose of the engineer's remark in the last paragraph is to

(A) advertise a new industrial-strength cleaner.
(B) illustrate the omnipresent abundance of iron ore in the area.
(C) call upon all citizens of the area to prevent pollution of lakes and reservoirs.
(D) encourage sanitation among the families of the engineers.

10. The writer of this passage probably had an interest in

    (A) physics.
    (B) mathematics.
    (C) chemistry.
    (D) geology.

11. For a society to function properly, everyone must function with everyone else. Individual effort is great—for the individual. Social scientists should devote less time to figuring out how and why the individual does what he does and should spend more time figuring out how to get people to do more of what everybody should do: cooperate.

    The author of this statement would probably approve most of a

    (A) psychological study of the determinants of behavior.
    (B) sociological study of why people go to war.
    (C) historical study of the communes that have failed.
    (D) psychological study of what makes people cooperative or antisocial.

12. The great thing about watching a sporting event is its unpredictability. No one knows what is going to happen next; at any point something may happen that has never happened before.

    Which of the following provides the most logical continuation of the paragraph?

    (A) When you read a good book, you do not know what is coming next.
    (B) Professional wrestling features "matches" that are really rehearsed acts.
    (C) Football is better suited to television than is baseball.
    (D) This compares favorably with such activities as watching television situation comedies and listening to political speeches.

Questions 13 and 14 refer to the following passage:

Sociologists claim that integrated schools are better for African-American students than are all-African-American schools. Their evidence is that reading and arithmetic scores of African Americans go up after two years of attendance at an integrated school. I suggest that perhaps African Americans are simply getting better teaching at the integrated school, and that integration *per se* is not beneficial.

13. Which of the following illustrates the way the author questions the sociologists' claim?

    (A) He calls them professionally incompetent.
    (B) He implies that they are blinded by ideology.
    (C) He offers a competing explanation of the evidence.
    (D) He proposes that perhaps they are only partially correct.

14. The author apparently believes that the sociologists he mentions

    (A) inferred too much from certain data.
    (B) failed to consider the correct explanation, which he mentions.
    (C) are " bleeding-heart liberals."
    (D) should have collected more data.

15. "Without innovation, society cannot progress. Yet without an intellectual tradition to follow, real innovation is not possible. A free-thinking society with no cultural heritage will flounder just as surely as a tradition-bound society with no independent thought."

    The author would be most likely to oppose a philosophy that

    (A) advocates building a new society upon the ashes of the old one.
    (B) advocates remedying historical wrongs by overturning the existing social order.
    (C) holds imagination to be more valuable than tradition.
    (D) venerates ancestors.

16. As one of the most common serious infectious diseases of mankind, malaria presents a considerable challenge to public health workers. The challenge is the more irresistible because of the complicated mode of transmission of the disease. Human beings can get infected only from the bite of an infected mosquito, which is itself infected by biting an infected human being. Interrupting the mosquito link in the chain would seem to present an ecologically sound, though expensive, way to clear large regions of the world of this scourge. More money should be spent on solving this problem right now.

    One of the author's assumptions is that

    (A) mosquitoes are dangerous insects.
    (B) the life cycle of the organism that causes malaria is completely known.
    (C) enough money is now being spent on cancer.
    (D) malaria is sometimes fatal.

17. "This little car is the best, the greatest, the most fantastic economy car on the market. I cannot begin to describe to you the praise, the cries of delight, the veritable enthusiasm that its buyers have expressed to me," the salesman spluttered.

    "Try more information and less pitch next time, fella," the woman said, and walked away.

    The customer criticizes the salesman because his remarks are too

    (A) detailed and circumstantial.
    (B) exact and specific.
    (C) verbose and unspecific.
    (D) general and philosophical.

Questions 18–21 refer to the following passage:

"I have considered the structure of all volant animals, and find the folding continuity of the bat's wings most easily accommodated to the human form. Upon this model I shall begin my task tomorrow, and in a year expect to tower into the air beyond the malice or pursuit of man. But I will work only on this condition, that the art shall not be divulged, and that you shall not require me to make wings for any but ourselves."

"Why," said Rasselas, "should you envy others so great an advantage? All skill ought to be exerted for universal good; every man has owed much to others."

18. The point of view of Rasselas is one that encourages

    (A) helping others.
    (B) military victory.
    (C) intellectual pursuits.
    (D) artistic pursuits.

19. The person to whom Rasselas is speaking is a(n)

    (A) tailor.
    (B) gambler.
    (C) bat.
    (D) artist.

20. The conversation is probably being held

    (A) in private.
    (B) at a cocktail party.
    (C) with many friends present.
    (D) in a movie theater.

21. The first speaker has studied animals that

    (A) resemble humans.
    (B) can fly.
    (C) are dangerous.
    (D) are nocturnal.

Questions 22–24 refer to the following passages:

(A) Here was buried Thomas Jefferson, author of the Declaration of American Independence, of the statute of Virginia for religious freedom, and father of the University of Virginia.

(B) Knowledge is the only instrument of production that is not subject to diminishing returns.

(C) Man is the only animal that blushes. Or needs to.

(D) Hence, loathed Melancholy. Of Cerberus and
    blackest Midnight born,
    In Stygian cave forlorn, 'Mongst horrid
    shapes and shrieks and sights unholy!

22. Which is written tongue-in-cheek?

23. Which uses mythical places to make its point?

24. Which uses economic terms to make its point?

Prepare for the NYSTCE: LAST and ATS-W

25. Which of the following is a prominent feature of the painting pictured above?

    (A) A strong horizontal emphasis within the painting.
    (B) Importance placed in the details of the figures.
    (C) The use of light and a stippling technique to emphasize the cathedral.
    (D) An abstraction concerned with geometric forms.

26. Which of the following provides the best description of the van Gogh painting shown at top right?

    (A) A surrealistic composition
    (B) A horizontally composed work
    (C) A work that stresses Cubist ideals
    (D) A self-portrait

27. The greenhouse effect of CO_2 is best opposed by

    (A) deep respirations.
    (B) water pollution.
    (C) X rays.
    (D) smog particles.

28. During a lunar eclipse, the

    (A) sun casts a shadow on the earth.
    (B) earth casts a shadow on the sun.
    (C) moon casts a shadow on the earth.
    (D) earth casts a shadow on the moon.

Question 29 is based on the following two graphs:

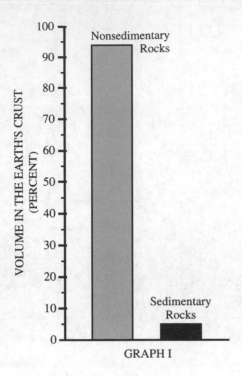

GRAPH I

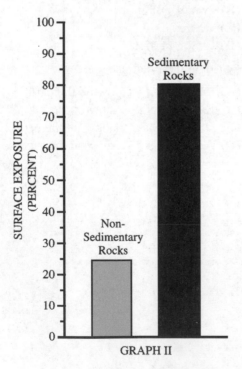

GRAPH II

29. Which of the following statements can be inferred from the data shown on the graphs?

   (A) The crust of the earth is composed mostly of sedimentary rocks.
   (B) Rock outcrops on the earth's surface are chiefly of the nonsedimentary type.
   (C) Most nonsedimentary rocks are composed of the melted remains of sedimentary rocks.
   (D) Most sedimentary rock is found at or near the surface of the earth.

30. The seasons on earth are a result of

   (A) the distance of the sun from the earth.
   (B) gravitational forces between the earth and the moon.
   (C) the tilted axis of the earth.
   (D) pulsations from the surface of the sun.

31. Organisms in temperate zones are able to time their activities by cues given by the photoperiod, since

   (A) all organisms need time to rest.
   (B) light is a limiting factor.
   (C) all organisms have a biological clock.
   (D) day length is always constant for a specific locality and season.

32. The cell seems to be the basic unit of life for the following reason(s):

   I. All cells are self-reproductive without a host.
   II. All cells have the same general size and shape.
   III. All cells are self-regulating.

   (A) I only
   (B) II only
   (C) III only
   (D) I and III only

Questions 33–36 refer to the following figures:

(A)

(C)

(B)

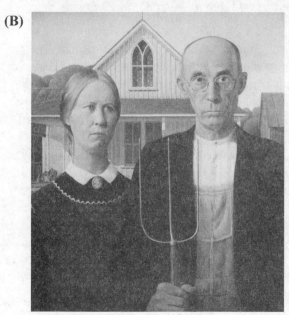

(D)

33. Which painting depicts the artist's view of rural America?

34. Which painting has a Biblical theme?

35. Which is an Impressionist painting?

36. Which portrays an abstract sculpture?

37. Judging from the tenor of the following statements and the apparent authoritativeness of their sources, which is the most reasonable and trustworthy?

    (A) Army Sergeant: "The men in my outfit are the best soldiers on this base."

    (B) Doctor: "Mrs. Jones, your baby is one of the brightest children I've ever seen."

    (C) Night Watchman: "I spotted a man trying to get out of the yard by climbing a barbed wire fence, at about three o'clock in the morning."

    (D) Car Dealer: "The new Sangusto V8 is probably the smoothest-riding car on the road."

38. Which of the following sentences indicates how the writer feels about the drafting of women?

    (A) Women one day may be required to serve in the Armed Forces.

    (B) It would be foolish to suggest that women should be part of the military.

    (C) A large majority of young people are opposed to the drafting of women.

    (D) Most people I know have mixed feelings concerning women serving in the Armed Forces.

39. "When is a man drafted for military service justified in refusing to serve? He cannot legitimately believe that the law that conscripts him is morally wrong unless he believes that the war for which he is drafted to fight is an unjust war. As a law-abiding citizen, he must presume the laws of his country to be just. If he merely doubts that the war is just, this doubt is not enough to justify his refusal to serve."

    The conclusion implied by the author's argument is

    (A) a man is never justified in refusing to serve his country.

    (B) a man may consent to serve but refuse to shed blood.

    (C) to be justified in refusing to serve, a man must be convinced that the war is unjust.

    (D) a man is justified in refusing to serve provided that he is prepared to suffer the legal consequences of his refusal.

40. "The tension and conflict between white and black people admits of a technological solution. Basically, all that is required is the discovery of a chemical that will transform skin color. Therefore, chemists should try to find a chemical that will turn dark skin white."

    The author's argument does NOT lead to his conclusion unless the following assumption is true:

    (A) There are black and white races.

    (B) There is tension and conflict between black and white people.

    (C) No black person can pass for a white person.

    (D) It is better in itself to have white rather than black skin.

Questions 41 and 42 refer to the following passage:

"It is commonly thought that we can single out each of our beliefs apart from the rest and discover if it is true or false. To have a belief, however, we must first have some idea of what it is we believe to be the case. But no single one of our ideas can exist in isolation from at least some of our other ideas. So, for example, if we believe that Fido is a spaniel, we must have some idea of what a spaniel is and this idea is obviously connected with other ideas: e.g., of an animal; of a canine animal; of a barking canine animal, etc. Therefore, for us to verify that Fido is a spaniel—our original belief—we must also verify the beliefs that Fido is an animal, a canine animal, etc."

41. The conclusion implied by the author's argument is

    (A) each idea we have is connected with every one of our ideas.

    (B) we cannot verify any single one of our beliefs unless we can verify every one of them.

    (C) no one of our beliefs can be verified without verifying some of our other beliefs.

    (D) we cannot be sure of anything because we would have to know everything.

42. The author's argument would be considerably weakened if which of the following statements were true?

   (A) To every idea connected with a given idea, there corresponds a belief requiring verification.
   (B) Ideas are connected with other ideas.
   (C) By verifying one belief, we at the same time verify several other beliefs that are connected with it.
   (D) To every belief there corresponds at least one idea, and to every idea there corresponds at least one belief.

43. "The importance of a liberal education has been greatly underestimated by those who downgrade the value of a traditional four-year education. Vocational schools are fine for those with little imagination, but a person should have exposure to many areas of learning. Not only is such exposure likely to make him a better person, but it is also likely to mean that he will earn more money."

   The author appears to believe that

   (A) people who attend vocational schools are unimaginative.
   (B) people cannot compete unless they attend a four-year liberal arts school.
   (C) people with higher IQs should get a liberal education.
   (D) a four-year vocational school does not provide a traditional education.

44. "Van Gogh felt that God should not be judged on this earth, which he felt represents one of His sketches that turned out badly."

   Which of the following may be inferred from the passage above?

   (A) Van Gogh felt that God created more than one universe.
   (B) Van Gogh felt that more evil than good exists on Earth.
   (C) Van Gogh felt that the only true art is that created by God.
   (D) Van Gogh felt that this Earth was created but not completed by God.

45. "During the past decade we have doubled our real expenditures on health, yet our life span has not increased at all. It seems clear that the country therefore needs fewer, not more, doctors, and that people should visit their doctors less frequently and have fewer tests performed."

   Which of the following statements represents an implication or assumption of the author?

   I. Better health is dependent upon increased life span.
   II. Decreasing the number of doctors would not lead to an increase in the average doctor's fee.
   III. Laboratory tests are unreasonably expensive.

   (A) I only
   (B) III only
   (C) I and II only
   (D) II and III only

46. Which of the following situations is NOT matched with the appropriate society?

   (A) Several generations of the same family live together: traditional society
   (B) The birth of many children ensures the economic survival of the family: modern technological society
   (C) Children generally follow the occupations of their parents: semi-industrialized society
   (D) Men and women may work at the same jobs: a modern technological society

47. An anthropologist working in a rural Native American village would most likely do which of the following activities?

   (A) Train farmers to plant new types of crops
   (B) Reform the local legal system
   (C) Persuade villages to accept family planning programs
   (D) Study the relationships/kinship of families

YEAR	WHEAT PRODUCTION (thousands of bushels)	PRICE OF WHEAT (cents per bushel)
1875	2,450	51.9
1880	2,706	49.0
1885	3,058	42.2

48. The data in this chart could best be used to illustrate which economic concept?

    (A) Recession
    (B) Inflation
    (C) Interdependence
    (D) Supply and demand

Questions 49–51 refer to the following graph:

U.S. BALANCE OF INTERNATIONAL PAYMENTS

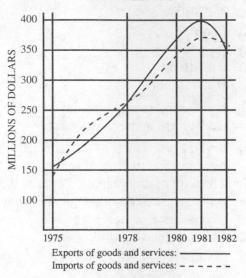

Exports of goods and services: ———
Imports of goods and services: – – – – –

49. According to the graph, the value of goods and services exported by the United States exceeded the value of goods and services imported during which of the following years?

    (A) 1976
    (B) 1977
    (C) 1980
    (D) 1982

50. The value of goods and services imported by the United States exceeded the value of goods and services exported during which of the following years?

    (A) 1975
    (B) 1979
    (C) 1980
    (D) 1982

51. By how many millions of dollars did exports exceed imports in 1980? (Answer in millions of dollars.)

    (A) 10
    (B) 30
    (C) 50
    (D) 70

UNEMPLOYMENT RATES AS A PERCENTAGE OF THE CIVILIAN LABOR FORCE, 1929–1968

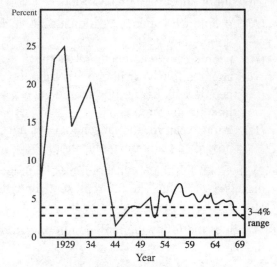

52. All of the following conclusions can be drawn from this graph EXCEPT

    (A) in 1933, almost a quarter of the civilian labor force was unemployed.
    (B) civilian employment increases in times of war.
    (C) employment dropped precipitously between 1938 and 1942.
    (D) in 1959, about 5 percent of the civilian population was unemployed.

Questions 53–55 are based on the map below and the following selection:

To make the federal government more accessible to the people who need its services, the Executive Branch is divided into ten geographical regions, as shown on the map that follows. The dots in each region locate the regional headquarters city.

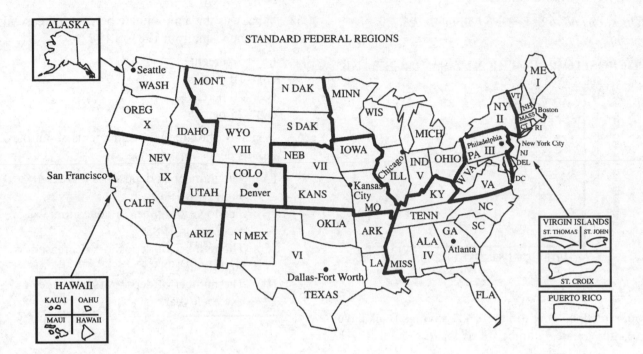

STANDARD FEDERAL REGIONS

53. If you are a resident of Puerto Rico, where is the regional headquarters for your area?

(A) Atlanta
(B) Miami
(C) Philadelphia
(D) New York City

54. What states does Region VII include?

(A) South Dakota, Iowa, Kansas, Missouri
(B) Arkansas, Illinois, Missouri, Iowa
(C) Iowa, Missouri, Kansas, Nebraska
(D) Iowa, Colorado, Missouri, Kansas

55. From the information presented on the map, which of the following best explains why Region II is so small?

(A) It is close to Washington, D.C.
(B) It is densely populated.
(C) It receives a great deal of federal assistance.
(D) It has powerful congressmen and senators.

56. Which one of the following types of tax is most regressive?

(A) Excise and sales taxes
(B) Property taxes
(C) Payroll taxes
(D) Personal income taxes

57. Which of the following processes is responsible for clothes drying on the line on a warm summer day?

(A) Melting
(B) Condensation
(C) Sublimation
(D) Evaporation

58. The primary purpose of these institutions is to make mortgage loans to their members. Which of the following best fits this description?

(A) Mutual savings banks
(B) Savings and loan associations
(C) Credit unions
(D) Life insurance companies

59. The citizen's constitutional right to protection from unwarranted arrest is provided by the

(A) right of eminent domain.
(B) writ of assistance.
(C) writ of habeas corpus.
(D) bill of attainder.

Questions 60–62 are based on the following graph:

DEPOSITORS IN THE XYZ SAVINGS BANK

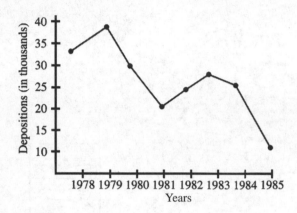

60. In which year did the XYZ Savings Bank have the greatest number of depositors?

(A) 1978
(B) 1979
(C) 1981
(D) 1982

61. In 1984 the bank had approximately how many depositors?

(A) 3,000
(B) 30,000
(C) 35,000
(D) 25,000

62. What was the approximate percent increase in bank deposits from 1981 to 1982?

(A) 5 percent
(B) 10 percent
(C) 20 percent
(D) 25 percent

63. Which of the following statements about the bank's depositors is false?

(A) The number of depositors increased slightly in 1982.
(B) The lowest number of depositors was recorded in 1985.
(C) The number of depositors decreased slightly in 1983.
(D) The number of depositors continues to rise each year.

Questions 64 and 65 refer to the following graph:

U.S. POPULATION BY AGE GROUP 1970 AND 1990

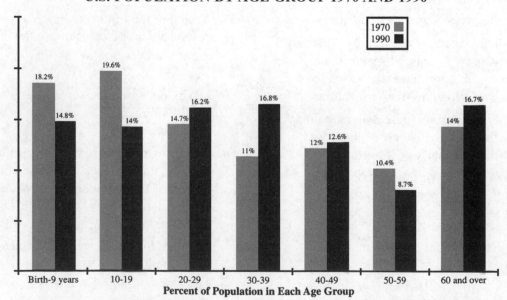

Prepare for the NYSTCE: LAST and ATS-W

64. From 1970 to 1990, the smallest change in the percent of population occurred within which age group?

   (A) Birth–9 years
   (B) 10–19 years
   (C) 20–29 years
   (D) 40–49 years

65. Which of the following statements is supported by the graph?

   (A) There were more children in the birth–9-year age group in 1970 than in 1990.
   (B) There were more people 60 and over in 1990 than there were in 1970.

   (C) The number of people in the 40–49-year age group was nearly the same in 1970 and 1990.
   (D) In 1970, more than half the population was between the ages of birth and 29.

66. The basic reason for the support of public education in the United States has been to provide

   (A) skilled workers for industry.
   (B) trained people for the professions.
   (C) educated leaders for government services.
   (D) informed citizens for a democratic society.

Questions 67 and 68 refer to the following graph:

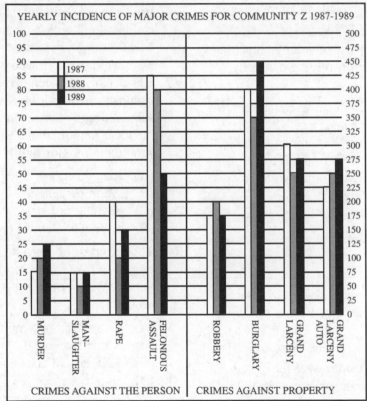

67. In 1989, the incidence of which of the following crimes was greater than in the previous two years?

   (A) Grand larceny
   (B) Murder
   (C) Rape
   (D) Robbery

68. The graph indicates that the percentage increase in grand larceny auto from 1988 to 1989 was

   (A) 5 percent.
   (B) 10 percent.
   (C) 15 percent.
   (D) 20 percent.

69. According to the theory of supply and demand, as the price of an article decreases, the quantity demanded will

    (A) usually fall.
    (B) fall and then rise.
    (C) not change.
    (D) usually rise.

70. The money supply of the United States is regulated by the

    (A) U.S. Department of the Treasury.
    (B) Treasurer of the United States.
    (C) U.S. Bureau of Engraving and Printing.
    (D) Federal Reserve System.

71. "When prices of conventional fuels rise sufficiently to match the cost of solar energy, then solar energy will be able to supply more than 10 percent of our needs."

    To bring about greater use of solar energy, the author of this statement is relying primarily upon

    (A) the market system to cause consumers to switch to solar energy.
    (B) government policy to encourage solar energy at the expense of other fuels.
    (C) technological breakthroughs to reduce the cost of solar energy.
    (D) changes in the attitude of big business toward solar energy.

Questions 72–75 refer to the following information:

In governing their various states, each governor receives administrative assistance from a variety of state officials, both elected and appointed. Most state governments typically include these officials:

Lieutenant governor—presides over the state senate; sits as acting governor when governor leaves the state

Attorney general—enforces state laws; represents the state in court as chief prosecutor or defense attorney; serves as legal advisor to the state government

Secretary of state—supervises the state's official business

State treasurer—collects taxes and pays bills

Superintendent of public instruction— supervises the administration of public schools and enforces the state education code

Each of the following items describes a situation in which a citizen or citizens would need to call upon the assistance of a state official. Choose the best official to deal with this problem.

72. A rapidly growing company decides to change its legal structure and become incorporated. Which official deals with this problem?

    (A) Lieutenant governor
    (B) Attorney general
    (C) Secretary of state
    (D) State treasurer

73. In the Fort Deeges School District, handicapped children are entitled to attend classes along with nonhandicapped children as much as is physically possible. Mr. and Mrs. Jenkins's son, who is confined to a wheelchair, has been denied the right to attend chemistry or physics classes at his high school, despite appeals to the principal and the local school board. To which state official should the Jenkins family turn for help?

    (A) Lieutenant governor
    (B) Attorney general
    (C) Secretary of state
    (D) Superintendent of public instruction

74. The governor of the state resigns in the middle of his term to run for a seat in the U.S. Senate. Which official deals with this problem?

    (A) Lieutenant governor
    (B) Attorney general
    (C) Secretary of state
    (D) State treasurer

75. A pyramid scheme, supposedly designed to make every participant rich in a short time, has collapsed. More than 100 people were victimized, and each one lost between $500 and $2,500. To whom should these victims turn for help?

    (A) Lieutenant governor
    (B) Attorney general
    (C) Secretary of state
    (D) State treasurer

76. "Whenever . . . government becomes destructive to these ends it is the right of the people to alter or abolish it, and to institute new government. . . ."

—Thomas Jefferson

". . . there comes a time when people get tired. We are here this evening to say to those who have mistreated us so long that we are tired—tired of being segregated and humiliated, tired of being kicked about by the brutal feet of oppression. We have no alternative but to protest. . . ."

—Martin Luther King, Jr.

Which statement best summarizes the main idea of both quotations?

(A) Violence is the only effective form of protest.
(B) Government is harmful to freedom and human dignity.
(C) Revolution is inevitable in a democratic society.
(D) The people may ultimately have to force the government to meet their needs.

77. The term *matrilocal* is most likely to refer to

(A) a mother's authority over her children.
(B) control over a child's choice of spouse.
(C) an individual's female descendents.
(D) a family's place of residence.

78. Which of the following best describes the sculpture shown in the figure at the top right?

(A) The pose suggests impending flight.
(B) The sculpture has uniform surface texture.
(C) The figure is lank and indistinct.
(D) The sculpture suggests pensiveness and meditation.

Questions 79 and 80 refer to the following passage:

"Such is the common process of marriage. A youth and maiden meeting by chance, or brought together by artifice, exchange glances, reciprocate civilities, go home, and dream of one another. Having little to divert attention, or diversify thought, they find themselves uneasy when they are apart, and therefore conclude that they shall be happy together. They marry, and discover what nothing but voluntary blindness had before concealed; they wear out life in altercations, and charge nature with cruelty."

79. The author's view of marriage is

(A) complacent.
(B) negative.
(C) sympathetic.
(D) indecisive.

80. The author feels that people marry

(A) without really knowing each other.
(B) too late in life.
(C) without family consent.
(D) outside their religious belief.

ESSAY

"A well-regulated Militia, being necessary to the security of a free state, the right of the people to keep and bear arms shall not be infringed."

—Second Amendment, U.S. Constitution

"If guns are outlawed, only outlaws will have guns."

—National Rifle Association

Comment on these two statements. Do you agree or disagree with gun-control legislation? Be as specific as you can to justify your argument. You can continue on a separate piece of paper.

_____

_____

_____

_____

_____

_____

_____

_____

_____

_____

_____

_____

_____

_____

_____

_____

_____

_____

ANSWER KEY

1. D	15. A	29. D	42. C	55. B	68. B
2. A	16. B	30. C	43. D	56. A	69. D
3. C	17. C	31. D	44. D	57. D	70. D
4. D	18. A	32. D	45. A	58. B	71. A
5. C	19. D	33. B	46. B	59. C	72. C
6. C	20. A	34. D	47. D	60. B	73. D
7. D	21. B	35. A	48. D	61. D	74. A
8. D	22. C	36. C	49. C	62. D	75. B
9. B	23. D	37. C	50. D	63. D	76. D
10. D	24. B	38. B	51. B	64. D	77. D
11. D	25. C	39. C	52. C	65. D	78. D
12. D	26. D	40. D	53. D	66. D	79. B
13. C	27. D	41. C	54. C	67. B	80. A
14. A	28. D				

ANSWERS AND EXPLANATIONS

1. **The correct answer is (D).** The first line states that Monseigneur is in his "grand hotel" in Paris.

2. **The correct answer is (A).** Sarcasm is a taunting or caustic tone, which is generally ironical.

3. **The correct answer is (C).** The allusion in the last line of the paragraph to the fact that Monseigneur may be "rather rapidly swallowing France" ultimately reveals his "profligate" or dissolute character.

4. **The correct answer is (D).** Starfish have the ability to regrow lost arms. In this example, many of the cut pieces were able to grow into new starfish.

5. **The correct answer is (C).** Grafting can produce seedless grapes, sturdy apple and orange trees, and, in this case, a pear tree that bears different types of pears.

6. **The correct answer is (C).** The atmosphere scatters optical energy, restricting optical astronomers, but it does not affect radio energy.

7. **The correct answer is (D).** Visual identification of a species leads to some sort of behavioral change; therefore, the correct answer is behavioral isolation.

8. **The correct answer is (D).** When the agar, which was in contact with a cut tip, is placed on a seedling, the seedling grows as if the tip itself had been replaced. The substance within the tip is a chemical that diffused into the agar.

9. **The correct answer is (B).** The engineer is proud of the abundance of iron ore in the area. In the last paragraph, he is bragging.

10. **The correct answer is (D).** To write a piece that is closely connected to the concerns of geology, the writer probably had an interest in geology, the science of the earth's crust.

11. **The correct answer is (D).** Choice (D) is correct because it suggests what the author is most in favor of: finding out how to make people cooperate.

12. **The correct answer is (D).** The author is praising sports for their spontaneity.

13. **The correct answer is (C).** The author proposes an alternate explanation of the evidence by saying that increased African-American academic achievement may be due to better instruction at white schools.

14. **The correct answer is (A).** By offering an explanation, which follows as logically from the experimental results as the sociologists' explanation does, the author implies that he feels that the sociologists inferred too much from their data.

15. **The correct answer is (A).** The author stresses the importance of tradition and thus would probably oppose destroying society.

16. **The correct answer is (B).** The third sentence of the passage indicates that the author is confident that the disease's mode of transmission is completely understood.

17. **The correct answer is (C).** *Verbose* is defined as "using too many words." *Best*, *greatest*, and *most fantastic* are verbose when used together.

18. **The correct answer is (A).** Rasselas states that he believes that "all skill ought to be exerted for universal good." Thus, one should use one's skill for the good of all.

19. **The correct answer is (D).** The man identifies himself when he asks that his "art shall not be divulged."

20. **The correct answer is (A).** The artist wants only Rasselas to know about his discovery, so the conversation is most likely being held in private.

21. **The correct answer is (B).** *Volant* means capable of flight.

22. **The correct answer is (C).** Mark Twain, one of the most famous American satirists, wrote this quotation.

23. **The correct answer is (D).** *Cerberus* is the mythical dog guarding the gate of Hades. *Stygian* refers to the mythical river Styx.

24. **The correct answer is (B).** *Instruments of production* and *diminishing returns* are economic terms.

25. **The correct answer is (C).** The use of light and a stippling painting technique emphasize the cathedral in this Luce Maximilien painting.

26. **The correct answer is (D).** This Vincent van Gogh painting is titled *Self-Portrait*.

27. **The correct answer is (D).** The greenhouse effect is the surface warming of heat reradiated back to the earth's surface. Atmospheric particles influence the temperature balance of the earth; therefore, the correct answer is choice (D).

28. **The correct answer is (D).** A lunar eclipse occurs when the earth positions itself between the sun and the moon.

29. **The correct answer is (D).** Using both graphs, it may be inferred that there is very little sedimentary rock, but much of what is present is at the earth's surface.

30. **The correct answer is (C).** The changing angle at which the sun's rays hit the earth as the earth moves around the sun causes the seasonal changes experienced in both the Northern and Southern Hemispheres.

31. **The correct answer is (D).** Choice (D) is directly related to cues, which are given by the photoperiod and encompasses all activities in all plants.

32. **The correct answer is (D).** Option II is not true; therefore, the correct answer is I and III.

33. **The correct answer is (B).** Grant Wood: *American Gothic* (1930) depicts the artist's dark view of American rural life.

34. **The correct answer is (D).** Rembrandt van Rijn: *Belshazzar's Feast* (1630s) shows a Hebrew king and others at a feast. Rembrandt's use of Hebrew letters adds to the Biblical theme.

35. **The correct answer is (A).** Alfred Sisley: *The Small Boat during the Flood* (1876).

36. **The correct answer is (C).** Alexander Calder: *Stabile* is a sculpture made in the abstract style.

37. **The correct answer is (C).** The night watchman has a vested interest in reporting accurately the events that occur during his tour of duty.

38. **The correct answer is (B).** The use of the words *It would be foolish* immediately suggests that the writer is opposed to those who favor the drafting of women.

39. **The correct answer is (C).** The argument is that the refusal must turn on strong conviction.

40. **The correct answer is (D).** It could just as well have been argued that chemists should try to find a chemical that will turn white skin dark.

41. **The correct answer is (C).** Choices (A) and (B) are too extreme. Choice (D) is wrong because it presupposes choice (B).

42. **The correct answer is (C).** The author argues that beliefs must correspond to ideas. Choice (D) is the best answer.

43. **The correct answer is (D).** The author contrasts a traditional four-year education with a vocational school's education, thereby implying that a four-year vocational school's education is not traditional.

44. **The correct answer is (D).** It may be inferred that van Gogh thought that the earth was a bad sketch. Sketches are incomplete paintings or drawings, and bad sketches are usually not completed even as sketches. Therefore, choice (D) is the best answer.

45. **The correct answer is (A).** The author equates the lack of increase in the life span with a lack of improvement in health in general; verification is required for every belief connected with a given belief. Thus, he tacitly assumes that one cannot verify these beliefs by verifying the given belief.

46. **The correct answer is (B).** Large families with many children are often an asset in agricultural societies, but families are generally small in modern technological societies.

47. **The correct answer is (D).** An anthropologist aims to observe other societies without altering them.

48. **The correct answer is (D).** The data shows that as the supply of wheat increased, the price decreased. This is an illustration of the concept of supply and demand.

49. **The correct answer is (C).** To find a year in which exports exceeded imports, find a section of the graph where the solid line appears over the dotted line. This happens in 1979, 1980, and 1981.

50. **The correct answer is (D).** Imports exceed exports when the dotted line is over the solid line: 1976, 1977, 1978, and 1982.

51. **The correct answer is (B).** Exports in 1980 were $370 million. Imports for 1980 were $340 million. The difference is $30 million.

52. **The correct answer is (C).** Unemployment dropped precipitously between 1938 and 1942; employment rose. The other answers are illustrated by the graph.

53. **The correct answer is (D).** New York City is headquarters for Region II, which includes Puerto Rico.

54. **The correct answer is (C).** Region VII includes Iowa, Missouri, Kansas, and Nebraska.

55. **The correct answer is (B).** It has a great many people in need of government services.

56. **The correct answer is (A).** Excise taxes tend to be the most regressive because a large portion of the commodities taxed—such as liquor, telephone service, and appliances—are commodities for which consumption does not increase in proportion to income.

57. **The correct answer is (D).** Evaporation is described by the following formula:

Water (liquid) > Water (gas)

58. **The correct answer is (B).** Savings and loan associations issue shares to savers, making them owners. The funds collected by the associations are usually spent to grant home mortgages.

59. **The correct answer is (C).** The writ of habeas corpus provides a safeguard against unwarranted arrest. It orders a law enforcement official to present a person in court so that a judge can determine whether that individual should be detained.

60. **The correct answer is (B).** The highest point of the graph is 1979.

61. **The correct answer is (D).** The dot for 1984 meets the scale for the number of depositors, at approximately 25,000 depositors in 1984.

62. **The correct answer is (D).** 1981 had 20,000 and 1982 had 25,000, which is an increase of 5,000 deposits. The percent increase is:

$$\frac{5,000}{20,000} = \frac{1}{4} \times 100 = 25\%$$

63. **The correct answer is (D).** The number of depositors has risen and fallen over the period shown, so choice (D) is false.

64. **The correct answer is (D).** The 40–49 category shows a mere 0.6 percent change.

65. **The correct answer is (D).** The graph indicated *percent* of population in each age group, not the *number* of people in any age group. Therefore, choices (A), (B), and (C) are wrong.

66. **The correct answer is (D).** Education has been viewed as an effective method for producing citizens who are capable of making intelligent decisions in a democratic way.

67. **The correct answer is (B).** The incidence of murder increased from 15 in 1987 to 20 in 1988 to 25 in 1989.

68. **The correct answer is (B).** The incidence of grand larceny auto went from 250 in 1988 to 275 in 1989, an increase of 25. The percent increase is: $\frac{25}{250} = \frac{1}{10} \times 100 = 10\%$.

69. **The correct answer is (D).** As the price decreases, demand will usually increase.

70. **The correct answer is (D).** The Federal Reserve System regulates the money supply. The Bureau of Engraving and Printing prints the money, but money is released at the discretion of the Federal Reserve.

71. **The correct answer is (A).** Solar energy will be used once its cost matches that of conventional fuels. If something is cheaper and just as good or better, the consumer will buy it. This is the market system at work.

72. **The correct answer is (C).** The secretary of state registers the state's official business, including the status of business corporations.

73. **The correct answer is (D).** Education is ultimately a state responsibility, and the state superintendent of public instruction is usually the final decision-maker in conflicts concerning the application of state education regulations.

74. **The correct answer is (A).** Most states have a lieutenant governor who would fill the job of the governor should he/she retire, resign, die, or be impeached.

75. **The correct answer is (B).** The attorney general, often regarded as the second most important office in state government, is highly visible and "political," as well as responsible for law enforcement within the state.

76. **The correct answer is (D).** Both Thomas Jefferson and Martin Luther King, Jr. supported the notion that a government is for the people and by the people. They believed that people could rebel against an oppressive government (Jefferson) or protest against a biased government (King).

77. **The correct answer is (D).** A matrilocal family lives in the residence of the wife's family or with the wife's tribe.

78. **The correct answer is (D).** August Rodin (1840–1917) sculpted *Le Penseur*, or *The Thinker*, in 1880. The piece has been suggested to imply that man cannot resolve all his concerns with strength alone; the sculpture suggests pensiveness and meditation.

79. The correct answer is (B). The author feels that people marry without really knowing one another; they merely see what they would like to see before marriage.

80. The correct answer is (A). See explanation for question 79.

ESSAY RESPONSE

The quotation above deals with our Second Amendment right to bear arms—a right guaranteed to us in the constitution for "the security of a free state." However, there is a wide gap between assuring the security of a country and allowing anyone and everyone to own a gun.

Gun control legislation is a provocative issue. Both adherents and detractors feel strongly about their positions. The National Rifle Association, a powerful national lobby, uses the axiom: "If guns are outlawed, only outlaws will have guns." Their point is that gun control legislation will force law-abiding citizens to give up their arms, while criminals will still possess them illegally. Although this maxim is catchy and seemingly reasonable, I disagree with the position of the National Rifle Association.

To prevent the widespread abuse of guns that we're currently seeing, we need to enforce some sort of regulation as to who can and cannot own a weapon. For example, there are currently no laws to prevent mentally unstable people from purchasing guns. It would help to require psychological assessments for prospective purchasers, to identify those with tendencies toward violence or other antisocial behaviors. Furthermore, studies show that most violence occurs within the household among people who know each other well. Gun ownership serves to escalate the number of cases of domestic violence; moreover greater injuries are the result of such violence than in incidents in which a gun was not present. If a gun is not available in the household, then people aren't able to "resolve" an argument or dispute by shooting.

Gun control legislation is necessary in American society. We are far too violent, with numerous injuries and deaths unnecessarily caused each year by the wanton use of guns. It is time to curb the ability to shoot indiscriminately.

Part III

ATS-W

Chapter 8

ATS-W REVIEW

ATS-W MULTIPLE-CHOICE QUESTIONS

The ATS-W is designed to assess a beginning teacher's knowledge obtained in undergraduate courses and experience in schools. The test consists of 80 multiple-choice questions and is based on four education-related subject areas. These areas are listed below along with the number of questions in each area:

Subject Area	Number of Questions
I—Knowledge of the Learner	20
II—Instructional Planning/Assessment	15
III—Instructional Delivery	25
IV—The Professional Environment	20

Since the subject areas are based more on concepts, theories, and experience and are not as straightforward as the LAST subjects, we are providing you with test objectives so you can review your course material as needed. This gives you the basics so you can determine your strengths and weaknesses. Once you are familiar with these test objectives, you can customize your preparation as needed.

Area I—Knowledge of the Learner

Objective: Test your understanding of the human developmental processes in the physical, social, emotional, moral, speech/language, and cognitive domains and variations. Test your use of this understanding and the theoretical foundations about how learning occurs to foster student learning.

Objective: Understand how factors in the home, the school, and the community may affect learners. Use of this knowledge to address these factors when making instructional decisions so all students can grow and learn.

Objective: Understand diverse student populations and use knowledge of diversity within the school and the community to address the needs of all learners. Foster a sense of community among students and an appreciation of and respect for all individuals and groups.

Objective: Understand the characteristics and needs of students with disabilities, developmental delays, visual and perceptual difficulties, special physical or sensory challenges, behavioral disorders, attention-deficit disorders, and exceptional abilities. Use this knowledge to adapt and implement strategies and environments that foster the development and learning of all students.

Objective: Understand learning processes and theoretical foundations about how learning occurs. Apply strategies that foster student learning, promote students' active engagement in learning, and encourage positive relationships and cooperation.

Area II—Instructional Planning and Assessment

Objective: Understand curriculum development and apply knowledge of factors and processes in curricular decision making.

Objective: Understand techniques for instructional planning (including addressing curriculum goals, selecting content topics, incorporating learning theory, etc.) and apply knowledge processes to design effective instruction.

Objective: Understand assessment strategies and how to use formal and informal assessment to learn about students, plan instruction, monitor student understanding, and make instructional adjustments.

Area III—Instructional Delivery

Objective: Understand principles and procedures for organizing and implementing lessons, and use this knowledge to help learners construct meaning and achieve intended outcomes.

Objective: Understand multiple approaches to instruction. Use this knowledge to create effective bridges between curriculum goals and student's experiences, facilitating learning in various situations.

Objective: Understand how motivational principles (such as promoting risk taking and problem solving, encouraging convergent and divergent thinking, stimulating curiosity) can be used to promote student achievement and participation.

Objective: Understand basic, effective verbal and nonverbal communication techniques and how to use them to promote student learning and to foster a climate of trust and support in the classroom.

Objective: Understand how to structure and manage a classroom to create a climate that fosters a safe and productive learning environment.

Area IV—The Professional Environment

Objective: Understand how to take advantage of various resources (such as professional literature, colleagues, professional associations, and professional development activities) to enhance professional development and effectiveness. Use personal reflection on teaching and learning practices as a basis for making professional decisions.

Objective: Understand how to foster effective home–school relationships and school–community interactions that support student learning. Develop and utilize partnerships among parents and guardians and community leaders to support the educational process.

Prepare for the NYSTCE: LAST and ATS-W

Objective: Understand shared ownership and shared decision making in situations involving interactions between teachers and students, parents, community members, colleagues, school administrators, and other school personnel.

Objective: Understand the structure and organization of the New York State educational system and the role of education in the broader society.

WRITTEN ASSIGNMENT

The ATS-W includes a written assignment. This may not be an essay but could be another writing assignment. Some examples include:

- Outline of a curriculum
- A lesson plan
- Response to a classroom situation
- Information/comments about other education-related situations

OVERVIEW OF THE WRITING PROCESS

Whether you are writing an essay or a few paragraphs, the writing process can be divided into three steps: *planning*, *drafting*, and *revising*. The following chart shows what each step means and how to spend your time wisely when completing the written assignment:

Step	Process
Planning	think of ideas
	arrange ideas into a rough outline
Drafting	write your first copy
	include details and examples
Revising	correct mistakes
	add more details, if necessary
	cut unnecessary information
	make a clean copy, if time permits

Here's a better look at each step in detail:

Step #1: Planning

When you plan, you think of ideas to include in your assignment. This is often called "brainstorming." You can brainstorm in many ways.

Here are some examples of ways you can brainstorm:

- Making a web or other graphic

- Listing subtopics

- Answering the questions: *Who? What? When? Where? Why? How?*

Before you do anything else, rephrase the writing prompt in your own words to make sure that you understand it.

To make all of this make sense, you should make a "web." To do this, draw a circle in the middle of a sheet of paper. Add lines going out from the circle. At the end of each line, draw a circle and fill it in with a subtopic. Here is a sample of what a "web" looks like:

Suppose you had the opportunity to give someone a tour of your town. In your essay, identify what parts of the town you would tour and why. Use your experience and knowledge to support your writing.

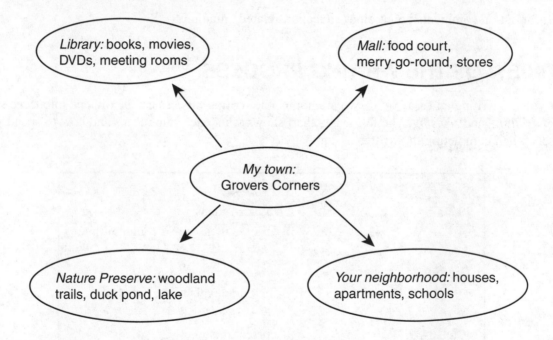

You do not have to use all these ideas in your writing. You may only use two, one in each paragraph of the body. However, making a web helps you get your ideas down on paper. This gives you the choice of subtopics to use. Always choose the subtopics that will best answer the question and appeal to your reader.

Step #2: Drafting

Follow these 6 steps as you write:

1. Be sure to write in ink.

2. It is natural to start at the beginning with the introduction, but if you are stuck for an opening, don't waste time. Instead, start where you can, in the middle; although, it is important that your writing is well organized and logical.

3. Keep writing. If you get stuck, skip some lines and keep on writing. If you can't keep on writing, take a few deep breaths and gather your thoughts. If you are still stuck, move on to another part. Staring at the paper only wastes time.

4. Write neatly. If your writing cannot be read, the scorer won't be able to grade your paper. If it is messy, your scorer might misread a crucial point. If you know your handwriting is hard to read, print neatly and carefully.

5. Be focused, serious, and mature in your writing.

6. Use a clock as you practice writing your assignment. This will teach you how to pace yourself so you can make sure that you finish within the time limits on the day of the test.

Step #3: Revising

When you revise, you do the following things:

- Correct mistakes in spelling, grammar, usage, punctuation, and capitalization
- Add more details, if necessary
- Cut unnecessary information
- Make a clean copy, if time permits

Assess Your Writing

You should always use the following Writing Evaluation Checklist as you assess your writing. Make copies and fill out a checklist each time you write a practice essay or practice written response.

WRITING EVALUATION CHECKLIST

1. Main Ideas

_____ Do my main points directly answer the question?

_____ Are my main points persuasive and logical?

_____ Will they convince my readers that my point is valid?

_____ Are my ideas linked in a logical way?

_____ Does my essay have unity?

2. Organization

_____ Does my essay have a clear beginning that introduces my main points?

_____ Does my essay have at least two body paragraphs?

_____ Do I start a new paragraph for each main point?

_____ Does my essay have a conclusion that sums up my main points?

3. Development of Ideas

_____ Do I include specific details to make my point? (_Details_ are examples, facts, statistics, reasons, definitions, and descriptions)

_____ Are my facts correct?

_____ Do my details really prove my point?

4. Skills

_____ Have I spelled all words correctly?

_____ Have I used correct grammar?

_____ Have I corrected all errors in punctuation and capitalization?

_____ Can my handwriting be read easily? Have I written in pen?

Answer Sheet for Chapter 9

ATS-W—PRACTICE TEST 1

1. Ⓐ Ⓑ Ⓒ Ⓓ   21. Ⓐ Ⓑ Ⓒ Ⓓ   41. Ⓐ Ⓑ Ⓒ Ⓓ   61. Ⓐ Ⓑ Ⓒ Ⓓ

2. Ⓐ Ⓑ Ⓒ Ⓓ   22. Ⓐ Ⓑ Ⓒ Ⓓ   42. Ⓐ Ⓑ Ⓒ Ⓓ   62. Ⓐ Ⓑ Ⓒ Ⓓ

3. Ⓐ Ⓑ Ⓒ Ⓓ   23. Ⓐ Ⓑ Ⓒ Ⓓ   43. Ⓐ Ⓑ Ⓒ Ⓓ   63. Ⓐ Ⓑ Ⓒ Ⓓ

4. Ⓐ Ⓑ Ⓒ Ⓓ   24. Ⓐ Ⓑ Ⓒ Ⓓ   44. Ⓐ Ⓑ Ⓒ Ⓓ   64. Ⓐ Ⓑ Ⓒ Ⓓ

5. Ⓐ Ⓑ Ⓒ Ⓓ   25. Ⓐ Ⓑ Ⓒ Ⓓ   45. Ⓐ Ⓑ Ⓒ Ⓓ   65. Ⓐ Ⓑ Ⓒ Ⓓ

6. Ⓐ Ⓑ Ⓒ Ⓓ   26. Ⓐ Ⓑ Ⓒ Ⓓ   46. Ⓐ Ⓑ Ⓒ Ⓓ   66. Ⓐ Ⓑ Ⓒ Ⓓ

7. Ⓐ Ⓑ Ⓒ Ⓓ   27. Ⓐ Ⓑ Ⓒ Ⓓ   47. Ⓐ Ⓑ Ⓒ Ⓓ   67. Ⓐ Ⓑ Ⓒ Ⓓ

8. Ⓐ Ⓑ Ⓒ Ⓓ   28. Ⓐ Ⓑ Ⓒ Ⓓ   48. Ⓐ Ⓑ Ⓒ Ⓓ   68. Ⓐ Ⓑ Ⓒ Ⓓ

9. Ⓐ Ⓑ Ⓒ Ⓓ   29. Ⓐ Ⓑ Ⓒ Ⓓ   49. Ⓐ Ⓑ Ⓒ Ⓓ   69. Ⓐ Ⓑ Ⓒ Ⓓ

10. Ⓐ Ⓑ Ⓒ Ⓓ   30. Ⓐ Ⓑ Ⓒ Ⓓ   50. Ⓐ Ⓑ Ⓒ Ⓓ   70. Ⓐ Ⓑ Ⓒ Ⓓ

11. Ⓐ Ⓑ Ⓒ Ⓓ   31. Ⓐ Ⓑ Ⓒ Ⓓ   51. Ⓐ Ⓑ Ⓒ Ⓓ   71. Ⓐ Ⓑ Ⓒ Ⓓ

12. Ⓐ Ⓑ Ⓒ Ⓓ   32. Ⓐ Ⓑ Ⓒ Ⓓ   52. Ⓐ Ⓑ Ⓒ Ⓓ   72. Ⓐ Ⓑ Ⓒ Ⓓ

13. Ⓐ Ⓑ Ⓒ Ⓓ   33. Ⓐ Ⓑ Ⓒ Ⓓ   53. Ⓐ Ⓑ Ⓒ Ⓓ   73. Ⓐ Ⓑ Ⓒ Ⓓ

14. Ⓐ Ⓑ Ⓒ Ⓓ   34. Ⓐ Ⓑ Ⓒ Ⓓ   54. Ⓐ Ⓑ Ⓒ Ⓓ   74. Ⓐ Ⓑ Ⓒ Ⓓ

15. Ⓐ Ⓑ Ⓒ Ⓓ   35. Ⓐ Ⓑ Ⓒ Ⓓ   55. Ⓐ Ⓑ Ⓒ Ⓓ   75. Ⓐ Ⓑ Ⓒ Ⓓ

16. Ⓐ Ⓑ Ⓒ Ⓓ   36. Ⓐ Ⓑ Ⓒ Ⓓ   56. Ⓐ Ⓑ Ⓒ Ⓓ   76. Ⓐ Ⓑ Ⓒ Ⓓ

17. Ⓐ Ⓑ Ⓒ Ⓓ   37. Ⓐ Ⓑ Ⓒ Ⓓ   57. Ⓐ Ⓑ Ⓒ Ⓓ   77. Ⓐ Ⓑ Ⓒ Ⓓ

18. Ⓐ Ⓑ Ⓒ Ⓓ   38. Ⓐ Ⓑ Ⓒ Ⓓ   58. Ⓐ Ⓑ Ⓒ Ⓓ   78. Ⓐ Ⓑ Ⓒ Ⓓ

19. Ⓐ Ⓑ Ⓒ Ⓓ   39. Ⓐ Ⓑ Ⓒ Ⓓ   59. Ⓐ Ⓑ Ⓒ Ⓓ   79. Ⓐ Ⓑ Ⓒ Ⓓ

20. Ⓐ Ⓑ Ⓒ Ⓓ   40. Ⓐ Ⓑ Ⓒ Ⓓ   60. Ⓐ Ⓑ Ⓒ Ⓓ   80. Ⓐ Ⓑ Ⓒ Ⓓ

Chapter 9

ATS-W—PRACTICE TEST 1

TIME: 4 Hours—80 Questions

> *Directions:* Each statement or passage in this test is followed by one or more questions. Read each statement or passage, and then answer the accompanying questions, basing your answer on what is stated or implied in the passage. Blacken the letter of your answer choice on the answer sheet.

1. A parent wrote a letter to Ms. Samuels, asking the teacher to call. When she did, the mother complained in an angry voice that she was upset that Ms. Samuels did not seem to defend her daughter from another girl who was picking on her. The student's mother wanted the situation resolved immediately and the girl who was bothering her daughter to be punished. How should Ms. Samuels respond to this mother?

   (A) Act surprised and tell the mother that it was her daughter who seemed to be instigating the conflict with the other student.
   (B) Thank the parent for making her aware of the problem and state that she will investigate the matter and deal with the problem between her daughter and this other student by the end of the day.
   (C) Immediately apologize to the parent and state that the other student would immediately be punished.
   (D) State to the parent that she was unaware of the problem because she was out of the classroom for several days.

2. In developing her reading program for the year, Mrs. Littell wants to assess the affective attitudes her fourth-grade students have about reading. Which type of instrument would be the least effective way to gather this information?

   (A) An oral interview with the students about their perceptions of reading and reading instruction
   (B) An interview with the students about their feelings about reading materials in the content area
   (C) A miscue analysis to see how the students react when words are mispronounced
   (D) A Likert-type scale that is filled out by the parents as to their perception about the reading habits of the student

3. Ms. Littell has decided to put together a reading interview so that she can determine how her students view the reading process. She has brainstormed a list of questions for the interview. Of the questions that follow, which one is most suitable in helping the teacher to understand her students' perceptions of what makes an effective reader?

  (A) When you do poorly on a reading test, what do you want to tell your parents?
  (B) What are three ways your teacher helps you to pronounce words?
  (C) When you read, what makes you like the story?
  (D) What makes your mother a good reader?

4. Mr. Schwartz, Ms. Littell's colleague, wants to adapt a reading attitude survey for his class of first-grade students. What advice should Ms. Littell give to Mr. Schwartz about developing a survey that will tap into the affective domain of his students in regards to reading?

  (A) The scale should be read orally, and the Likert choices should be in terms of various expressions made by the face of a cartoon character.
  (B) The questions should focus on the academic aspects of reading done in kindergarten and first grade.
  (C) The students should read the questions that are formatted using a rebus approach to facilitate the child's ability to read the scale.
  (D) Many CVC words should be used in the questions on this inventory, and Mr. Schwartz should observe the student's facial expressions as he tries to read the words.

5. When Ms. Littell conducts a reading lesson, she divides her class into three small groups. Jimmy is in a group made up of 5 students. When this group must engage in an independent reading activity while Ms. Littell works with another group, Jimmy often kicks the student that sits next to him. When this happens, the other student tells Jimmy to stop. Jimmy responds with curses and hits the student on the head. When this happens,

Jimmy is asked to sit by himself for the rest of the period. Which may be a motivating factor in this situation on the part of the student?

  (A) The reading material is too easy, and Jimmy often finishes first and has nothing to do.
  (B) The material is too hard, and he is trying to avoid doing the work in a basal reader.
  (C) The actions of this child show that he needs to be involved in psychotherapy.
  (D) He dislikes reading because he constantly fails the standardized tests.

6. Mrs. Fenichal is a new third-grade teacher. During orientation, the principal stated that social studies in his school is supposed to be taught as a multidisciplinary unit. Mrs. Fenichal has never created such a unit before. In addition, she has never taught third grade and has no knowledge of the curriculum at that grade. Which of the following items should the teacher do to gain enough skills to create a third-grade multidisciplinary unit in social studies?

  I. Mrs. Fenichal should see several units created last year by a more experienced third-grade teacher.
  II. The teacher should adapt a unit she created three years earlier in college as part of a course in the teaching of social studies.
  III. Mrs. Fenichal should try to find a similar unit in an Internet lesson plan database.
  IV. She should review the third-grade curriculum manual in social studies.

  (A) I and III only
  (B) II, III, and IV only
  (C) I and II only
  (D) I and IV only

7. According to state guidelines, Mrs. Fenichal must create a unit on communities. In this unit, she must discuss that people in the United States move from one part of the country to another part of the country to begin new communities. In addition, she must explain that immigrants have come to the United States and often influenced community development. Finally, she must discuss how changes in transportation and communication have affected the lives of people in different

communities in the United States. Which of the following may NOT be an appropriate objective for this unit?

(A) Students should know how various societies were affected by contacts and exchanges among diverse people.

(B) Students should understand the impact of scientific and technological developments on individuals and societies.

(C) Students should know the characteristics, location, distribution, and migration of human populations.

(D) Students should be able to identify the different contributions made by various immigrant groups.

8. Mrs. Fenichal wants to create a unit on communities that will have a lot of hands-on experiences. She wants to create many multi-sensory activities so that as many students as possible can be actively involved. She wants her class to learn by doing. Which list does NOT contain appropriate materials for such an approach?

(A) Oregon Trail CD-ROM, inflatable map of the world, videotape of Little House on the Prairie

(B) Nineteenth-century photographs, a desk map of the United States, colored markers

(C) Construction paper, map of pioneer trails in the United States, access to a computer laboratory

(D) Social studies textbook, graph paper to chart marks, a library book on immigrants containing many photographs

9. Mrs. Fenichal spends ten days teaching the first lesson of her unit. The title of the lesson is "Building New Lives." She must incorporate English and language arts into this part of the unit. Which item incorporates English concepts into this lesson?

(A) Students will pretend to be late nineteenth-century European immigrants and write a letter back to relatives in their respective countries about life in New York.

(B) Students will create a graph about changes in immigration patterns from 1900 to 1990.

(C) Students will study the different types of engines found in steam ships that crossed the ocean during the first half of the twentieth century.

(D) Students will create a blueprint of a tenement in New York City and label different parts of the building.

10. Mrs. Fenichal has created a group project for the unit. Students must work in groups of four or five. Half the class must research and present information on the Italian, Irish, and Jewish immigrants in New York City during the year 1900. The other half of the class must discuss how these groups exist today.

The groups will build and present displays containing maps, pictures, charts, or anything of interest to the students depicting these immigrant groups and the types of technology they used to travel and communicate. These two groups will provide the class with a handout relevant to their display.

The teacher must create a rubric to grade the two group presentations. She is taking into consideration cooperative learning methodology in her creation of a group mark for these projects.

Which one of these items would be least relevant to the grading of this cooperative project?

(A) The number and relevance of the student handouts

(B) The distribution of the contributions for each member

(C) Whether the display contained the most information in the curriculum guidelines

(D) The organization and number of items within the display

11. Mr. Charles is an eighth-grade math teacher in a middle school situated in an upper-middle-class neighborhood. Susan, one of his best students, received failing grades on her last two quizzes. During his preparation period right after Susan's class, Mr. Charles decides to talk with her about this matter. During the conversation, Susan bursts into tears and tells him that she is being molested by her new stepfather. What is Mr. Charles' next course of action?

    (A) He should tell Susan that this is a private matter and end the conversation immediately.

    (B) He should offer to tutor the student in his subject area because he should focus only upon her academic and not her personal problems.

    (C) He should call up Susan's mother and request that she come in for a conference, in which he will bring up the matter.

    (D) He should immediately inform the principal of the discussion.

12. The reading scores of the students in PS 155 have been declining for the past three years. Therefore, the principal has formed a teacher/administrative committee to come up with another standard to assess the reading achievement of the students in the school. The principal feels that mitigating factors are contributing to this decline. The committee is made up of seven teachers. Two teachers are from the upper grade, two are early childhood teachers, two are special educators, and the seventh is a learning disabilities consultant. Mr. Weingarten, a resource room teacher in the school, told the committee that he feels a standardized reading score on a single test is not a valid measure for determining the reading progress of a student. He feels that other factors impact upon the reading score of standardized tests.

    What might the specialist say are some variables that may affect reading scores on a standardized test?

    I. The number of immigrant students in the school
    II. The socioeconomic status of the area

    III. The condition of the school's physical plant
    IV. The number of students who attended preschool programs

    (A) II and III only
    (B) I, II, and III only
    (C) I, II, and IV only
    (D) I only

13. Mr. Weingarten and the other members of the committee must come up with other ways to measure the reading ability of the students in their school. The committee is in agreement that they no longer want to rely on the state and citywide reading tests as the primary measures of reading ability. The committee wants to rely on informal measures of reading ability. The group decided to brainstorm many informal measures. All of the following are informal measures of reading ability EXCEPT

    (A) portfolios.
    (B) IRIs.
    (C) diagnostic/prescriptive measures.
    (D) interest inventories.

14. The committee decided that there would be a standard literary portfolio for the school to assess the reading skills of their pupils. The portfolio would consist of lists of books read, sample books, student drawings, samples of writing, photographs, and the student's report card. This portfolio would help the inner-city students in this school build their self-esteem. The portfolio would contain many nonschool items because many of the students have a nonacademic involvement with literature. The portfolio would be shared with their parents and next year's teacher. However, there was heated debate in the committee about whether to implement such a portfolio assessment. Several members were against portfolios. Which of the items is a significant criticism against portfolios?

    (A) Items chosen for the portfolio by the student may not be a true measure of reading ability.

    (B) If too many people share in viewing and analyzing the portfolio, the items it is supposed to measure may be compromised.

(C) Written critiques by the student about various stories are not relevant to the reading process.

(D) When portfolios are used in the classroom, there is a decrease in independent seat work during structured reading lessons.

15. On the other hand, the principal on the committee feels that portfolios are more comprehensive and more accurate than regular types of assessments. He feels that portfolios help students make and achieve appropriate goals. In his discussion favoring portfolios, which of the following items might be mentioned?

   I. Because the items in the portfolio are important to the student, pupils use this approach to learn about themselves.
   II. Students have the ability to plan a relevant, authentic curriculum for themselves, and this will help them expand their learning horizons.
   III. Portfolios help at-risk students stay in school because they motivate them to attempt new tasks.
   IV. A more relevant curriculum will help students increase their scores on standardized tests.

   (A) II and III only
   (B) III and IV only
   (C) I, III, and IV only
   (D) I, II, and III only

16. During a parent-teacher conference, Mrs. Smith must tell Leroy's parents that he is a management problem in the classroom. The teacher has not discussed this matter previously with Leroy's mother and father in the hope that she would be able to remedy the situation herself. However, she can no longer tolerate his constant drumming on the desk and singing. During the conference, which is the most effective manner that Mrs. Smith could relate this situation to his parents?

   (A) Mrs. Smith could describe the student's strengths before anecdotally describing his behavior in a factual manner.
   (B) Mrs. Smith could tell the parents that he may possibly need a referral for special education because of his management needs.

(C) The teacher should immediately discuss and describe the child's management problems.

(D) The teacher could describe how the child is preventing the rest of the class from learning.

17. Mrs. Fields is developing a communication arts curriculum for the early childhood classes in her elementary school. She is developing a curriculum with the awareness of the logical order in which students develop language skills. According to her research, communication skills develop according to which sequence?

   (A) Listening, speaking, reading, and writing
   (B) Speaking, listening, reading, and writing
   (C) Listening, speaking, writing, and reading
   (D) Writing, reading, listening, and speaking

18. Mr. Williams is a sixth-grade general education teacher of 33 students. Chuck is a sixth-grade student in his class. Although attentive, Chuck has handwriting that is so sloppy and illegible that he is unable to copy notes, read his own work, or accurately copy his homework. As a result, he received failing grades on a literature test and a social studies test. What is the first thing Mr. Williams should do to remedy Chuck's problem?

   (A) The student should be referred to the Committee on Special Education so that he can receive occupational therapy.
   (B) Because the teacher does not have the time, Mr. Williams should assign Chuck a peer tutor to work on handwriting.
   (C) The student's difficulty should be sent to the school's Pupil Personnel Committee, who will come up with interventions that the teacher may be able to implement.
   (D) Notes should be sent home to the parents stating that the child needs two hours of handwriting practice every day.

19. Even though a peer tutor has been assigned to help Chuck with his handwriting, several problems remain. His inability to copy his homework and hand in legible assignments are negatively affecting his grades. Even though Chuck is working hard, there is a possibility that he might fail several subjects. Mr. Williams consults the learning disability specialist, who is a member of the Pupil Personnel Committee, for a solution. What can Mr. Williams do to remedy the situation?

    (A) He should no longer assign this student written homework but instead should allow the student to answer questions through drawing.

    (B) All class notes should be written in print instead of script.

    (C) Another student should write the notes with carbon paper and then give the notes to Chuck.

    (D) The student should use a computer to copy his homework and notes in class.

20. After several months, even with adaptations authorized within general education by the school's Pupil Personnel Committee, Chuck is still failing most tests because of his handwriting. The teacher cannot read his essays and often gives him lower grades in English and social studies. The teacher asks the Child Study Team that assesses special education students for help. What should be the result of this request?

    (A) Chuck should be tested by the team to see if he needs any special educational services.

    (B) The team should tell the teacher that this seems like a 504 issue and that more formal adaptations have to be authorized.

    (C) The team, with parent consent, will exempt the child from all formalized citywide and state tests.

    (D) The Child Study Team will not evaluate a child that is brought up before the Pupil Personnel Committee.

21. Chuck's parents, the principal, and the 504 coordinator of the district have a meeting to discuss different adaptations that can be done to help the student compensate for his handwriting problem. Which item will NOT help Chuck compensate for his handwriting difficulty in school?

    (A) The student will learn to utilize a laptop computer to copy his notes and homework in a quick and accurate manner using spell-checker and word-prediction software.

    (B) He will be able to record his written responses to classroom, citywide, and state tests in any manner.

    (C) He will record answers to essay-type questions on examinations.

    (D) He will learn to write slower when he copies his homework and class notes from the board.

22. If during this 504 meeting the school district or its representative and the parents cannot reach agreement as to the type of adaptations Chuck may need, what is the next course of action that should take place?

    (A) His parents will withdraw him from the school district to find another district that will provide the services.

    (B) There will be either mediation or a due process hearing by an impartial officer.

    (C) The school district will pay for the student to receive educational services at home or in a private school that will provide the adaptations.

    (D) State law mandates that any adaptation requested by a parent be implemented by the district within ten days.

23. To convince a hearing officer that Chuck needs adaptations in regular education to compensate for inability to perform the physical act of writing, his parents need evidence that will back up their claims. Which of the following assessments could convince a hearing officer to give Chuck various adaptations on his terminal IEP?

I. A portfolio containing the student's class work and homework
II. A report from an occupational therapist
III. A progress report from his physical education teacher
IV. A recommendation for services by the student's pediatrician

(A) I and II only
(B) III and IV only
(C) II only
(D) I and III only

24. Timothy has been a major problem in the school since he arrived in kindergarten two years ago. He has a history of touching other students inappropriately. When Timothy does not get his way, he throws violent temper tantrums. The principal told the teacher that she must keep anecdotal records to justify any potential evaluation of the student. Following are four examples of anecdotal records. Which of these statements represents an appropriate format when writing anecdotal materials?

(A) This afternoon, Timmy acted out and threw a temper tantrum that resulted in a suspension.
(B) 2 p.m.—Timothy constantly bothered three students that sat next to him and was generally bad all afternoon.
(C) Next, Timothy cursed much of the time. He left the room to sit in another teacher's class.
(D) During the 35-minute math period after 1 p.m., Timothy left his assigned seat four times and hit Jamie on the head when he vacated his desk for a second time.

25. Dr. Jenkins specializes in teaching unit concepts in interesting ways. He is presently working on various games and activities to teach sixth-grade social studies concepts. For his present unit, he made up a fable contest hosted by Mr. Ted Aesop. Four cooperative groups make up fables; the most interesting one wins an all-expense-paid trip to a pizza parlor.

A second activity is called Cardboard Columns. Paper towel rolls are decorated and pasted together to make an interesting building. Next, illustrated cards are made to play a game called Young Venus. If someone is left with Venus after matching pairs of cards, then that person wins something. The unit this class is studying is focusing on which country?

(A) Ancient Greece
(B) The Roman Republic
(C) The Roman Empire
(D) The Assyrian Empire

26. The geography of the ancient Greeks had to be taught by Dr. Jenkins over the next several weeks to the class. Geography today focuses more on social history; geography today is social geography. All of the following are basic themes in the teaching of geography today EXCEPT

(A) understanding the reasons for and the importance of human migration.
(B) understanding the interaction between humans and the natural environment through time.
(C) understanding the world regions and the interrelated impact of cultural and global interdependence.
(D) understanding the difference among various symbols within maps of countries in conflict.

27. Dr. Jenkins assigned the reading of Antigone, Socrates, an anthology of myths, and excerpts from the history of the ancient world by Herodotus. The reason these books were assigned was to

(A) make history more interesting.
(B) use literature to teach social studies.
(C) cover issues in depth.
(D) teach the difference between fiction, plays, philosophy, and nonfiction.

28. When Dr. Jenkins was being observed, the assistant principal took many notes. In their post-conference, the administrator asked the teacher why he was devoting so much time to ancient European history in this world history course he was teaching. What would be an appropriate response by the teacher?

- **(A)** There is too much emphasis on multiculturalism in the curriculum guide.
- **(B)** Ancient history is a celebration of our diversity as a people.
- **(C)** There are many Greek words in our language as a result of immigration.
- **(D)** This will help the students learn about the origins of many beliefs and principals.

29. John Witcomb began teaching two months ago in Seneca Valley Middle School. In Mr. Witcomb's science class, a student called out a response to a question instead of raising his hand. The teacher told the student that he was giving him three extra chapters to read for homework because of the outburst. When he collected the homework, he saw that Charles' homework was not complete: he missed two questions. The teacher yelled to the student that he was going to lose five points off his report card grade. A girl in his class started to giggle, and the teacher responded by saying that the class would have to write 400 times, "I will be quiet." Only one student started to write, and the rest began to yell and scream that it was not fair. The teacher screamed to the class to be quiet and wrote on the board that they had to now read three chapters instead of one chapter. At this point, three students uttered profanities and walked out of the room.

Which factors were causing discipline problems in Mr. Witcomb's class?

- I. He punished the whole class when one student misbehaved.
- II. He maintained no personal distance from the students.
- III. He used schoolwork as punishment.
- IV. He did not give the students any privileges.

- **(A)** IV only
- **(B)** III and IV only
- **(C)** I and III only
- **(D)** II and III only

30. Mr. Witcomb became upset because of his lack of management skills. For half the time every period, he must deal with behavior problems. Therefore, after an informal observation, the principal gave him a mentor to help him develop better management skills.

After the mentor observed Mr. Witcomb, he made several suggestions to improve the management of the class.

Which of the following would be a worthwhile suggestion the mentor would make to improve Mr. Witcomb's class?

- **(A)** If a student forgets to do part of his homework, have him complete the assignment during lunch and hand it in by the end of the day.
- **(B)** If a student talks, have him write, "I will not talk" only 100 times instead of 400 times.
- **(C)** If five kids talk during a lesson, give the class a 3-minute time out.
- **(D)** If a student has no pencil, send a letter home asking the parent to buy 10 pencils to keep in class.

31. The mentor gives Mr. Witcomb several suggestions to be more consistent in developing and implementing class rules. Which of the following actions by Mr. Witcomb is NOT inconsistent?

- **(A)** He extended the deadline for writing "I will not talk" four times.
- **(B)** Mr. Witcomb continued to warn the class to be quiet or there would be more homework.
- **(C)** The teacher gave the students a surprise quiz; when many students could not answer the questions, he stated that he would give them one more day to study.
- **(D)** When a student missed three homework assignments, his report card mark was reduced by 5 points.

32. Which of the following would NOT be a probable suggestion made by the mentor to help Mr. Witcomb improve his classroom management?

    (A) After a 50-question midterm, allow them to watch a movie the next day.
    (B) Just before Christmas, give each student a no-homework certificate as a present.
    (C) If a student has incomplete homework, keep him after class for 5 minutes to go over the problems that were left out.
    (D) Ask the student to choose her failing grade after class is over so as not to embarrass her in front of her peers.

33. The mentor shows Mr. Witcomb a film on appropriately ignoring misbehavers. According to the film, which of the following is an appropriate way to avoid trouble by not rewarding behaviors you want to eliminate?

    (A) If a student utters an expletive, go over to the student and say, "That's nasty! Shame! Don't ever say the word again!" in a loud voice so that the other students will hear the reprimand.
    (B) If a student is chewing gum, send the student out of the room to stand in the hall.
    (C) If a student gets up without permission to sharpen a pencil, talk to the student in a low voice about staying focused in her seat.
    (D) If a student is playing with a paper clip, take it away and ask all the students to clear out their desks to inspect if other students have similar objects.

34. Mr. Jamison is a ninth-grade global studies teacher. He is teaching a unit on the role of religion in history. This teacher knows that this may be a very sensitive topic and that religion has to be taught in a comparative manner. All are appropriate topics for his unit EXCEPT

    (A) contrasting the differences between the Moslem, Jewish, and Christian religions.
    (B) exploring the role of religion in the development of educational institutions.

    (C) exploring the origins of the three major Western religions.
    (D) exploring the role the prophets played in predicting events that happened in the future.

35. The chairperson of Mr. Jamison's social studies department went over several objectives for teaching comparative religion. One of the major objectives in teaching comparative religion is probably the

    (A) development of tolerance of different religious beliefs.
    (B) ability to determine which religion is the most valid expression of human needs.
    (C) understanding that religion is static and has not evolved since the end of the seventeenth century.
    (D) understanding that religion is the prime motivating factor in creating harmony in multicultural societies.

36. Mrs. Marlow is taking several education courses for a master's degree. One of her courses is entitled "Theoretical Thoughts in Education." In the course, she read four books by different educational theorists. Which of the following authors would most likely help Mrs. Marlow to understand the underlying effects of poverty on academic achievement?

    (A) Dewey
    (B) Maslow
    (C) Piaget
    (D) Ravitch

37. In this course, Mrs. Marlow reads several studies by Schlesinger and Ravitch pertaining to multicultural education. In their study, these two authors reviewed various textbooks. Mrs. Marlow had to summarize their conclusions in a terse and concise manner. Which of the following statements would best represent a summary of the conclusions reached by these two authors?

(A) Multicultural social studies textbooks contain faulty empirical research. Many of these books contain mythological stories about various ethnic groups that are now being passed off as fact.

(B) These textbooks now give a clearer view of American history because they include information about many important Americans that were passed over during earlier eras. Present textbooks are, as a result, less Eurocentric.

(C) Multicultural textbooks focus more on class distinctions rather than on race in and of itself. Many of these books reflect a wide divergence of political thought.

(D) Modern textbooks are less biased than during previous eras. They reflect a truer picture of American history. The shortcomings as well as the great strides within American society are discussed.

38. Mr. Foley, a sixth-grade regular education teacher, receives a copy of Timmy Steward's IEP. Timmy has been recommended for a consultant teacher. On the IEP, several testing modifications are mentioned. Timmy is supposed to be given double time in a minimally distracting environment for doing tests. Passages, questions, and directions are all to be read to the student. Timmy is also allowed to record answers using a tape recorder.

The assistant principal instructed Mr. Foley to implement this IEP in the classroom.

This is the first time Mr. Foley must implement an IEP in his class. He is told he has a week to submit a written plan of how he will make these adaptations in the classroom.

What would be an appropriate course of action for Mr. Foley?

(A) He will make sure that the resource room teacher in his school will give the students all citywide and state tests.

(B) He will ignore the IEP because only the consultant teacher will implement the adaptations.

(C) He will talk with the consultant teacher to develop strategies to implement the adaptations in a collaborative manner.

(D) He will have the child reevaluated by the school's Child Study Team for placement in a special education class so that it will be easier to implement the various modifications.

39. Mr. Foley asks the assistant principal which tests must be modified. Which statement would probably be the response of this building administrator?

(A) All quizzes, classroom tests, state tests, and citywide tests

(B) Only such pivotal tests as midterms, finals, and citywide examinations

(C) All short answer tests in which the student must fill in a computer grid

(D) Those tests deemed appropriate by the consultant teacher

40. Mr. Foley is unsure how to reduce the distractions in the classroom when giving a test. He discusses this with the consultant teacher. Which of the following would NOT be an appropriate recommendation?

(A) The student should sit at a carrel while taking classroom tests.

(B) During test time, the student's desk should face an area of the class that has few stimulating displays and posters.

(C) The student should take the test out of the classroom in the hall.

(D) As the student takes the test, he should uncover the parts he has to read one line at a time.

41. Referring back to question 38, based on the previous test modifications, this child most likely has

    (A) a perceptual handicap.
    (B) attention deficit disorder.
    (C) a visual deficit.
    (D) mental retardation.

42. Mrs. Jeroky is preparing her seventh-grade science class for a science fair. She is giving her class four weeks to prepare for the fair. She feels that the science fair should be fun and educational. She wants her students to pick something they are interested in because these projects take a lot of time and effort.

    John is interested in music. However, he cannot think of any type of science fair project that can incorporate his interest. Mrs. Jeroky enlists the help of the rest of the class to brainstorm different science fair projects that are related to music.

    Which of the items listed here would be an appropriate science fair project related to music?

    I. Comparing the sound from different CDs to try to determine which one is the loudest.
    II. Determining the effect music has on emotions.
    III. Determining whether the price of different CDs is dependent upon the complexity of the music.
    IV. Determining the effect of different types of music upon common houseplants.

    (A) I and II only
    (B) I, II, and III only
    (C) IV, II, and I only
    (D) I, II, and IV only

43. Mrs. Jeroky has the class come up with some generalizations about developing an effective science fair project. One generalization is that the students should not wait until the last minute to start a project. All the reasons here would be mentioned by the students as to why a project should be started early EXCEPT

    (A) taking measurements require you to repeat your experiment more than once.
    (B) you must research reasons for your experiment.
    (C) it takes time to prepare a concise display for your experiment.
    (D) you must choose a different project if your hypothesis is disproved.

44. Mrs. Jeroky decided that she would give approval only for projects that are appropriate for middle school. The project should have background information, use the scientific method, use controls, and have data that is graphed and charted on some type of exhibit or display. Which of the following projects is NOT appropriate, according to the teacher's guidelines?

    (A) A project on pollution in plants in which different pollutants are mixed in the soil of perennial plants. The student has to prove which pollutant limited the most growth in plants.
    (B) A project set up to determine which battery lasts longest in relation to its price. The project is supposed to determine which battery is the best deal economically.
    (C) A project set up to determine which brick is most resistant to erosion over an extended period of time when cement is mixed with different amounts of plastic.
    (D) A project set up to compare a series circuit to a parallel circuit in terms of determining how much wiring must be used to produce a light in a small bulb.

45. John's science fair project was to find out whether plants grew in sand or dirt. He wanted to see if plants put in sand would grow taller, or would grow at all. He thought that plants would grow taller in dirt. He used a 20-pound bag each of sand and dirt, two planting containers, and a package of beans. He put sand in one container and dirt in another. Then he put three bean seeds in each container. John watered the plants every other day. After the end of a month, the plants in the sand and dirt were the same height.

Which of the following statements is probably the hypothesis for this science fair project?

(A) Plants in dirt will grow taller.
(B) Plants will not grow if there is too much rain.
(C) The lack of nutrients has no effect on plants.
(D) Seawater has an effect on the growth of plants.

46. The staff at Midwood Elementary School is taking a mandated in-service course on the writing process. The course is being conducted by Mrs. Roberta Herly. In the course, Mrs. Herly tells her teachers that students should free write, jot down notes, and collect journal entries. These exercises are important to the writing process because they lead to

(A) the first draft.
(B) the rehearsal stage.
(C) the publication stage.
(D) more refined editing.

47. In her course, Mrs. Herly describes the composing stage of the writing process for grades 3 to 5. Which of the following items would least help a student compose some type of writing at this level?

(A) Explore the factual and fictional works of professionals to become familiar with different literary techniques in order to replicate them
(B) Use a variety of forms, such as narrative, expository prose, and poetry

(C) Focus on writing multiparagraph compositions to develop the readiness skills to write content area compositions
(D) Learn to write for various audiences and purposes by changing style, tone, expressions, and formality

48. In her course, Mrs. Herly gives out the essay of a sixth-grade student for everyone to read and analyze.

"Mr. Jamison has been a dusty, old liberal Senator since the stone age. He has ideas of the past. The time has come for a new generation. We do not need a '60s peacenik to represent us in the upper House. We do not need someone who supports red unions and incompetent and indecent teachers protected by tenure. He wants to spend our hard-earned money on giveaways and boondoggles. It's time we had a Senator for our generation. Vote for Tim Smith, a leader of the '90s."

Which type of writing style is the teacher illustrating by this essay?

(A) Glittering generalities
(B) Bandwagon
(C) Testimonial
(D) Loaded language

49. The paragraph in question 48 is an example of propaganda. Mrs. Herly states that propaganda can be either positive or negative. In discussing the passage with the class, the instructor wants the class to generate a useful follow-up activity for this lesson. All of the following are examples of effective follow-ups EXCEPT

(A) to rewrite the paragraph in an objective manner.
(B) to ask the students to circle and define all loaded words.
(C) to use the writing process to check for syntactical and grammatical errors.
(D) to have the other senator write a reply to this letter.

50. During the last part of the course, Mrs. Herly discusses how teachers could use the writing process to help middle-school students present their written material. For example, students could reflect on their collected writings over time to develop personal writing goals in the future. Which items are appropriate presentations that can be used in her class?

 I. Preparing oral presentations in terms of a debate
 II. Showing their writing to different audiences
 III. Encouraging neat handwriting when presenting their work
 IV. Storing written material in manila folders

(A) I only
(B) III and IV only
(C) II only
(D) I and II only

51. A cluster of fourth-grade teachers at Smithville Elementary School is working together to improve the math curriculum of the school. They are using the NCTM standards as a basis. They want students to learn to value math, become confident in their math ability, become math problem solvers, and communicate and reason mathematically.

In developing a curriculum using fractions, these fourth-grade teachers will focus on which of the following goals, according to the NCTM?

(A) Discuss fraction problems using the correct terminology
(B) Solve fractional problems by trying to build a model town
(C) Increase the speed at which students are able to reduce common fractions
(D) Develop a long-term project involving fractional concepts

52. The fourth-grade teachers developed a list of fractional and decimal goals at Smithville Elementary, such as:

• Develop concepts of fractions, mixed numbers, and decimals
• Use models to find equivalent fractions
• Use fractions and decimals to solve problem situations
• Use fractional numbers in developing correct algorithms

Which of the following would NOT be an effective goal according to NCTM standards?

(A) Use models to find equivalent fractions
(B) Use fractions and decimals to solve problem situations
(C) Use fractional numbers in developing correct algorithms
(D) Develop the concepts of fractions, mixed numbers, and decimals

53. One fourth-grade teacher developed a card game in which the students had to match different fractions. The shapes contained within each card were the same, while the number of parts shaded was different. In this rummy-type game, the student that was left with the most pairs won the game. This activity is being used to teach the concept of

(A) proper and improper fractions.
(B) equivalent fractions.
(C) sequencing fractions.
(D) converting fractions.

54. According to Ms. Wilson, who teaches an accelerated fourth-grade program, symbols, such as $\frac{1}{4}$ and $\frac{2}{3}$ should be

(A) introduced immediately so that students will be able to write the answers to fractional examples.
(B) memorized in their correct order so that students will gain an understanding of number sequence.
(C) converted into fractions containing their like denominators so that students will understand that all fractions are equivalent.
(D) introduced only after children have developed the concepts and oral language necessary for these forms to have meaning and to be connected to language.

55. When doing exploratory work in adding and subtracting fractions, solving problems, and finding fractional parts of sets using real-world problems, students will gain a better understanding if

    (A) physical materials are used to explain the concepts.
    (B) decimal concepts are used first in explaining these concepts.
    (C) the concept is explained using algebraic expressions.
    (D) fractions are converted to whole number operations.

56. Mrs. Grey teaches a lesson in which students must recognize that $\frac{1}{4}$ is the same amount as 0.25. They use this relationship to determine that .15 and .20 are slightly less than $\frac{1}{4}$ and that 0.30 and 0.38 are a little more than $\frac{1}{4}$.

    Which of the following concepts is being taught in this lesson?

    I. Numeration skills for decimals
    II. Relationships between fractions and decimals
    III. Fractional conversions
    IV. Place value of decimals

    (A) III only
    (B) I only
    (C) II and IV only
    (D) I and II only

57. The superintendent of the Roland Independent School District has asked building administrators to set up inclusionary structures for special education students. In this district, more than 70 percent of the high-incidence students were educated in self-contained classrooms or sent to regional programs.

    Dr. Wilkerson, the principal of Hewbard Elementary, developed a needs assessment concerning the establishment of an inclusion structure in his school. When he got back the results, they were in accordance with many recent studies in this particular area.

His needs assessment probably showed that most

    (A) general education teachers do not support the inclusion of students with disabilities in regular classes.
    (B) teachers feel there is enough time during a school day for collaboration.
    (C) teachers feel that guidance counselors are supportive in the process.
    (D) teachers feel they need additional training to develop expertise in helping atypical students.

58. In setting up an inclusion program, the principal gave teachers a list of practices that increase the success of such a program. All of the following will be included in the list EXCEPT

    (A) adapted curriculum.
    (B) increased planning time.
    (C) teacher-directed lessons.
    (D) reduced class size.

59. When the program was set up in the school, teachers began to engage in collaborative problem solving. In this way, special and regular education teachers worked together in a systematic way to identify problems or barriers to successful inclusion, and ways to develop solutions to the problems. During one collaborative problem-solving session, it was perceived that several students were disruptive or distracting to others. Which of the following types of problems could this situation be identified with?

    (A) Attitudinal problems
    (B) Instructional problems
    (C) Peer acceptance problems
    (D) Social problems

60. Timothy is an 11-year-old boy in sixth grade. He has gross motor delays, cognitive deficits, and problems with articulation. He walks with a pronounced limp because the structure of his hip was damaged at birth.

    Timothy's latest IEP has placed him in an inclusion program. He is in an integrated class of 23 students in which 8 students have various disabling conditions. He receives adaptive physical education, physical therapy, occupational therapy, and speech therapy. His general education teacher collaborates with a special education consultant and a paraprofessional who is available three periods per day.

In his class, Timothy sits alone at a carrel because he has slight attention problems. In lunch, he sits at the end of the table by himself. The computer cluster teacher noticed that other students make fun of his gait and speech patterns. The student has made no friends in his inclusion class. The guidance counselor reports that Timothy stated that he no longer likes to go to school. Recently, his attendance has become problematic. He has stayed home several times due to stomach and throat problems. His mother reports that the student is resistant to going to the doctor.

Which of the following would be a possible solution to this problem?

(A) Timothy's peers will stop teasing him.
(B) Timothy will improve his attendance.
(C) Peer tutors will work with Timothy in his inclusive class.
(D) Timothy will progress in an adapted curriculum in his inclusive class.

61. In Mr. Smithson's eighth-grade social studies class, his students read a story about a man who was imprisoned with his wife by the Nazis. The Nazi commander asked the man to give him the names of various Jewish residents from his Polish town. The commander told the man that if he did not tell him who was Jewish, he would kill his wife. Mr. Smithson then asked the students in his class what they would do in this situation.

Using this technique, Mr. Smithson is making application of a theory developed by

(A) Kohlberg.
(B) Bruner.
(C) Piaget.
(D) Bandura.

62. Dr. Haliwell, the assistant principal of the middle school, observed another moral development lesson by Mr. Smithson. The lesson was about saving a child from drowning in rough surf. Mr. Smithson asked his students if they would attempt to save a drowning child in the wake of a hurricane's approach. The teacher orally presented the scenario, and the students responded with various answers. This particular moral dilemma generated a lot of student–student interaction. Then the students had to write an essay outlining what they would do about this matter.

Dr. Haliwell praised the lesson for being motivational and generating a lot of pupil–pupil interaction. However, one major criticism would be that

(A) the lesson is too controversial for a conventional social studies class.
(B) the dilemma is not a realistic situation.
(C) the lesson is not part of the social studies curriculum for the grade.
(D) moral development teaching does not generate group social identities within students.

63. Several members of the school board got upset that Mr. Smithson was teaching these moral development lessons. At a school board meeting, several members demanded that this type of instruction be stopped. They questioned the ethics of the teacher's moral development curriculum. Which of the following would be a reason for the board to vote against the use of this instructional technique?

(A) Mr. Smithson is of poor moral character, according to a report by a private investigator hired by the district.
(B) Such a lesson cannot be made part of a thematic curriculum on ethical development.
(C) An investigation by the board into Mr. Smithson's credentials revealed that he did not take the appropriate course work to teach such a curriculum.
(D) Such lessons may violate the beliefs of most board members that morality should be taught at home and not in school.

64. To extend these moral development lessons, Mr. Smithson asked the class to write their own moral dilemmas. This is a hard task for many students in the class. Where would the students find an interesting tale that reflects a moral dilemma?

    (A) Articles in newspapers and magazines
    (B) A novel about a family's dilemma of which side to support during the Civil War
    (C) Articles in scholarly journals
    (D) An article about a scientific investigation discussing the different uses of cobalt

65. Mrs. Jaclin, Mr. Smithson's colleague, has been trying to integrate moral development into her social studies curriculum. However, unlike Mr. Smithson, Mrs. Jaclin has been unable to generate any type of lively debate between her students. All of the following would be suggested by Mr. Smithson to generate student–student interaction EXCEPT

    (A) generating active listening skills.
    (B) arranging the class in face-to-face groupings.
    (C) being an accepting model.
    (D) evaluating the veracity of each student's opinion.

66. Mr. Smithson placed on the board as an objective: "Is believing in war morally right or wrong?" He instructed the class to use the Internet to find quotes by various authors about war. He had the class divide the quotes into those quotes favoring war and those quotes that were in opposition to war. Then he threw out to the class the question: "Are you in favor or opposed to war? Why?"

    How could Mr. Smithson have improved this lesson?

    (A) He wasted time having the students find the quotes. He should have presented the quotes as a motivation and then followed up the information in the form of a class discussion.
    (B) His moral question about war should have been a part of a lesson on the anti-war movement during the Vietnam War era.

    (C) The teacher should have used the question as a motivation in a lesson discussing the philosophy of pacifism.
    (D) This question should not have been asked of an eighth-grade social studies class because most of the students are not formal thinkers at this age.

67. Mr. Smithson gave a workshop on teaching moral development to a group of elementary school teachers. He stated that younger children respond to moral conflicts differently than older children. What is his rationale for this statement?

    (A) A younger child feels that the physical consequence of an action determines whether it is right or wrong.
    (B) A younger child develops insight into universal ethical principles.
    (C) A younger child understands that to maintain social order, fixed rules must be established and obeyed.
    (D) A younger child understands that order is maintained by mutual agreement so that the rights of an individual are protected.

68. In Mr. Jensen's seventh-grade science lab, he gives the students wires, bulbs, switches, and dry cells. He asks them to come up with a circuit that will increase the brightness of each individual bulb. Before the lab experience, he discusses how electricity flows through wires and what generates the electric charge.

    How would you describe Mr. Jensen's approach to instruction?

    (A) He is using taxonomy of basic thinking skills.
    (B) He is using a cooperative learning approach.
    (C) He is using a constructivist approach.
    (D) He is helping his students understand scientific methodology.

69. The following week, Mr. Jensen develops another lesson using the constructivist approach. Which of the following lessons incorporate this approach?

    (A) The students look up in encyclopedias or on line a list of various laboratory instruments.

(B) The students must explain and describe other instruments that serve the same purpose as a compass.

(C) The students are given a sheet on which they must classify chemicals that generate electric currents.

(D) The students must research varying scientists who furthered the investigation of electromagnetism.

70. Mr. Jensen understands that when he uses the discovery approach with seventh-grade students, their thinking is in which mode of representation, according to Jerome Bruner's constructivist theory?

(A) Enactive
(B) Iconic
(C) Symbolic
(D) Metabolic

71. As a follow-up, Mr. Jensen shows the students schematics of different types of circuits that generate different degrees of heat. How would he proceed in using this information using a constructivist approach?

(A) He would discuss how people in the Middle Ages generated heat in their environment.

(B) He would tell the class which circuit generates the most heat.

(C) He would ask the students to decide which circuit generates a high level of energy.

(D) He would have the class research different types of heat-generating circuits.

72. Mrs. Diamond is a third-grade teacher who is presented with a student from Papua-New Guinea. The student speaks only pigeon English; he has no word recognition skills and cannot write his name. He also has trouble staying in his seat. During the lesson, the student gets up and wanders around the room, touching various books and objects. The teacher had four apples on her desk, and he began to eat them. When they were taken away from him, the student pushed the teacher away. Then he started to cry. The teacher had to decide on a course of action in dealing with this new student.

What would be the most realistic action Mrs. Diamond would take concerning this student?

(A) She would set up a behavior modification program for the student.

(B) She would consult the guidance counselor.

(C) She would immediately have the student suspended for hitting her.

(D) She would bring the student extra food for lunch.

73. The guidance counselor gives Mrs. Diamond a form in which she must broadly describe the problem. He then brings this form to a collaboration team within the school, made up of various support personnel and administration. The team meets in the principal's office once every two weeks to deal with at-risk students. All of the following personnel would probably be on this team EXCEPT

(A) the assistant principal.
(B) a paraprofessional.
(C) the consultant teacher.
(D) a nurse.

74. This Child Study Team engages in collaborative problem solving. Different members of the team have a role in this collaborative process. Besides using their professional skills, the various members enhance the effectiveness of this collaborative approach to problem solving. Which of the following roles would NOT enhance the effectiveness of this collaborative process?

(A) A facilitator
(B) A time-keeper
(C) A recorder
(D) A leader

75. Mrs. Diamond was invited to discuss the problem with her immigrant student with the Child Study Team. At the end of the discussion, Mrs. Diamond noticed that one of the members asked the others if everyone participated, stayed within the time frame, and accomplished the goal of the meeting. This person was probably the

(A) timekeeper.
(B) observer.
(C) recorder.
(D) facilitator.

76. The collaboration team must come up with a plan to help Mrs. Diamond's immigrant student. Which of the following would be the most realistic plan to help this student?

(A) A member of the team would be assigned to have a meeting with the parent and the teacher. The parent would give some background information prior to a referral for special educational services.
(B) A member of the team would be assigned to have a meeting with the parent and the teacher. This team member would probably ask that some type of translator be present. The psychosocial history would be taken prior to engaging the parent in some type of agency intervention.
(C) A member of the team would be assigned to further investigate the problem. She would call the parent. If the parent had difficulty with English, the team member would attempt to find a translator. The parent would be called in to a meeting to get some background information and discuss school-based interventions.
(D) A member of the team would be assigned to further investigate the problem. She would call the parent. If the parent had difficulty with English, the team member would attempt to find a translator. The parent would be called in to meet with this team member and the classroom teacher. After some discussion, the team member would set up a behavior modification program for the teacher to deal with the problem.

77. After the consultant teacher met with the parent and teacher, a course of action was decided upon. An intervention was proposed to facilitate socialization and the development of readiness and literacy skills in this student who had never attended school in his native country. Which of the following would NOT be a probable intervention?

(A) Participation in a Little League and a YMCA program
(B) School-based group counseling by the guidance counselor
(C) Cross-age tutoring with a sixth-grader
(D) Placement in a bridge class

78. Mrs. Arista is a first-grade teacher at Park Hill Elementary. Each week she sends students home with a backpack containing three books on a particular literary theme. The student is supposed to either read the book or have the parent read the book to him. The student or the parent then writes a sentence or two giving his impression of one of the books. Finally, the child must choose from about five or six different activities that illustrate or depict a part of the book.

This reading strategy is derived from which of the following reading approaches?

(A) A linguistic approach to reading
(B) The Gattegno approach to reading remediation
(C) A whole language approach to reading
(D) The application of whole word methodology

79. Mrs. Arista has two students who are having difficulty reading repetitive picture books that contain words in which initial consonants must be blended. These two students usually pronounce blends as single consonants even when the words are used over and over. Using the whole language approach, how would this teacher develop decoding skills in these students?

   (A) She would teach a lesson on blending *bl*, *sl*, *cl*, and *fl* words to the whole class, so as not to embarrass these students.

   (B) She would have the students recognize blends by having them pick out similar blended words in children's magazines.

   (C) She would teach a mini lesson on blending to these students, using the words in the picture book they are reading.

   (D) She would totally avoid teaching phonics because the development of sound/symbol relations is not taught within this philosophical approach.

80. By the end of the year, many of the students in Mrs. Arista's class were reading complex stories. However, she discovered that when she would ask them questions about such stories, they would become confused about how the plot develops. Sometimes diversions in the story would make them go off on tangents. Which of the following procedures would be an effective way to help her students make sense out of the stories?

   (A) The teacher would develop a story map to visually display the major characters and events in the story.

   (B) She would show an animated version of the story to the class and ask questions about each part.

   (C) She would have the students make mental images of the story and discuss these images after reading.

   (D) She would have the students relate alternate endings to the story to enhance plot focus.

ESSAY

You have been assigned to teach either middle or secondary school students in a subject you are prepared to teach. Three students have been recertified to your general education class from a small special education class. Under recent reforms, your district has placed all high-incidence learning-disabled students in regular classes. The educational report on one of these students shows that she has average comprehension skills, but that she only decodes at the beginning of the second-grade level. In addition, a math assessment shows that her computational skills are at the third-grade level, while her conceptual skills are at the eighth-grade level. Describe three ways in which you will help this student access the general education curriculum and enable her to eventually achieve a state-mandated regent's diploma.

Your audience in writing is a group of New York State educators. Be sure to specify an instructional context (e.g., subject area and grade level) that will help clarify your response, but frame your response so that any educator certified at the elementary or secondary level will be able to understand the basis for your decision. You can continue on a separate piece of paper.

_____

_____

_____

_____

_____

_____

_____

_____

_____

_____

_____

_____

_____

_____

_____

_____

_____

ANSWER KEY

1. B	15. D	29. C	42. D	55. A	68. C
2. C	16. A	30. A	43. D	56. D	69. B
3. D	17. A	31. D	44. D	57. D	70. C
4. A	18. C	32. D	45. A	58. C	71. C
5. B	19. C	33. C	46. B	59. D	72. B
6. C	20. B	34. D	47. C	60. C	73. B
7. D	21. D	35. A	48. D	61. A	74. D
8. D	22. B	36. B	49. C	62. B	75. B
9. A	23. A	37. A	50. D	63. D	76. C
10. C	24. D	38. C	51. C	64. A	77. A
11. D	25. A	39. A	52. C	65. D	78. C
12. C	26. D	40. C	53. B	66. C	79. C
13. C	27. B	41. B	54. D	67. A	80. A
14. A	28. D				

ANSWERS AND EXPLANATIONS

1. **The correct answer is (B).** When handling complaints, a teacher should thank the parent, apologize, and then let the parent know that she will immediately follow up on the problem. Choice (A) is wrong because a teacher should never act surprised when talking to a parent about what is happening in her classroom. Choice (C) is wrong because you should always thank the parent before apologizing. Choice (D) is incorrect because her statement lets the parent think that the teacher is avoiding all responsibility.

2. **The correct answer is (C).** The least effective way to assess the affective domain is through a cognitive-type test. A miscue analysis focuses on decoding skills, not on the affective domain. Choices (A), (B), and (D) are all instruments that assess the feelings of her students about reading.

3. **The correct answer is (D).** This response helps the teacher understand how a student determines what makes someone a good reader. The other three choices focus more on how the students feel about learning how to read and their feelings about achievement.

4. **The correct answer is (A).** Young students best comprehend Likert scales if they are in the form of pictures. Numbers relating to feelings are too abstract for young children. Choice (B) is incorrect because the questions should focus on recreational as well as academic reading. Choices (C) and (D) are wrong because the inventory should not focus upon how the student reads.

5. **The correct answer is (B).** The student may be acting out because the work is too difficult for him and he does not want the teacher and the class to find out. Choice (A) is wrong because, if the student had good skills, he would probably find some independent seat work to do. Choice (C) is not a realistic service that the school would offer to a child who may be

acting out. Choice (D) cannot be inferred from the question.

6. **The correct answer is (C).** Teachers learn best when they are not isolated and can learn collaboratively from more experienced teachers. In addition, the teacher could adapt similar information she acquired in a curriculum course. With option III, by using the work of someone else, she will not learn to create a unit on her own. Furthermore, this Internet unit may not be congruent with her state's curriculum. Option IV is incorrect because reviewing the curriculum will not help her learn how to create a multidisciplinary unit.

7. **The correct answer is (D).** This is a unit on communities, and the contributions of different immigrants are not relevant. It would be relevant only if the objective discussed the contributions of immigrants to changes in communication and transportation in the United States. Choices (A), (B), and (C) are all relevant objectives for this unit on communities.

8. **The correct answer is (D).** The other three choices list very detailed curriculum areas that have to be focused upon. Choices (A), (B), and (C) use a variety of media to teach this unit.

9. **The correct answer is (A).** This is the only choice that incorporates language arts into the lesson. Choices (B) and (D) incorporate mathematical concepts into the lesson, while choice (C) focuses upon scientific concepts.

10. **The correct answer is (C).** This is a cooperative learning task, and the mark should not be based upon some outside criteria. Choices (B) and (D) focus upon the quality of this group work. Choice (A) in the rubric rightly focuses on how the group worked together in this cooperative learning task.

11. **The correct answer is (D).** The school is mandated to report to the state any suspected incident of abuse. When a teacher finds out such information, he must inform an administrator, who will delegate guidance services to investigate the matter and decide if protective services should be contacted. Choice

(C) is incorrect because a teacher may not have the clinical skills to discuss such a matter with the child's parent. Choices (A) and (B) are incorrect because if a teacher does not inform anyone of suspected abuse, he could be held liable by the state.

12. **The correct answer is (C).** A score on a standardized reading test may be affected by the English language ability of a student, his economic status, and his prior educational experience. Option III will probably not affect the score of a student; the physical condition of a school is not necessarily related to the cognitive ability of a student, whereas the other three factors are.

13. **The correct answer is (C).** Diagnostic/ prescriptive measures are most often norm reference tests in which the student is compared to other students. Portfolios, informal reading inventories, and interest inventories are all informal measures of reading ability.

14. **The correct answer is (A).** The student, with some teacher consultation, decides which items should be within the portfolio. Therefore, many of the items may not be relevant to reading instruction, as is the case in the current scenario. Choice (B) makes no sense because the number of people who view a portfolio has no impact on its contents. Choice (C) can be a measure of reading ability. Written critiques tap into the comprehension skills of the students. With choice (D), the opposite is true. When portfolios are used, there is often an increase in independent work.

15. **The correct answer is (D).** The only inappropriate answer is option IV. Portfolios are supposed to be used in lieu of standardized tests. The first three choices relate to how portfolios focus upon the affective domain. Portfolios are supposed to improve the feelings students have about the reading process.

16. **The correct answer is (A).** When discussing a child, strengths should always be brought up first and any discussion of management should be factual. If you picked choice (B), the teacher would probably no longer be able to

communicate with a defensive parent. Choice (C) is wrong because the discussion is wholly negative about the child. Choice (D) is very negative and would probably end communication with the parents.

17. **The correct answer is (A).** Receptive language must develop before expressive language. Then reading skills develop before written expression.

18. **The correct answer is (C).** When a student has learning difficulties that cannot be resolved in the classroom, the child must be referred to the Pupil Personnel Committee, which will set up interventions within regular education, not special education. The purpose of the PPC is to prevent students from being labeled. Choice (B) is a possibility but should be implemented only after an intervention meeting by the PPC. Choice (D) is wrong because the primary responsibility for helping the child is placed on the parents. Choice (A) is wrong because a referral to special education is the last resort.

19. **The correct answer is (C).** This is an appropriate adaptation within regular education to prevent special educational services. Choice (A) is wrong because the student should not have a different standard than everyone else in the class. Choice (B) is wrong because the student is probably able to read both forms of writing because he attempts both forms of written expression. Choice (D) is a form of assistive technology that can be authorized only at a CSE level.

20. **The correct answer is (B).** This is a 504 issue. The child needs adaptations because of his inability to write within regular education. Choice (A) is wrong because the child probably does not need an educational service that would be authorized under IDEA. Choice (C) is wrong because only students who have severe developmental disabilities are exempt from testing. Choice (D) is wrong because any child referred must be evaluated.

21. **The correct answer is (D).** The key word in this question is "compensate." These adaptations are not meant for the student to overcome his problem. Instead, the student is supposed to have adaptations to help him get around his writing difficulty. Choice (D) is a remedial method, not compensation. Choices (A), (B), and (C) are ways for the student to do the work without performing the physical act of writing.

22. **The correct answer is (B).** According to Federal 504 statutes, if agreement cannot be reached at a 504 conference, there must be a due process hearing. Choice (A) is incorrect because if the parents went to another district, the same 504 procedures would have to be followed. Choice (C) is wrong because the student needs adaptations within regular education, not special educational services. Federal 504 statutes do not specify a timeline for implementation by a district.

23. **The correct answer is (A).** A clinical report and supporting evidence will ascertain that the student has a potential handicapping condition and can have adaptations under Section 504 of the Vocational and Rehabilitation Act of 1973. Option III is incorrect because a report from a PE teacher will focus on gross, not fine, motor skills. Option IV is incorrect because physician reports usually lead to an evaluation, which is not the terminal reason for providing services.

24. **The correct answer is (D).** This anecdotal record is appropriate because it is made up of factual details using nonbiased language. All the other choices contain sentences that are too general or are biased.

25. **The correct answer is (A).** Fables, the goddess Venus, and columns are all items that refer to ancient Greece.

26. **The correct answer is (D).** Understanding the symbols within various maps attunes students to traditional geographic concepts. The first three choices can create a social understanding of the ancient Greeks. Choice (A) can help students determine how the Greeks migrated to different regions. Choice (B) can help students understand the resources the Greeks used in their city-states. Choice (C) can help students understand the spread of Greek culture throughout the ancient world.

27. The correct answer is (B). The teacher is using literature to teach social studies. Choice (A) is incorrect because literature is not the only way to make history more interesting. Choice (C) is wrong because the literature being read covers many issues. Choice (D) is wrong because students in sixth grade should understand the difference among these various types of literature.

28. The correct answer is (D). Choice (C) is not a good justification for teaching Greek history. In addition, these words came into English during modern times. Choice (B) is wrong because multiculturalism celebrates our diversity. Choice (A) is incorrect because it may be considered a biased remark.

29. The correct answer is (C). Option II is incorrect because the teacher is socially distanced from the students. Option IV is incorrect because we do not know if the students had any privileges. The teacher did punish the whole class for the transgression of one student, and he used homework as a punishment.

30. The correct answer is (A). In the first choice, the punishment fits the crime and is a natural consequence of the action. In choice (B), the punishment does not fit the crime. With choice (C), the whole class is being punished in addition to the perpetrators. In choice (D), there is no consequence to the student if his parents must buy him the supplies.

31. The correct answer is (D). The consequence for choice (D) is being consistently applied. With the other three choices, the teacher keeps giving the students more chances. He postpones following through with the consequences.

32. The correct answer is (D). Choosing a failing grade, even in private, will reduce the self-esteem of the student. One of the key tenets in improving classroom management is treating students with love and respect. Some ways to do this include giving the students a surprise treat, choice (A), or giving them a reward for no reason at all, choice (B). Choice (C) makes the students feel that the teacher is their friend.

33. The correct answer is (C). This answer is correct because the class was not drawn to focus on the minor infraction that took place. Choice (A) is wrong because the public reprimand may cause other students to test the teacher by saying the same expletive. Choice (B) is an example of rewarding a student for inappropriate behavior; the student may want to leave the room. Choice (D) also makes a public display of a minor infraction.

34. The correct answer is (D). This answer is correct because such a topic should not be taught in social studies. This concept is part of the theology of several religions, not comparative history. The other three examples look at different religions comparatively and analyze the similarities and differences of many religions.

35. The correct answer is (A). The main reason to teach comparative religion is to help students develop tolerance and a comprehension of one of the primary motivating factors governing human history. Choice (B) is incorrect because it gives preference to a particular religion. Choice (C) is incorrect because a major curriculum objective is the concept that religions evolve over time and are not static. Choice (D) is wrong because religions in multicultural societies often contribute to ethnic conflict.

36. The correct answer is (B). Maslow's needs theory would help this teacher understand the effects poverty has on learning. Dewey would help the teacher understand progressive education. Piaget would help the teacher understand the different stages of learning. Ravitch would help the teacher have a better understanding of multicultural education.

37. The correct answer is (A). These two authors view multicultural textbooks as biased. Therefore, they would disagree with choice (D). They would also disagree with choice (B) because these authors feel that many modern textbooks contain irrelevant information. Choice (C) is also incorrect because many multicultural textbooks focus on a racial view of American society.

38. **The correct answer is (C).** The teacher will work with a special education expert to discuss implementation within his general education class. Choice (A) is wrong because the child is not receiving part-time services. With a consultant teacher, he is in general education full-time. Choice (B) is wrong because the consultant is in the classroom only two or three times a week, but many of these modifications must take place during several periods. Choice (D) is wrong because it would be inappropriate to ask for a re-evaluation when the original IEP has not yet been implemented.

39. **The correct answer is (A).** Test modifications are meant for every test the student takes in the class. The IEP would explicitly state that quizzes, classroom tests, state tests, and citywide tests all would have to be modified.

40. **The correct answer is (C).** The purpose of keeping this student in regular education is so that he can be a participating member of the class. The other three choices are appropriate recommendations to reduce distraction.

41. **The correct answer is (B).** The key phrase is "a minimum of distraction." The student probably has a severe attention problem that may have contributed to a severe reading deficit. However, the fact that he can function in a regular class shows that his intellectual ability is probably at least within the average range. Therefore, choice (D) is out of the question. Based on the information at hand, we cannot determine the validity of either choices (A) or (C).

42. **The correct answer is (D).** Statement III cannot be turned into a scientific experiment; the two factors have no relationship to each other. The other three choices have scientific factors. Options II and IV have to do with sound and biology; Option I is an experiment relating to a physical aspect of sound.

43. **The correct answer is (D).** If an experiment does not prove the hypothesis, this is also valid. It may lead to a different line of research at another time. The other three choices show that a project must be started early because a lot of planning is involved.

44. **The correct answer is (D).** The last project is not trying to prove a hypothesis; this experiment is just a comparison of two known scientific facts.

45. **The correct answer is (A).** This choice is a logical outcome of the description of the experiment. Choices (B) and (C) are both variables a plant needs to grow. Choice (D) has nothing to do with the description of the experiment.

46. **The correct answer is (B).** Free writing, writing notes, and journal writing are some ways students get ideas prior to their first draft. This is called the rehearsal stage of writing; choices (A), (C), and (D) come after this stage in the writing process.

47. **The correct answer is (C).** Students must learn how to compose using a variety of writing forms, such as fantasies, fiction, news articles, and persuasive essays. The other three choices are all part of the composing process.

48. **The correct answer is (D).** The student is writing using emotionally toned words that express a political bias. Choice (A) involves writing positively about someone or something without any proof. Choice (C) involves a famous person advocating a project. Choice (B) involves stating that "everyone" is buying something.

49. **The correct answer is (C).** This choice does not extend the concept of writing either objectively or by using propaganda. Choices (A), (B), and (D) are all examples of using bias in writing. Even objective articles can have some type of gross bias.

50. **The correct answer is (D).** Options I and II are unique ways to present written material. Option IV is wrong because students should be given more unique ways to display their work, either by using audio, video, or graphics. Option III is wrong because students must get used to using different tools, such as word processors, computers, and other technology.

51. **The correct answer is (C).** The NTCM standards put less emphasis on rote learning and more emphasis on problem solving. Therefore, choice (C) is incorrect because it emphasizes rote learning. According to the standards, the students are supposed to emphasize communicating mathematically, choice (A), as well as solving realistic, long-term problems, choices (B) and (D).

52. **The correct answer is (C).** There should be less emphasis on doing examples using fractions. The emphasis must be on developing concepts, choices (A) and (D), and on solving problem situations, choice (B).

53. **The correct answer is (B).** This activity is helping the student identify which fractions are the same. Choice (D) means changing a fraction to a decimal. Choice (C) means determining the size order of various fractions. Choice (A) means determining what type of fraction is being used.

54. **The correct answer is (D).** The fractional symbols must be connected to the concept for them to have any meaning. Choice (A) is meaningless if the student has no understanding of fractions. Choice (C) is similarly meaningless if the student has no concept of equivalence on the concrete level. Choice (B) is wrong because the student needs to have a concrete concept of equivalence.

55. **The correct answer is (A).** When exploring problems, teachers should present physical, concrete materials before algorithms. Choices (B) and (D) are incorrect because students must be taught that these two concepts are related to each other. Choice (C) is wrong because math must be taught from the concrete to the abstract.

56. **The correct answer is (D).** The students are developing a number sense for decimals and how decimals and fractions are related. Option III is wrong because this lesson shows students how to convert fractions to decimals. Option IV is also wrong because place value does not come into play during this lesson.

57. **The correct answer is (D).** General education teachers feel that they need additional training and support in dealing with such students. Choice (A) is wrong because most studies show that a majority of general education teachers are supportive of inclusion. Choice (B) is also wrong because general and special education teachers feel that there is too little time for collaboration. Choice (C) is incorrect because research shows that most teachers are looking for support from special education personnel.

58. **The correct answer is (C).** This choice is incorrect because research shows that a cooperative learning approach is more effective for these children. The other three choices all contribute to the success of an inclusive classroom.

59. **The correct answer is (D).** This is a behavioral problem in which the included child may be lacking appropriate social skills associated with general education students. Choice (A) is incorrect because it is not a problem regarding the teacher's feelings about students having a disability. Choice (B) is also wrong because it is not a problem in which the teacher lacks skills developing appropriate curricula adaptations. Choice (C) is incorrect because the problem is not a result of the student being rejected, teased, or isolated.

60. **The correct answer is (C).** This sentence is a solution; choices (A), (B), and (D) are long-term objectives.

61. **The correct answer is (A).** Using discussion techniques to develop moral reasoning comes from Kohlberg. Choice (B) is mostly associated with constructivism. Choice (C) is concerned with Piaget's learning stages, and choice (D) is associated with Bandura's social learning theory.

62. **The correct answer is (B).** A major criticism of Kohlberg is that his dilemmas are not realistic enough for the students. The dilemmas should be based on real-life situations. Choice (A) cannot be determined because the question does not give us any information about the community. There is also no information that

will allow us to determine whether choices (C) or (D) are correct.

63. **The correct answer is (D).** Many communities are opposed to moral development lessons because they feel that such ethics should be taught outside of school. Choice (A) is illegal, and choice (C) is not relevant. Most education programs usually teach Kohlberg's theory of moral development. Choice (B) is wrong because ethics is usually taught as part of a theme.

64. **The correct answer is (A).** They would find a relevant dilemma in a newspaper or magazine. Choice (B) is incorrect because the novel discusses an incident that happened a long time ago. A scholarly journal, choice (C), would not have an article discussing a moral dilemma. There also is no moral dilemma in an article discussing the scientific use of cobalt, choice (D).

65. **The correct answer is (D).** In discussing moral dilemmas, there are *no absolute* right or wrong answers. Choices (A), (B), and (C) are all techniques that would encourage student–student interaction. Suggesting that certain answers are more correct will have the effect of limiting the interaction of some students.

66. **The correct answer is (C).** Recent research shows that students best develop an awareness of moral issues if the issues are integrated into the curriculum; therefore, there should not be a "moral education period" within the social studies curriculum. Choices (A) and (B) are incorrect because the lesson is not incorporated into the general social studies curriculum; it remains a separate moral development lesson. Choice (D) is wrong because, at this age, formal operational skills are beginning to develop.

67. **The correct answer is (A).** Children up to age 9 exhibit preconventional morality in which the physical consequence of an action determines whether it is right or wrong. The other choices reflect higher stages in Kohlberg's theory of moral development.

68. **The correct answer is (C).** The teacher is using the discovery approach and the constructivist view of learning. He is guiding students so that they discover or construct a scientific concept. Choice (B) is wrong because the scenario does not mention whether the students are working in small groups; they could be working individually. Choice (A) is incorrect because we do not know whether the teacher is using lower- and higher-level questions in this lesson. Choice (D) may be incorrect because, by doing experiments, the students already understand scientific theory.

69. **The correct answer is (B).** Here the students must discover from past knowledge instruments that serve the same purpose as a compass after structured information is given about the purpose of this instrument. Choices (A) and (D) involve simply looking up information in a reference source; the students are not using any structure to discover a concept. Choice (C) is wrong because no structure is given to the student to do the sheet. The instructor will probably have to give the student the needed information.

70. **The correct answer is (C).** According to Bruner, in late childhood and early adolescence, students represent ideas in terms of verbal propositions, mathematical formulas, and logical symbols. Choice (A) represents the thinking of preschool children, and choice (B) represents the thinking of children during the early school years. Choice (D) is incorrect because it is not one of Bruner's stages of thinking.

71. **The correct answer is (C).** The constructivist approach encourages informed guessing. Choices (B) and (D) are incorrect because these approaches do not allow the students to participate in the discovery process; they are basically being told the information. Choice (A) is wrong because the teacher is not comparing and contrasting information. Emphasizing contrast is a basic element of this approach to learning.

72. **The correct answer is (B).** The most appropriate response is to contact the guidance counselor for advice about handling the student. Choice (A) is incorrect because the teacher may not understand the real needs of the student. Choice (C) is wrong because a suspense hearing would not solve the social and academic problems of this frightened, immigrant student. Choice (D) is also incorrect because bringing in food also does not address the real needs of this student.

73. **The correct answer is (B).** A paraprofessional would not be on a child study team because she may lack the skills to investigate a problem, consult with a teacher, and propose or implement a possible solution. The other three choices have the professional skills to develop and implement a plan to help this student.

74. **The correct answer is (D).** On a collaborative team, there is no leader. Leadership is a shared responsibility; choices (A), (B), and (C) are roles that are often found on collaborative teams.

75. **The correct answer is (B).** This person was asking questions to determine whether the group remained on task. Therefore, choice (A) is incorrect. The timekeeper would focus only on the time. Choice (C) is wrong because this person did not record any information during the meeting, and choice (D) is incorrect because this person did not facilitate the meeting.

76. **The correct answer is (C).** School-based interventions would be developed and discussed in collaboration with the classroom teacher and parent. Choice (A) is incorrect because it is inappropriate to offer special educational services to recent immigrants under state and federal law. Choice (B) is wrong because a social history is usually given when a child is referred for special educational services. Choice (D) is not a collaborative approach; this professional is dictating to the teacher and parent the intervention that should be done.

77. **The correct answer is (A).** The teacher, parent, and collaboration team member would propose school-based interventions. The parent may not have the skills or resources available to join a Little League or YMCA. School-based counseling would be proposed because it would develop socialization skills. Cross-age tutoring with a sixth-grade child would be monitored to develop some readiness or literacy skills. The student would be put in a smaller bridge class made up of second- and third-graders, if available in the school.

78. **The correct answer is (C).** One application of the whole language approach is being illustrated. This approach uses children's literature to develop reading skills. Choices (A), (B), and (D) illustrate other methods used in the teaching of reading.

79. **The correct answer is (C).** Phonics is taught on an as-needed basis in the whole language approach. Choice (A) is incorrect because formal phonic lessons are not taught in this approach. Choice (B) is incorrect because the lesson is isolated from the literary content. Choice (D) is wrong because phonics skills are taught using this approach when necessary.

80. **The correct answer is (A).** The key concept in this question is "complex." Students can comprehend complex information better if they create a visual semantic or concept map of the story. Though the other choices are comprehension development activities, they would probably be used with less complex literary works or short passages.

ESSAY RESPONSE

As a ninth-grade math teacher, I have to help a learning-disabled student learn the concepts and skills for Sequential I mathematics even though her computational skills are at the third-grade level. To help me do this, my class has been assigned to an inclusion program. A consultant teacher comes into my class twice a week for direct instruction of the student. In addition, we meet each week to collaborate on strategies to help this student achieve the goals of her Individual Educational Program (IEP).

According to her IEP, the student has to learn how to solve verbal problems utilizing a variety of algebraic concepts. This is a difficult task because the student not only has severe computational problems, but she also has severe decoding problems and has difficulty reading the questions at hand. As a result of a discussion with the consultant teacher, we decided that the first strategy that the student needs to achieve this task is to have a reconvened IEP meeting to help her access computer technology. The student needs computer access for two reasons. She needs word/number-recognition reading software. This software, used in conjunction with a scanner, enables the computer to read textbook pages to the student. In this way, examples, written directions, and verbal problems can be read and reread to the student within the classroom through the use of earphones and a laptop. The student will be working with the same curriculum material as her regular education counterparts. In addition, the student will work out algebraic examples using math software so that columns and lines can be neatly arranged to help her avoid careless errors.

A second strategy will allow the student to use a calculator to do the basic computations. The student still does not know her basic addition, subtraction, and multiplication facts without relying on her fingers, drawings, sets, and charts. It is impossible to use a calculator to find the answer to a complex algebraic problem. Therefore, a calculator will not give her an unfair advantage over the other students. However, she will utilize the calculator for doing basic operations when solving such problems to help her avoid making careless errors. The calculator could be used as a tool to help her develop higher-level math concepts by freeing her from concentrating on computational skills.

Finally, to enable the student to pass examinations, extensive test modifications have to be placed on the IEP for this student. Because the student needs to use assistive technology to answer test questions, she needs twice as much time to do any classroom, citywide, or state examinations. In addition, the student needs to be allowed to utilize the computer and calculator when doing all tests. Lastly, the student needs to be allowed to give her answers on the computer, not through paper and pencil, to help her avoid making careless errors.

Using these strategies, the student will be able to pass Sequential I. Because the student does not have any difficulty understanding grade-level concepts, she just needs help in the nuts and bolts of working out answers to problems. Not having to focus on computations will free her mind to develop the conceptual and application skills to pass this course. Utilizing assistive technology will prevent this student from making careless mistakes and will help her stay organized. Therefore, she will develop the skills necessary for her to pass the regents requirements for a high school diploma.

Answer Sheet for Chapter 10

ATS-W—PRACTICE TEST 2

1. Ⓐ Ⓑ Ⓒ Ⓓ   21. Ⓐ Ⓑ Ⓒ Ⓓ   41. Ⓐ Ⓑ Ⓒ Ⓓ   61. Ⓐ Ⓑ Ⓒ Ⓓ

2. Ⓐ Ⓑ Ⓒ Ⓓ   22. Ⓐ Ⓑ Ⓒ Ⓓ   42. Ⓐ Ⓑ Ⓒ Ⓓ   62. Ⓐ Ⓑ Ⓒ Ⓓ

3. Ⓐ Ⓑ Ⓒ Ⓓ   23. Ⓐ Ⓑ Ⓒ Ⓓ   43. Ⓐ Ⓑ Ⓒ Ⓓ   63. Ⓐ Ⓑ Ⓒ Ⓓ

4. Ⓐ Ⓑ Ⓒ Ⓓ   24. Ⓐ Ⓑ Ⓒ Ⓓ   44. Ⓐ Ⓑ Ⓒ Ⓓ   64. Ⓐ Ⓑ Ⓒ Ⓓ

5. Ⓐ Ⓑ Ⓒ Ⓓ   25. Ⓐ Ⓑ Ⓒ Ⓓ   45. Ⓐ Ⓑ Ⓒ Ⓓ   65. Ⓐ Ⓑ Ⓒ Ⓓ

6. Ⓐ Ⓑ Ⓒ Ⓓ   26. Ⓐ Ⓑ Ⓒ Ⓓ   46. Ⓐ Ⓑ Ⓒ Ⓓ   66. Ⓐ Ⓑ Ⓒ Ⓓ

7. Ⓐ Ⓑ Ⓒ Ⓓ   27. Ⓐ Ⓑ Ⓒ Ⓓ   47. Ⓐ Ⓑ Ⓒ Ⓓ   67. Ⓐ Ⓑ Ⓒ Ⓓ

8. Ⓐ Ⓑ Ⓒ Ⓓ   28. Ⓐ Ⓑ Ⓒ Ⓓ   48. Ⓐ Ⓑ Ⓒ Ⓓ   68. Ⓐ Ⓑ Ⓒ Ⓓ

9. Ⓐ Ⓑ Ⓒ Ⓓ   29. Ⓐ Ⓑ Ⓒ Ⓓ   49. Ⓐ Ⓑ Ⓒ Ⓓ   69. Ⓐ Ⓑ Ⓒ Ⓓ

10. Ⓐ Ⓑ Ⓒ Ⓓ   30. Ⓐ Ⓑ Ⓒ Ⓓ   50. Ⓐ Ⓑ Ⓒ Ⓓ   70. Ⓐ Ⓑ Ⓒ Ⓓ

11. Ⓐ Ⓑ Ⓒ Ⓓ   31. Ⓐ Ⓑ Ⓒ Ⓓ   51. Ⓐ Ⓑ Ⓒ Ⓓ   71. Ⓐ Ⓑ Ⓒ Ⓓ

12. Ⓐ Ⓑ Ⓒ Ⓓ   32. Ⓐ Ⓑ Ⓒ Ⓓ   52. Ⓐ Ⓑ Ⓒ Ⓓ   72. Ⓐ Ⓑ Ⓒ Ⓓ

13. Ⓐ Ⓑ Ⓒ Ⓓ   33. Ⓐ Ⓑ Ⓒ Ⓓ   53. Ⓐ Ⓑ Ⓒ Ⓓ   73. Ⓐ Ⓑ Ⓒ Ⓓ

14. Ⓐ Ⓑ Ⓒ Ⓓ   34. Ⓐ Ⓑ Ⓒ Ⓓ   54. Ⓐ Ⓑ Ⓒ Ⓓ   74. Ⓐ Ⓑ Ⓒ Ⓓ

15. Ⓐ Ⓑ Ⓒ Ⓓ   35. Ⓐ Ⓑ Ⓒ Ⓓ   55. Ⓐ Ⓑ Ⓒ Ⓓ   75. Ⓐ Ⓑ Ⓒ Ⓓ

16. Ⓐ Ⓑ Ⓒ Ⓓ   36. Ⓐ Ⓑ Ⓒ Ⓓ   56. Ⓐ Ⓑ Ⓒ Ⓓ   76. Ⓐ Ⓑ Ⓒ Ⓓ

17. Ⓐ Ⓑ Ⓒ Ⓓ   37. Ⓐ Ⓑ Ⓒ Ⓓ   57. Ⓐ Ⓑ Ⓒ Ⓓ   77. Ⓐ Ⓑ Ⓒ Ⓓ

18. Ⓐ Ⓑ Ⓒ Ⓓ   38. Ⓐ Ⓑ Ⓒ Ⓓ   58. Ⓐ Ⓑ Ⓒ Ⓓ   78. Ⓐ Ⓑ Ⓒ Ⓓ

19. Ⓐ Ⓑ Ⓒ Ⓓ   39. Ⓐ Ⓑ Ⓒ Ⓓ   59. Ⓐ Ⓑ Ⓒ Ⓓ   79. Ⓐ Ⓑ Ⓒ Ⓓ

20. Ⓐ Ⓑ Ⓒ Ⓓ   40. Ⓐ Ⓑ Ⓒ Ⓓ   60. Ⓐ Ⓑ Ⓒ Ⓓ   80. Ⓐ Ⓑ Ⓒ Ⓓ

Chapter 10

ATS-W—PRACTICE TEST 2

TIME: 4 Hours—80 Questions

> *Directions:* Each statement or passage in this test is followed by one or more questions. Read each statement or passage, and then answer the accompanying questions, basing your answer on what is stated or implied in the passage. Blacken the letter of your answer choice on the answer sheet.

1. Mr. Williamson teaches a ninth-grade global studies class at Midville High School. The students are studying the Neolithic period. The teacher is dividing his class into cooperative learning groups. Each group must report on social, economic, and political changes during this period.

   This is the first time that Mr. Williamson is using a cooperative approach to do a social studies project. He has done some preliminary research and has attended several seminars on the approach. During the last seminar, he was given a bibliography of recommended readings.

   All the following authors are associated with this process EXCEPT

   (A) Johnson and Johnson.
   (B) Slavin.
   (C) Vygotsky.
   (D) Berliner.

2. Mr. Williamson has decided that each group will write a joint paper. One person will be responsible for social change during the Neolithic period, another will be responsible for political change during the Neolithic period, a third will be responsible for economic change during the Neolithic period, and a fourth student will write an analysis of these developments as a conclusion to the paper.

   In his classroom of 20 students, the teacher is using five groups. Each group will be divided along the same lines. Then members of each group responsible for the same subpart will form expert groups that will gather the necessary information. Finally, these experts will return to the original group and teach that particular section to their original teammates.

   This cooperative process is most associated with which method?

   (A) TGT
   (B) Jigsaw
   (C) STAD
   (D) Learning Together

3. Mr. Williamson evaluated his cooperative groups based on several rubrics he learned in the seminars he took. His groups were all seated in a circle. Students often taught one another information that was acquired in the expert groups. Once the material was gathered, they all worked together to synthesize the information into a cohesive paper. At the end of the process, the teacher asked each group to reflect about what was learned, how it was learned, and the skills used to process and meet the goal. Finally, a group grade was given to each cooperative learning unit.

How could Mr. Williamson have improved upon his use of the cooperative approach if he took into consideration the basic elements of Johnson and Johnson's rubric?

(A) He could have increased each group from 4 to approximately 8 students.

(B) He could have evaluated the students individually.

(C) He could have given students who worked harder in the group a higher group grade.

(D) He could have critiqued how each group worked together.

4. During a meeting of the social studies department of his high school, Mr. Williamson told his chairperson what he was doing in the class. Mr. Smith, the chairperson, is a traditionalist. He feels that students should study individually and that each student should have written his own paper. Mr. Smith also feels that some students probably did very little work, while more intelligent students probably did the bulk of the work.

Which of the following reasons would Mr. Williamson have used to justify the benefits of the cooperative approach to his chairperson?

I. Research has shown that this approach helps students develop better social skills and higher-level thinking.

II. In the corporate world today, projects are often done in cooperative groups.

III. It is more important that social skills be developed rather than a high grade earned.

IV. Students need to improve their communication skills by teaching and sharing with one another.

(A) I, II, and III only

(B) II and IV only

(C) I, II, and IV only

(D) II, III, and IV only

5. Mr. Williamson tells his department head that cooperative learning is not a new concept, but is built upon educational ideas that have existed over the last 200 years. Cooperative learning was central to the teaching ideas of all of the following theorists EXCEPT

(A) Rousseau.

(B) Pestalozzi.

(C) Dewey.

(D) Flavell.

6. During this meeting of social studies teachers, one of Mr. Williamson's colleagues asks him how his groups are made up. This teacher wants groups that will work well together because every time he attempted a group project, he met with resistance. Certain students did not want to sit or work with other students. Mr. Williamson would give as advice all of the following EXCEPT

(A) start cooperative groups as dyads working together before trying a larger working group.

(B) allow the teacher to set up cooperative groups to determine which students can best work together.

(C) allow for homogeneous grouping because only students of like intelligence can work well together.

(D) allow high-achieving students to help low-achieving students to reinforce their remedial instruction.

7. Mr. Williamson also advised his colleague that students in cooperative learning groups need to be taught procedures to develop group skills. They need to learn how to move quickly into groups, respond to the teachers' signals for attention, and so on. They also need explicit instruction and regular practice in the interpersonal skills that this method requires. Which of the following items represent active group skills that students must learn for this approach?

    I. Reaching consensus
   II. Evaluating the ability of team members
  III. Practicing active/reflective listening
  IV. Using competitive motivation

  (A) I and III only
  (B) II and IV only
  (C) I and II only
  (D) II and III only

8. Mr. Williamson tells each group in the class that when they discuss what should be contained in the paper, all members must agree. He states that if someone disagrees, that person should hold up his hand to the group. If the student holds up his hand using one finger, it means that he is not happy with the decision but can live with the group's decision. If he holds up five fingers, this means that the student is unhappy with the decision and will actively work against the decision. Therefore, the group will have to decide to do something else.

Which cooperative learning technique is being illustrated here?

  (A) Positive interdependence
  (B) Face-to-face interaction
  (C) Post-group reflection
  (D) Social interaction behaviors

9. Mr. Williamson receives a telephone call from a concerned parent who was surprised when she saw the report that was written on the Neolithic period. She stated that her son has a long history of learning problems, and she knows that this could not be his work. The student told his mother that he worked in a group to write this report. This upset the parent greatly, and she feels that the teacher does not realize that her son has limitations. She wants Mr. Williamson to help her son develop the skills that he will need, not have other students do the work for him.

How should Mr. Williamson respond to this parent?

  (A) Mr. Williamson should tell this parent that she should not concern herself about the methods he uses because she has limited understanding of what is going on in the classroom.
  (B) Mr. Williamson should give the student another project to complete on his own so that the pupil can get an independent grade.
  (C) Mr. Williamson should meet with the parent and promise that the student will no longer participate in any cooperative groups so that the student's instructional needs will be met.
  (D) Mr. Williamson should meet with the parent to go over the rationale for the cooperative approach and explain how her son could benefit from the procedure.

10. Mrs. Gardner is a kindergarten teacher at Linfield Elementary. She has 21 students in her class, and supplements her academic approach with many socialization activities. She has close to twenty years of experience, and understands the needs of atypical children because her own son has attention deficit disorder.

    By the end of the second day of school, Mrs. Gardner realized that one of her new students, Carl, was having great difficulty. He was unable to concentrate on a task for more than 3 or 4 seconds, and he constantly left his seat. He would gravitate to items that spun or spilled in a controlled manner. He would go to a certain closet to find a little hourglass from a learning game; he liked to watch the sand move from one part to another. When the teacher locked the closet, he threw a temper tantrum and wailed like a 6-month-old child.

    Carl is echolalic and engages in telegraphic speech. Eye contact is very sporadic. When Mrs. Gardner tells him to look at her, his focus is very fleeting. He holds all writing instruments in his fist and tends to scribble all over any drawing paper or book in an impulsive manner. When he leaves his seat, which has been changed to be near the paraprofessional, Mrs. Gardner or her assistant tries to grab him. When this happens, Carl is resistant and often begins to hit his head with his own fist.

    What should Mrs. Gardner do to deal with this problematic student?

    (A) After informally discussing the problem with the parents, she should call them in to have them observe the child's behavior in the class prior to a more formal conference.

    (B) She should assign the paraprofessional to work individually with the student for the full day so that she can engage the rest of her students.

    (C) She should have this student expelled from the kindergarten class because kindergarten is not mandatory within her school system.

    (D) She should tell the parents that the child needs an immediate evaluation because she suspects he has a handicapping condition that should be addressed immediately.

11. After the initial meeting, there was little or no contact with the parent. The parents stated that they would get the child help; however, it was not stated what this help would be. Homework was not complete, and the parents did not respond to several notes. At this point, Mrs. Gardner contacted the guidance counselor, who consults with the school psychologist and learning specialist.

    What is the most likely outcome of this consultation?

    (A) The guidance counselor will probably take the child for individual counseling.

    (B) The psychologist will put the child in a group therapy session.

    (C) There will be a meeting with the parents in which the school psychologist and guidance counselor will be invited.

    (D) After this consultation, the principal will expel the child because kindergarten is not mandatory.

12. The principal invites the parents to a meeting. The school psychologist, the guidance counselor, and the learning specialist also attend the meeting. The parents are upset because they feel that the kindergarten teacher does not want to work with their child. The child's mother states that her older children had Mrs. Weinblock as a kindergarten teacher, and they would like the child moved into her class. They feel that their child is being picked on. They state that they are aware that he has a problem with self-control, but that he is able to do most of the work. They do not want him in special education because they feel that it is a dumping ground for retarded children. The child's father states that he works with the children every night at home. As a result of this meeting, an action plan is developed.

    Which of the following choices represents the most realistic plan for this student?

    (A) The student will remain in his present class, and the paraprofessional will work individually with the child all day. After two months, the situation will be monitored to see if a special education referral is necessary.

(B) The student will be placed on a truncated day, and the school psychologist will set up a behavior management program. The student will be moved to the other kindergarten class, and academic modifications will be implemented in collaboration with the learning specialist. The parents will agree that they will take the child for a psychoneurological evaluation at the children's hospital and that they will present the results to the school in about two months.

(C) The parents will volunteer to remove the child from kindergarten because of the optional nature of this program. During this time, they will take the child for a psychoneurological evaluation at the request of the school psychologist, who writes a referral to the hospital stating that the child exhibits autistic-like behaviors. If the result is a possible handicapping condition, only private school recommendations will be made.

(D) The parents will come into the classroom each day to work individually with the child because the school has a shortage of paraprofessional personnel. The child will be placed on a truncated day so that the parent can have a full 8 hours of employment in the afternoon. When the child goes home at noon, he will be placed in a daycare program for autistic children.

13. In collaboration with the new general education teacher, Mrs. Gardner sets up an individualized behavior management program with the student. Based on the behavioral description of the child stated in question 10, such a program would include all of the following EXCEPT

(A) consistent social praise after a certain amount of tokens the child would get for acting appropriately.

(B) pretzels given after every 3 minutes the student works on or concentrates on a given task.

(C) the teacher consistently ignoring the student's screaming, and the giving of edible rewards after every half-hour the student does not scream.

(D) the pairing of high-interest activities with low-interest activities to increase the child's concentration and attention.

14. After two months, the child still exhibits problems with self-control. The teacher has not been consistently applying the behavior management program because she must devote time to the other students in the class. Though screaming has decreased, the child still has not made any academic progress. He scribbles impulsively. He has no number or letter recognition. He has difficulty responding to verbal stimuli. Echolalic and perseverative behaviors are evident.

The principal calls the parents to a follow-up meeting. Attending the meeting are the teacher, guidance counselor, and school psychologist. The principal tells the parents that the paraprofessional must be removed because he was assigned to another school. He asks the parents about the results of the psychoneurological evaluation. They state that they have not had any time for this evaluation because the child is not exhibiting the type of screaming and tantrums that he had at the first meeting. They want him to remain in his present program and to go on to first grade next September.

As a result of the meeting, what will be the most likely recommendation by the school?

(A) The teacher will continue to work with the student in the regular education environment.

(B) The child will be placed in the at-risk tutorial program to further develop skills he will need next year for first grade.

(C) The teacher will write up a formal evaluation for special services because the parent did not follow through with the neuropsychological evaluation.

(D) The assistant principal will set up an inclusion class for next year for the student.

15. If the parents do not consent to a formal evaluation of the student after a referral document is generated by the school, the general education teacher should

    (A) stop all classroom modifications for the student unless an Individual Educational Program (IEP) is written.
    (B) keep anecdotal records of the student's behavior and all parental contacts because the principal might have to request an impartial hearing or mediation to force the issue of a formal assessment.
    (C) call the city's children's services agency to report the parents for educational neglect.
    (D) call the parents to another conference to discuss the possibility of keeping the child in kindergarten next year, and discuss management techniques to be used in the home.

16. Mrs. Schuster was assigned to a low-functioning second-grade class in an inner-city school. The class has twenty-four children. Nine of the children are repeating second grade. Most of the children in her class are reading at the first-grade level. About half are at the beginning of the preprimer level. Mrs. Schuster must develop a program that will help these children learn how to decode words and comprehend the material they are reading. Which of the following remedial adaptations would be an effective start in teaching Mrs. Schuster's children how to read?

    I. The extensive use of repetitive stories
    II. Shorter stories and passages during the reading lesson
    III. Memorization of sight words on a weekly basis
    IV. The teaching of individual phonemes

    (A) I and II only
    (B) I, II, and IV only
    (C) II and III only
    (D) I only

17. Mrs. Schuster has divided her class into two reading groups. She has one group working at the primer level and a second group on the preprimer level. She wants to reinforce the skills of the higher reading group while developing skills in the lower reading group. Her lower reading group is not only having problems reading the words, but they also are having trouble comprehending the material. Which is the least effective measure in facilitating reading comprehension?

    (A) Having the students in the preprimer group read the material slowly to better identify the organization of the passage of the text
    (B) Devoting lessons to finding specific types of information in a story
    (C) Pairing students in the lower reading group with those in the higher reading group to find and summarize the main idea of a passage
    (D) Having the students discover the meaning of a story through the use of context clues

18. Because poor readers have difficulty identifying the organization of a passage of text, comprehension is suffering. How can Mrs. Schuster increase her students' ability to structure the passage to increase reading comprehension?

    (A) She can have them look up new vocabulary concepts in a simplified children's dictionary.
    (B) She can create a semantic concept map of the story.
    (C) She can have the students read the passage with their parents at home for reinforcement.
    (D) She can create an extensive list of comprehension questions using an overhead projector that the students will have to answer after the passage is silently read in class.

19. One particular way of improving comprehension is to have the students develop skills in visual imagery. All of the following ways will develop visual imagery in reading impaired students EXCEPT

    (A) having the students arrange comic illustrations of a story in sequential order.
    (B) having the students role-play various parts of a story.

(C) having the students close their eyes to create a mental image of the important events in the story.

(D) having the students interview the teacher, who is playing the role of one of the characters in the story.

20. One of Mrs. Schuster's students, named Sarah, came to school with a note from her mother. Although Sarah is reading at the primer level, the parent is concerned that her daughter has not brought home a second-grade reader after four weeks of school. In the child's book bag was a library book that her mother picked out for the student. Sarah's mother wants the teacher to read this book to her on a regular basis. According to a readability formula, this story is really at the fourth-grade level. How should Mrs. Schuster respond to this parent?

(A) After praising the parent for her concern about the child's academic needs, the teacher should choose stories containing a controlled vocabulary and direct, straightforward syntax.

(B) Longer passages should be given to the child at the parent's request so that engage time in reading will increase in the school.

(C) Stories with no illustrations should be given so that the impaired students can concentrate on the text of the material.

(D) Stories with many difficult words and concepts should be given so that comprehension will increase by the end of the marking period.

21. Mrs. Schuster was chosen by her principal to speak to the parents of kindergarten students about preparing preschool children for reading success. In her workshop, she described all of the following predictors of success EXCEPT

(A) preschoolers' ability to recognize and name letters of the alphabet.

(B) preschoolers' awareness of phonemes.

(C) literacy preparation, such as playing with refrigerator letters, being read to, or watching Sesame Street.

(D) a wide range of concept development and information.

22. During her discussion with one kindergarten parent, Mrs. Schuster surprised her with a little known fact about learning how to read. According to the latest research, which statement is true about learning how to read?

(A) Children with no experiences with print have just as good a chance to learn how to read as children whose parents read with them every day.

(B) Differences in reading potential are shown not to be strongly related to poverty, handedness, dialect, gender, IQ, and mental age.

(C) Musical ability is positively correlated to reading ability.

(D) All children who value reading as a means of entertainment, information, and communication learn how to read at the same rate.

23. Mr. Robertson, a seventh-grade teacher, just graduated from college last year. He is having his first parent/teacher conference. When Lisa's parents came to his classroom, he sat them down in front of his desk. He immediately described the student's negative behavior in his class. He also stated that she is about a year behind in reading. Mr. Robertson told Lisa's parents that they must not be lazy and that they should work with their daughter. After he made his statement about Lisa, he thanked them for coming and told them that he had to see the next parent. However, he said that they could call him if they had any further questions.

After Lisa's parents left the classroom, they immediately went to the principal. They had several complaints.

Which is NOT a legitimate complaint they could discuss with the principal?

(A) The teacher used his authority to intimidate them.

(B) The teacher did not listen to anything they had to say.

(C) The teacher implied that the student had some type of disabling condition.

(D) The teacher was very negative about the child.

24. At the close of his meeting with Mr. Robertson, the principal offered several suggestions on how the teacher could improve his parent conferences. Which of the following would be possible recommendations?

    I. He should show specific examples of the student's work to the parents.

    II. He should use more technical language to better explain the educational needs of the child.

    III. He and the parents should develop a plan to help the child in the next few months.

    IV. He must set a more positive tone in his conversations.

  (A) I and IV only
  (B) III and IV only
  (C) I, II, and III only
  (D) I, III, and IV only

25. Mr. Robertson also had a conference with the parents of Rachel, another student. Mr. Robertson stated that Rachel was "very messy." He began to talk about her messy desk, messy writing, and messy pencil case. He also stated that she is totally disorganized. What can the parents of this child conclude as a result of this meeting?

  (A) They must help Rachel develop organizational skills.
  (B) The teacher may not like their child for some reason.
  (C) They must talk to a special education consultant to help their child develop study skills.
  (D) The teacher has told it like it is, with legitimate criticism of their daughter.

26. Mr. Borestein's fourth-grade class spends each day examining the rules and fundamentals of scoring a particular sport. Research skills are used to locate information concerning the sport's history. Then the students are placed in groups of four. The group is given box score material for each sport. In addition, a game's attendance and the length of time the game was played are also noted. For example, in baseball, such information as at-bats, runs batted in, hits, errors, innings pitched, outs, and walks are given in the box scores. From these box scores, the students create word problems in their learning groups.

According to the NCTM, which goal is being best expressed during this lesson?

  (A) Increasing confidence in making sense of the world around them using mathematical ideas
  (B) Using complex problems that have no right or wrong answer
  (C) Developing the ability to communicate mathematically using signs, symbols, and terms
  (D) Developing good reasoning skills to make conjecture and build arguments to support various given notions

27. Which of the following would be a good follow-up activity for the lesson described in the previous question?

  (A) Groups solve their own problems at home and convene the next day to determine appropriate responses.
  (B) Scientific notation is used to solve the most complex problems developed by the group.
  (C) Students are given problems on index cards with the box scores, and work with them independently at a learning center.
  (D) The groups vote the next day to determine which group came up with the most unique problem.

28. The teacher states that composing word problems gives students the opportunity to reinforce their expressive skills. Also, composing the problems stresses correct capitalization and punctuation skills. Students are evaluated on the clarity of the information being given. Which discipline is the teacher tying himself into?

  (A) Physical education
  (B) Language arts
  (C) Mathematics
  (D) History

29. How can the teacher expand the theme of this lesson on sports problem solving to incorporate social studies concepts?

(A) The areas of different major league stadiums could be compared and contrasted.

(B) Maps could be used to determine where major league stadiums can be found.

(C) Students could orally describe the directions to a particular stadium.

(D) Students could read a newspaper article about their favorite team and write a short critique.

30. Mr. Farley has students research information on the Internet about the founding of county fairs in the United States. He wants the students to know the history of these fairs and to understand their original purpose. He also wants the students to understand the various types of shows and events found at such fairs. He wants the students to compare county fairs, trade fairs, and national and international exhibitions and expositions. How should Mr. Farley structure the class to find out about this information?

  I. He should tell the students what county fairs are like through a teacher-directed lesson.

  II. He should have each student find out information about different nineteenth-century county fairs through a variety of research techniques prior to going to a local county fair.

  III. He should have different cooperative groups research the differences among county fairs, trade fairs, and national and international exhibitions during the nineteenth-century.

  IV. He should have the students read an article about the history and politics of the Marin County Fair from an article found in a search engine.

(A) I and II only
(B) II and III only
(C) III and IV only
(D) II only

31. One group is researching fairs using the Internet. All of the following are some preliminary skills needed to do Internet-based research EXCEPT

(A) the ability to touch-type effectively to enhance the productivity of the process.

(B) understanding how to effectively use a search engine to find information from key words.

(C) the ability to use a multimedia encyclopedia to find supplementary articles on the Internet.

(D) understanding the strengths and limitations of some of the commercial Internet databases, such as Research-It or the Encarta Online Library.

32. Mrs. Waters is a first-grade teacher who is serving on a committee in her school to streamline the instruction of reading from kindergarten to third grade. The committee must determine whether the emphasis should be on whole language or phonics. Prior to being part of this committee, Mrs. Waters attended several workshops on phonic instruction. In these workshops, the whole language approach was critiqued. Which of the following is NOT a legitimate critique of whole language?

(A) Whole language instruction teaches children to guess at words by looking at pictures on a page.

(B) Whole language instruction depends more on memorization of common words than on decoding.

(C) Whole language instruction does not teach phonics in the early childhood grades.

(D) Whole language instruction depends more on word prediction.

33. Mr. Landsman, on the other hand, is in favor of the whole language approach to instruction. He states that Mrs. Waters' arguments do not take into consideration that

    (A) the self-esteem of the student as a reader is just as important in whole language as developing specific reading skills.
    (B) whole language instruction usually does not commence until third grade.
    (C) many state legislatures have praised whole language instruction and have earmarked money for textbook conversation and the training of all teachers in this approach.
    (D) most assessment tests used in high school and higher education are dependent upon this approach.

34. Mrs. Waters countered Mr. Landsman by stating that whole language is not really a new technique. It is based upon the "whole word" or "look and say" method that dominated the public school after the 1930s. She cites the following book in critiquing this mid-twentieth century approach to reading:

    (A) Flesch, *Why Johnny Can't Read*
    (B) Silberman, *The Open Classroom*
    (C) Wiig and Semel, *Language Assessment and Intervention*
    (D) Roswell and Natchez, *Reading Disability*

35. Mr. Landsman relates a story about a 3-year-old boy who was taught using a phonetic approach to reading. He was able to sound out most of the words in a Hemingway novel. He even used context clues to figure out how to pronounce some unknown words. He was easily able to read some very difficult multisyllable words. However, when asked questions about the novel, he was unsure what the book was about. He even had difficulty recalling basic facts.

    This story illustrates that

    (A) phonics does not focus on language arts because it is felt that those who learn by this method have good language skills.
    (B) when using phonics, more difficult reading material is often used.

    (C) whole language instruction has a focus on remedial instruction.
    (D) if a child has poor language skills, learning to decode will not make him an effective reader.

36. After a month, the committee with Mrs. Waters and Mr. Landsman came up with some recommendations:

    I.   Phonics instruction should be sequential, explicit, and based on the current text being read.
    II. Language experiences should be incorporated into reading to enhance comprehension skills.
    III. Spelling and grammar should be emphasized more in the lower grades.
    IV. Readability should include a richer vocabulary to teach phonic skills.

    (A) II, III, and IV only
    (B) I, II, III, and IV
    (C) I, II, and III only
    (D) IV only

37. Mrs. Waters must choose appropriate reading material for her first-grade class to implement the school's new reading program. She went through various catalogues and got free samples. In setting up an eclectic approach to the teaching of reading, all of the following are appropriate materials EXCEPT

    (A) books with realistic and motivating stories containing controlled phonetic elements.
    (B) picture books containing repetitive sentences or vocabulary words.
    (C) trade books containing common sight words.
    (D) linguistic workbooks containing structured exercises in the teaching of phonetic skills.

38. Mrs. Waters is working with Polly, a student teacher from a local college. Polly, who is interning in Mrs. Waters' classroom is preparing to teach a directed reading lesson, Mrs. Waters gives Polly the following summary of this approach:

   - Develop an experience background or readiness
   - Develop needed concepts
   - Develop words that may cause difficulty
   - Develop the aim or purpose for reading
   - Encourage independent reading activity
   - Extend interpretation

   Which of these statements does NOT fit in with this reading method?

   (A) Develop words that may cause difficulty
   (B) Extend interpretation
   (C) Encourage independent silent reading
   (D) Develop needed concepts

39. During her first lesson, Polly asked the following questions after reading the story "Stone Soup."

   "Why do you think the boy was wearing ragged clothes?"
   "What was the boy really doing to the old lady?"
   "Why do you think the boy chose this old lady?"

   What is the teacher asking the students to do with these questions?

   (A) Predict outcome
   (B) Draw conclusions
   (C) Use cause and effect
   (D) Sequence information

40. When Polly did a guided reading activity with Mrs. Waters' class, she used a variety of questions. As she asked questions, the students read in a round-robin fashion one paragraph at a time. She then had students reread certain parts to find the most interesting parts of the story, locate certain descriptive words, and contrast and compare ideas.

After the lesson, Mrs. Waters critiqued the lesson. Which of the following is the weakest part of her student teacher's guided reading activity?

(A) Round-robin reading
(B) Rereading of different parts
(C) Finding interesting parts of the story
(D) Analyzing descriptive words

41. In Mrs. Waters' school, the first two periods are mandated reading periods for the class. Another teacher in the school, Mr. Simon, a second-grade teacher, has Mrs. Waters as a mentor. Last year, during his first year of teaching, no matter how hard he worked, the reading scores of Mr. Simon's class made no significant improvement.

   Mr. Simon asked Mrs. Waters to observe the first two periods of his class. When the class came in, he put up a do-now exercise that took up both boards and in which twenty synonyms had to be matched. Then he went around collecting the homework. Six children had to be sent to the bathroom. Then Mr. Simon began his reading lesson. He noticed that the text the students were reading had many contractions. Therefore, he taught a lesson on contractions before the class began to read. In the middle of the guided reading activity, the bell rang for the third period.

   According to this description, what seems to be a problem with Mr. Simon's lesson?

   (A) He has poor engage time.
   (B) Academic learning time is poorly utilized.
   (C) Mr. Simon has poor expectations for the students.
   (D) The lesson has poor structure.

42. Seth is a sixth-grade student in a middle school. He has been struggling in school for years, and has been diagnosed as having visual-spatial problems. Diagnostic testing revealed that the student's comprehension is at the seventh-grade level, and decoding skills are at the fourth-grade level. Seth has difficulty spelling and organizing his written work. Though he understands which operations he must use to do word problems, he makes many careless mistakes in his written work. His understanding of many social studies and science concepts are above grade level.

On his first report card, Seth failed English, math, social studies, and science. His mother was called into a conference with the classroom teacher, the principal, the resource room teacher, and the Child Study Team. When she came to the conference, Seth's mother brought various hospital-based evaluations outlining his problems. Seth's mother did not want any special educational services because the one small class that was available in the school was out of control. The children were always walking the halls, and she felt that her son's needs might not be met in that class. Instead, she wanted adaptations made in the regular classroom through the 504 process.

What is the likely result of this conference?

(A) The child will be placed in a small class because of his severe decoding problem.
(B) Adaptations will be made in the regular classroom to meet his needs.
(C) Outside tutorial services will be recommended.
(D) The student will be retested in six months to see if he has made any academic progress in decoding.

43. A team of professionals sits with the student's mother to come up with a 504 plan for the student. Many academic adaptations are recommended. All of the following are probable recommendations EXCEPT

(A) questions and directions should be read to the student.

(B) the student should develop self-correcting skills using a computerized grammar- and spell-checker so that he can focus on creative writing rather than being bogged down by mechanics.
(C) photocopies of other students' notes should be prepared so that the pupil does not waste valuable academic learning time on such a task.
(D) the student will undergo intensive practice in penmanship and legibility.

44. Mr. Weiss, Seth's math teacher, was sent a copy of the 504 plan. In addition to having questions and directions read to him, the student also needed extended time and was allowed to record his answers in any manner because of his visual-organizational problems. In addition, when doing verbal problems, he was allowed to use a calculator.

This teacher reacted negatively to this plan. He believes that the student is spoiled and lazy. He believes that Seth just does not want to concentrate and do the work appropriately. He does not see the student as being motivated, and he feels that Seth should not be given these adaptations.

What is the most appropriate action this teacher should take?

(A) He should refuse to implement the 504 plan because he has too many students in the class, and this would take away time from his other pupils.
(B) He should not implement a voluntary plan he is opposed to.
(C) He should write a referral for special education so that this needy student can be placed in a small class that could better meet his needs.
(D) He should attempt to implement the recommendations; if he is having difficulty, he should ask for technical support.

45. Ms. Williams is Seth's English teacher. She wants to implement the adaptations in the 504 plan in regards to reading and writing, but does not know how. Which of the following are appropriate remedial strategies to help a student with visual-perceptual problems?

I. Give the student shorter assignments.

II. Have the student read words within a stencil template.

III. Phase out reading questions as the student's decoding ability improves.

IV. Have an LD specialist come into the room and implement the plan.

(A) II and III only
(B) I only
(C) I and II only
(D) III and IV only

46. The assistant principal called the major subject area teachers together to discuss Seth's 504 adaptations. She gave the teachers some research materials about teaching students with visual-perceptual-spatial problems. Which of the statements here represents current research in the field?

(A) These students need to enhance their visual skills through perceptual training. They need to work on pattern boards and do visual exercises that will enhance their tracking of various objects.

(B) These students usually need a small class environment to develop individual learning tasks in which visual stimuli are presented in small units of time. This enhances the attention of the students.

(C) These students need intensive remediation to develop language concepts to compensate for their lack of reading skills. They also need a stress-free environment so that they can concentrate on visual tasks.

(D) These students need to develop compensatory strategies that are based on tasks being taught in the classroom environment. They need alternate approaches to academic tasks.

47. Which of the following are appropriate strategies to help a child with a visual-perceptual problem adapt to the general education classroom?

I. Have the student write a two-paragraph composition in an organized manner.

II. Have the student keep his place during a guided reading lesson by using a sentence window.

III. Have the student format a 20-page spelling test appropriately.

IV. Have the student fold paper into 16 boxes and put one example in each box.

(A) I and III only
(B) II and IV only
(C) IV only
(D) III only

48. Mrs. Winters is a remedial math teacher who instructs five different grades. In her second-grade class, she wants to instruct the students in estimation. She decides to use money to teach this skill. She has the students work in six cooperative groups to guess the number of pennies in a jar. The students are asked to submit a group guess, and the group guesses are recorded on the board. The students are then asked to arrange the pennies in piles of approximately ten, but are instructed not to count the pennies as they arrange the piles. Then the group is asked to take another guesstimate on the number of pennies.

Which is an appropriate skill that can be taught using this technique at this grade level?

(A) Write the guesses in Roman numerals
(B) Round the numbers to the nearest ten
(C) Tell the number that comes before each guess
(D) Identify the guessed numbers using place value

49. Mrs. Winters must then set up various activities to teach estimation to a fifth-grade class. She increases the number of pennies in the jar. All of the following are grade-level activities EXCEPT

(A) find the mean, mode, and median of the guesses.
(B) show the fractional part of the whole group.
(C) estimate your bill in a fast food restaurant.
(D) tell if the guesses are odd or even.

50. Mrs. Winters decides to use corn to teach place value to her third-grade remedial math class. The students must group large amounts of corn by tens and ones and then write the total in standard form. She structured this lesson using Bloom's *Taxonomy*. Which of the following procedures represent "analysis" according to Bloom?

  (A) Students will count the number of corn kernels they have.

  (B) Students will categorize their corn according to given numbers.

  (C) Students will defend their reasons for grouping kernels.

  (D) Students will develop a plan to count all the kernels in an estimation jar.

51. Mrs. Winters used a variety of learning modalities to teach her various remedial lessons. In her teaching of place value using corn, which of the following represents the use of a kinesthetic approach to teaching?

  (A) Students will use place value mats, overheads, recording charts, individual recording sheets, corn, and Dixie cups.

  (B) Students will listen to teacher directions and choral reciting.

  (C) Students will manipulate corn kernels by sorting them into cups in groups of ten.

  (D) Students will sort corn by texture.

52. Mr. Shawn is a high school English teacher in a school that is 60 percent African American, 25 percent Hispanic, 10 percent Caucasian, and 5 percent Asian. His tenth-grade class had to analyze five Shakespearean plays in a term. The students read from the fourth- to eighth-grade level. Most students were from poor or working-class backgrounds. The teacher's first goal was for the class to understand the play *The Taming of the Shrew*.

  This teacher had to find a way for all the students to read the play, even though many still had significant decoding problems. However, he also realized that decoding would be an issue even for those students near grade level. He realized that he would have to make adaptations from a standard reading lesson.

All of the following are alternate strategies for these students EXCEPT

  (A) having the students play the parts of different characters as they read the play orally.

  (B) reviewing a summary of a scene prior to the reading.

  (C) having the students read silently to find specific information.

  (D) reviewing the meanings of archaic words.

53. When the students read the play, many were confused about the various characters that appeared in the scenes. They seemed to confuse one character with another. They were also unable to interpret the personalities of the different characters. Jon, a student who stuttered and had a severe decoding problem, stated that all the different people in the play seemed to blend in with each other. Which is an appropriate strategy to help these students analyze the different characters in the play?

  (A) The teacher should develop a character map with the class.

  (B) In cooperative groups, the students should create coherent outlines.

  (C) The students should look up words that describe different personality traits.

  (D) After every scene, the teacher should develop a quiz asking literal questions about different characters.

54. Which of the following answers given by students represents a very high level of comprehension according to Bloom's *Taxonomy*?

  (A) "Kate should not have gone along with Petruchio when he admired the moonlight in the afternoon because it showed she was weak."

  (B) "Kate is not really a shrew, but someone who has a mind of her own."

  (C) "Petruchio is making believe that he is a shrew also."

  (D) "This play represents the battle of the sexes."

55. At first, the teacher decided to read the play orally to the class himself because, as even the best readers took turns playing various characters, they exhibited halting fluency. As a result, many of the students lost attention. They stared out the window or played with pens on their desk. There was even some mild conversation. Which of the following methods would be most effective in increasing the students' understanding of the play?

(A) Watching a movie of the play

(B) Having the teacher help the students decode as they read

(C) Doing mini lessons reinforcing various skill weaknesses during the reading

(D) Having only the best readers recite the play

56. During lunch, Mr. Shawn and Mrs. Williams were talking. That morning, the Principal made an announcement that all students had to remove their coats and place them in a locker. In Mr. Shawn's homeroom, a student refused and was sent to the dean. He came back in 5 minutes with his coat still on. Ten minutes later, an assistant principal looked into the class and criticized the teacher in front of the class for not forcing the student to remove his coat. This scenario represents

(A) a lack of consequences.

(B) administrative control.

(C) a subjective interpretation of events.

(D) a lack of structure.

57. Every Tuesday, Mr. Shawn takes his class to the computer room for vocabulary development. Using dictionary software, the students look up twenty words, print out the definitions, and then write sentences using the words. The students usually write sentences like the following:

- My mother is glib.
- My mother has forbearance.
- My mother has finesse.

Mr. Shawn feels that learning vocabulary out of context and printing definitions is not effective. How can Mr. Shawn make this lesson more challenging for his students?

(A) The students could match full-sentence definitions with the words.

(B) The students could write a paragraph using the vocabulary words in sentences that convey their meanings.

(C) The students could write sentences conveying different definitions of a given word.

(D) The students could put the vocabulary words in a modified Cloze passage.

58. As part of the unit on *The Taming of the Shrew*, Mr. Shawn brings in some children's books and articles in which women are in more traditional male occupations. The class discusses whether boys should go into more traditional female occupations. Finally, the class discusses whether a girl should ask a boy out on a date. The teacher is trying to relate this to Kate's character in the Shakespearean play.

The next day, Mr. Shawn is brought into the principal's office. In the room is the mother of one of the students in his class. When they sit down, the parent says that Mr. Shawn is trying to poison her son's mind with feminist propaganda. The parent demands that the teacher stop teaching this play.

Which scenario is an appropriate outcome of this meeting?

(A) As a result of the meeting, Mr. Shawn stops teaching *The Taming of the Shrew* and replaces it with another play.

(B) The teacher explains to the parent that he was teaching this lesson so that the male students would examine their preconceived notions to develop higher-level thinking skills.

(C) The teacher no longer discusses such matters in class at the request of the parent and the principal.

(D) The teacher brings in a union representative because this meeting may result in disciplinary action.

59. At the end of one of his lessons, Mr. Shawn notices two students shredding notebook paper into tiny pieces of confetti. The teacher walks over to them and states, "There are pieces of paper all over the floor." The boys reply, "I didn't do it." Which of the following is the most appropriate response for this teacher?

    (A) "You had better pick up this paper, or I am calling the dean."
    (B) "I am sending home a note for your parents to come in about this matter."
    (C) "Let's try to pick up this paper together to keep this school clean."
    (D) "You are picking up this paper, and you will not be going to your next class until it is done."

60. Mrs. Jensen is a seventh-grade middle school science teacher. She has been assigned to mentor a new teacher in the school. During a preconference, the new teacher decides that he wants to improve his classroom management skills. Mrs. Jensen tells this new teacher that she wants to observe him when the kids come in on the first day. Mrs. Jensen states that the first day usually sets the stage about whether the class will have significant management problems.

    She tells Mr. Southwell that adolescent students have specific first-day needs. All of the following are specific needs of bright middle school students EXCEPT

    (A) discussing grading practices.
    (B) understanding how a teacher will treat them.
    (C) understanding the rules of this classroom.
    (D) understanding who will work with them in cooperative groups.

61. All of the following items are appropriate classroom activities that must be discussed during the first few weeks of school EXCEPT

    (A) explaining classroom rules and procedures as well as the consequences for breaking the rules.
    (B) discussing course content and grading procedures.

    (C) taking roll call, organizing the seating, and establishing a seating chart.
    (D) stating that the bell will dismiss the class and not the teacher.

62. There are five basic types of rules, according to the latest research on classroom management: entry, interactive, attention, exit, and classroom. The rules must not be confusing, ambiguous, or irrelevant. Which of the following is an example of an attention rule?

    (A) Put away your coats upon entering the room.
    (B) Raise your hand when requesting to go to the bathroom.
    (C) Request water only during lunch.
    (D) Listen silently while your neighbor is reading.

63. Mrs. Devlin has a second-grade student, Janet, who, in November, is still reading at the first-grade level. The teacher decides to call Janet's parents in for a conference to discuss intervention strategies. She tells Janet's parents that they must do more reading with Janet at home. Her parents reply that they are very busy. They do not come home until late at night and are often very tired.

    Which of the following strategies would be ineffective in increasing Janet's reading time at home with her parents?

    (A) The child should listen to a movie of the story they just read.
    (B) The child should read to the parent and tell the parent about the story.
    (C) Whenever the parent takes the child somewhere and has to wait, he or she should bring along some magazines or books.
    (D) The parent should provide tape recordings of books when no one is available to read to the child.

64. Mrs. Devlin must provide systematic phonics instruction in combination with word meaning and sentence structure in her class. She must place this instruction within a literature-based reading program and choose books that reflect word analysis skills. Which of the following types of books would she choose for her reading program?

    I.   Poetry
   II.   Nursery rhymes
  III. Myths
  IV. Song books

  (A) I only
  (B) IV only
  (C) I, II, and IV only
  (D) I and II only

65. Mrs. Devlin's neighbor, Ms. Herman, is a sixth-grade teacher. She understands that even in sixth grade, systematic phonic instruction still must be taught. However, she feels uncomfortable teaching older children how to sound out words. Mrs. Devlin agrees that sounding out words is inappropriate for the sixth-grade level. She gives Ms. Herman some ideas about how to teach sound/symbol relations appropriately at this grade level. Which is an appropriate phonic skill to teach at the sixth-grade level?

  (A) Teaching the blending of vowel digraphs with consonant blends and digraphs
  (B) Having the students isolate vowel diphthongs in one-syllable words
  (C) Having the students identify and pronounce English words derived from foreign languages
  (D) Having the students make up alliterations using consonant blends

66. As part of her reading program, Mrs. Devlin reads to her students for 20 minutes just after lunch. Which of the following are valid reasons for reading aloud to children?

    I.   Exposing children to more classic types of literature
   II.   Modeling effective reading practices
  III. Quieting and calming students after a high level of activity
  IV. Filling in a transitional period of time between two low-interest activities

  (A) I, II, and III only
  (B) I and IV only
  (C) II, III, and IV only
  (D) I and II only

67. During a teacher-directed reading lesson, Mrs. Devlin asks the following questions:

    "What is this whole story about?"
    "What is the author's purpose in writing this story?"
    "What can we learn from this story?"

The teacher is using these questions to

  (A) confuse the students.
  (B) engage in structured comprehension.
  (C) engage the students in answering different drawing-conclusion questions.
  (D) increase question comprehension skills.

68. Mr. Saunders' high school physics class is working on understanding the physics involved in different types of machines. After reading about various types of levers and pulleys, the teacher divides his laboratory class into various groups. Each group is given weights, cords, pulleys, boards, and platforms. Their assignment is to create a machine that will perform a simple task, such as pour water in a bottle, in a complex manner. The approach he is using corresponds to a theory espoused by

  (A) Bettleheim.
  (B) Piaget.
  (C) Erikson.
  (D) Bruner.

69. Which of the following statements are true of the discovery approach to learning science?

    I.   Students do less well on standardized science tests using this approach.
   II.   Students do not have to discover every fact, principle, and concept they need to know.
  III. Students do not understand how ideas are connected using this method.
  IV. Most schools cannot use this approach because the materials needed are very expensive.

  (A) III and IV only
  (B) II only
  (C) IV only
  (D) I and III only

70. Mr. Saunders proposes a problem to his high school physics class. He states that a large boulder weighs 500 pounds and asks the class, "What are all the ways it can be moved?

One student states that it could be moved by using multiple pulleys on a hoist. Another states that it could be moved by prying it up with a first-class lever, placing logs under it, and then rolling it. A third states that it could be pulled up on an incline plane by a tractor onto a trailer.

The teacher then asks the class which would be the best machine to move the boulder. A student states that he would use a lever and the log because it would be the cheapest way.

This interaction between the teacher and his students represents an example of

(A) propositional thinking.
(B) hypothetical-deductive thinking.
(C) reflexive thinking.
(D) evaluative thinking.

71. Mr. Saunders is developing an in-service course on modern science instruction. He wants teachers to understand the difference between discovery teaching and inquiry teaching. All of the following items are components of inquiry EXCEPT

(A) synthesizing knowledge.
(B) testing ideas.
(C) formulating hypotheses.
(D) predicting outcomes.

72. Mr. Saunders discusses Bruner's rationale for using a discovery approach to learning. He tells his class that the only way a person learns the techniques of making discoveries is to have opportunities to discover. Through discovering, the student then learns how to organize and carry out investigations. Saunders is describing Bruner's concept of

(A) learning the heuristics of discovery.
(B) intellectual potency.
(C) intrinsic rather than extrinsic motives.
(D) conservation of memory.

73. Mr. Saunders has a prelaboratory discussion about a physics experiment that taps into energy conservation. He explains to the class the materials they will need. He outlines the procedures for the experiment and outlines the different hypotheses that can be tested by this experiment. He asks a variety of questions to focus the students toward appropriate conclusions. To conclude, he asks open-ended questions for which the students must design a follow-up investigation.

Which type of process is being described here?

(A) Guided discovery and inquiry
(B) Free discovery and inquiry
(C) Modified discovery and inquiry
(D) Experimental discovery and inquiry

74. Here are four questions:
   I. "What can you tell me about black holes?"
   II. "What did you find out about black holes?"
   III. "How does the natural world create a black hole?"
   IV. "Answering in one or two sentences, how are black holes made?"

Which of these sentences helps the students summarize the learning experiment?

(A) I only
(B) II only
(C) III only
(D) IV only

75. Mr. Saunders is developing questions for a test on heredity. He is using the "Taxonomy of Educational Objectives" as a guide in writing the questions. According to Bloom, questions can be of six different skill levels: knowledge, comprehension, application, analysis, synthesis, and evaluation.

Following are 4 questions from this test. Which of these questions is an analysis question?

(A) "Should people who are planning to marry consider the heredity of their families?"
(B) "What do most recessive genes have in common?"
(C) "What is Tay Sachs Disease?"
(D) "What are four ways to detect genetic diseases?"

76. Mr. Saunders wants the essay questions on his test to tap into divergent thinking. He wants creative, critical-thinking answers. Which of these 4 questions tap into divergent thinking skills?

(A) "How can PKU be detected?"

(B) "What improvements can you suggest for the environment in which you live?"

(C) "Why is it that no two people have the same fingerprints?"

(D) "Why do most states require newborn infants to have urine tests to detect PKU?"

77. Mr. Saunders had this as one of his test questions: "When will a cell decide to stop mutating?" When he read over his test, he decided to take out the question because he felt it was technically flawed. How may this question be flawed?

(A) It was too abstract for this particular grade level.

(B) It was anthropomorphic.

(C) It was teleological in nature.

(D) It would lead to a convergence of response.

78. Mrs. Schneider is an eighth-grade English teacher at Fairville Middle School. She has a class of twenty-seven children who are grouped heterogeneously. Mr. Simpson, a consultant teacher in the school, has asked this teacher to confer with him. They discuss the fact that John, one of Mrs. Schneider's students, is bright but has difficulty dealing with abstract verbal tasks. When facing verbal tasks, he becomes fidgety and cannot remain in his seat.

One of John's IEP goals is to pass the eighth-grade English Language Arts Test that has been mandated by the state. The student must read two pieces of literature and use writing skills to interpret these passages.

After talking with one another, the consultant and Mrs. Schneider come up with several short-term objectives and strategies for success. Which of the following strategies can help John acquire the skills needed to pass this test?

I. The consultant teacher should have John write compositions during the teacher-directed reading lesson.

II. The consultant teacher should sit next to John during the teacher-directed lesson and point to each line during guided silent reading to keep him focused.

III. The consultant teacher should help John develop plot maps as the story is read and discussed in class.

IV. The consultant teacher should drill John on irregular and nonphonetic spelling patterns.

(A) I and II only

(B) II only

(C) III only

(D) II and IV only

79. Mrs. Schneider wishes to make the best possible use of the consultant teacher's service in the classroom. Which of the following is the most effective use of a consultant within a regular classroom, according to the latest research?

(A) The consultant should walk around the room and work with any student who may need help.

(B) The general education teacher should pinpoint at-risk students and put them in an ad hoc group with the consultant. This group should work on the same skills being taught to the seventh-grade student in which the service is mandated.

(C) The consultant should work individually with other students in the back of the room on a variety of needed skills when John requires no help or is absent.

(D) The consultant should monitor the test-taking skills of some of the other students and work with them individually on test preparation.

80. The consultant and Mrs. Schneider have to decide at an annual review of the IEP which test modifications would best meet John's needs. All of the following are needed modifications for John EXCEPT

    (A) doubling the time necessary to generate a written response to a short passage.

    (B) responding in an alternate manner so that the student will attend to the answer, not the mechanics of writing.

    (C) taking the test in a quiet, less distracting environment.

    (D) having the entire test read orally to the student.

ESSAY

You have been assigned to teach a class of students in a subject area and at a grade you have been prepared to teach. You have been assigned to a class in which the students have heterogeneous academic skills. Although the students can comprehend literary texts, they are having difficulty comprehending content area material in such areas as social studies and science. On the last social studies test you gave, 60 percent of the students received grades of less than 70 percent. In addition, the students could not summarize orally any written information in either of these subject areas. Describe two (2) strategies you would use to improve your students' content area comprehension skills. Explain why you would choose these strategies and how they would improve content area comprehension.

Your audience in writing is a group of New York State educators. Be sure to specify an instructional context (e.g., subject area and grade level) that will help clarify your response, but frame your response so that any educator certified at the elementary or secondary level will be able to understand the basis for your decisions. You can continue on a separate piece of paper.

_____

_____

_____

_____

_____

_____

_____

_____

_____

_____

_____

_____

_____

ANSWER KEY

1. D	15. B	29. B	42. B	55. A	68. D
2. B	16. A	30. B	43. D	56. A	69. B
3. B	17. D	31. A	44. D	57. B	70. B
4. C	18. B	32. C	45. C	58. B	71. D
5. D	19. C	33. A	46. D	59. C	72. A
6. C	20. A	34. A	47. B	60. D	73. A
7. A	21. D	35. D	48. C	61. D	74. D
8. D	22. B	36. C	49. D	62. D	75. B
9. D	23. C	37. D	50. B	63. A	76. B
10. A	24. D	38. C	51. C	64. C	77. C
11. C	25. B	39. B	52. C	65. C	78. C
12. B	26. A	40. A	53. A	66. D	79. B
13. A	27. C	41. B	54. D	67. B	80. D
14. C	28. B				

ANSWERS AND EXPLANATIONS

1. **The correct answer is (D).** Berliner is associated with the effective teaching movement. Johnson and Johnson, choice (A), have done research on the composition of cooperative groups. Slavin, choice (B) has done extensive research in the field. Vygotsky, choice (C), has done research in group influence in relation to cognitive development and laid the foundation for this approach to learning.

2. **The correct answer is (B).** This basically describes the Jigsaw method of cooperative learning. Choice (D) is incorrect, even though Jigsaw can have elements of this method in which the whole group does one project together. Choice (C) is incorrect because this approach uses a variety of methods to teach a topic and is evaluated at the end by some type of test. Choice (A) is incorrect because the Teams–Games–Tournament approach uses tournaments instead of tests. Winning groups earn points that can be cashed in for a variety of rewards.

3. **The correct answer is (B).** According to Johnson and Johnson, the students still should be assessed individually. Choice (A) is incorrect because the maximum group size is from about 2 to 6 students. Choice (C) is obviously wrong because assessment is still individualized using this approach. Choice (D) is wrong because the students themselves should critique their cooperative group.

4. **The correct answer is (C).** Choice (C) is the correct answer because these three choices put academic achievement and real-world social experiences in the primary focus. Option III would not convince the chairperson because this statement puts academic achievement in a secondary position.

5. **The correct answer is (D).** Flavell is mostly associated with metacognition. The other three

educational theorists widely used cooperative learning within their theories during the eighteenth century to the early twentieth century.

6. **The correct answer is (C).** Research shows that groups should be heterogeneous so that students can bring different skills and abilities to the group. Choices (A), (B), and (D) represent advice based on relevant research about cooperative learning.

7. **The correct answer is (A).** Two group skills that need to be developed in the cooperative approach are consensus building and active/reflective listening. Option II is incorrect because in cooperative learning, students must support and accept individual differences. Option IV is wrong because the goal of this approach is teamwork, not competition.

8. **The correct answer is (D).** The scenario represents positive social interaction behaviors and attitudes in which the students have learned to manage conflicts, negotiate, and compromise. Choice (A) represents the structuring of tasks so that students believe that they have to sink or swim together. Choice (B) represents the fact that groups need to be arranged so that all the students face one another. Choice (C) represents students reflecting on how well they worked together as a team.

9. **The correct answer is (D).** The teacher needs to explain to the parent why the procedure is being used and how it can increase the boy's research skills and social interactions. He will explain that even though it is a group project, each student is marked individually. Choice (A) is incorrect because the teacher does not respect the wishes and need of the parent. Choices (B) and (C) are incorrect because the teacher did not explain the rationale for his cooperative approach to the parent. Instead, he changed the assignment to one that may not be beneficial to this student.

10. **The correct answer is (A).** When a teacher discovers that a student is at risk, she should first contact the parent to discuss the problem and create awareness about the situation.

Choice (B) is incorrect because, by assigning a paraprofessional to work with this child, the other children in the class will not be getting the individual instruction they need. Choice (C) is wrong because a kindergarten child cannot be expelled once he is registered without some form of due process. Choice (D) would cause the parents to possibly become resistant to help if they felt that the teacher had already diagnosed the needs of their child.

11. **The correct answer is (C).** The most likely outcome will be an educational meeting with school personnel to discuss the educational needs of this at-risk student in an attempt to maintain his regular education class. Choices (A) and (B) are incorrect because a child who exhibits autistic-like behaviors may not respond to therapy situations. Choice (D) is wrong because once a child is enrolled in the school, he cannot be expelled without due process.

12. **The correct answer is (B).** The most likely outcome will be a new teacher, a truncated day, behavioral interventions, and an outside assessment because the parent is opposed to special education and may not trust the Committee on Special Education. Choice (A) is wrong because the teacher will no longer be able to use the paraprofessional with the remainder of the class. Also, the parent will be turned off by an immediate special education referral. Choice (C) is wrong because the child has the right to stay in school, and the parent will be given public and private school choices during any evaluation procedure. Choice (D) is unrealistic because the parent may not be able to devote this much time to the student to the detriment of his or her work.

13. **The correct answer is (A).** Such a child may not respond to "only" social reinforcers. The reinforcer must be more concrete, such as edibles. Choices (B), (C), and (D) are all aspects of operant conditioning techniques applied to classroom instruction.

14. **The correct answer is (C).** The teacher will now have to write up a formal evaluation of the student because the parents did not follow up with an outside assessment. Choice (A) is wrong because remaining in regular education

is not completely effective due to the lack of academic progress. Choice (B) is wrong because a part-time program will not meet this child's academic needs. Choice (D) is wrong because the structure of the inclusion class is not mentioned.

15. **The correct answer is (B).** Evidence must be gathered for a due process hearing to force a consent for testing. Choice (A) is wrong because the teacher must continue all modifications to reinforce appropriate behaviors pending an evaluation. Choice (C) will create an extreme adversarial relationship with the parent. Choice (D) is wrong because leaving back a student with this problem will not increase his academic achievement.

16. **The correct answer is (A).** The students would have more success if they could read shorter, repetitive passages to reinforce either phonetic skills or certain vocabulary concepts. Option III is incorrect because many students who have difficulty reading have memory problems. Option IV is wrong because phonetic elements should not be taught in isolation.

17. **The correct answer is (D).** Preprimer readers will have a difficult time utilizing context clues because they are unable to read most of the words of a passage. Choice (A) is effective because by reading slowly, the students can concentrate more on the story's structure. Choice (B) is effective because the teacher focuses on a particular piece of information, making the material more manageable. Choice (C) is effective because paired learning enables each student to focus on a particular skill area to be developed.

18. **The correct answer is (B).** A visual representation of a story can help a learning-disabled student comprehend the structure of a story. Choice (A) is incorrect because these students are unable to read a very simple dictionary. Choice (C) is wrong because there is no guarantee that having a parent teach the child will be effective. Choice (D) is incorrect because there is no guarantee that these reading-impaired students will comprehend the questions on the overhead.

19. **The correct answer is (C).** Reading-impaired students cannot do this task. Choices (A), (B), and (D) are all tasks that help students create a mental image of the story. These procedures are being utilized because the students cannot read a story and create a mental summary.

20. **The correct answer is (A).** A controlled vocabulary will increase the achievement of reading-disabled youth. Choice (B) is incorrect because longer passages reduce concentration and attention, especially if a child makes decoding errors. Choice (C) is wrong because comprehension will increase if there are illustrations in a story. Choice (D) is incorrect because difficult words decrease comprehension.

21. **The correct answer is (D).** Students who exhibit good language concepts and oral comprehension may still have problems decoding words. Research shows that the other three choices, developed through several thousand hours of literacy training before reaching first grade, are effective in learning how to read.

22. **The correct answer is (B).** Research shows little correlation between many variables and learning how to read. Choices (C) and (D) are wrong because there is no correlation between reading and these other variables. Choice (A) is wrong because children who read with parents usually do better in school.

23. **The correct answer is (C).** The teacher did not imply any handicapping condition. Choices (A), (B), and (D) are all legitimate complaints. He arranged the desk in an authoritarian manner. He did not let the parents give him any input. Finally, all his statements about the child were negative.

24. **The correct answer is (D).** All are legitimate recommendations except for option II. Teachers should not use technical language or jargon; these words and acronyms can be chilling to parents. Instead, teachers must use clear and descriptive terms and must adjust the words used to the parent's needs and levels of understanding. If the teacher has to use a technical term, he must define it.

Prepare for the NYSTCE: LAST and ATS-W

25. **The correct answer is (B).** The only logical choice is that the teacher may not like their child because he found nothing positive to say about her. Choice (A) is wrong because total responsibility is put on the parent for the student's problem. Choice (C) is incorrect because the problem is not severe enough to warrant special education intervention. Choice (D) is wrong because the criticism seems out of proportion to the problem at hand.

26. **The correct answer is (A).** Using problem situations, the students use math to make sense of their world. They have to understand that doing math is a common human activity that is not really separate from other activities. Choice (B) is wrong because these sports questions do have right or wrong answers. Choice (C) is incorrect because few abstract symbols are being used to solve these problems. Choice (D) is wrong because these questions are not open-ended.

27. **The correct answer is (C).** The students not only create unique problems, but they also solve similar problems developed by others. Choice (A) is not a learning experience if the groups are solving the problems they made up. Choice (B) is usually not taught at the fourth-grade level. Choice (D) does not discuss any type of evaluation criteria to help students critique the work of others.

28. **The correct answer is (B).** This answer stresses language arts in the development of the writing process even though math problems are being used. Choice (C) is wrong because math is not being taught in isolation. Choices (A) and (D) are disciplines not being touched upon in this particular lesson.

29. **The correct answer is (B).** Map skills is the only legitimate social studies concept being taught in this lesson. Choices (A) and (C) involve broad math concepts. Choice (D) is a language arts activity, such as written expression.

30. **The correct answer is (B).** The teacher would structure the class so that the students could do independent and cooperative research comparing different types of fairs as part of a theme about the United States in the nineteenth century. Options II and IV are incorrect because the teacher is not developing independent study skills or making comparisons between concepts.

31. **The correct answer is (A).** The ability to type will not facilitate a student's skill in doing effective research. Choices (B), (C), and (D) are all legitimate techniques that must be taught to find clear and concise information from the Internet.

32. **The correct answer is (C).** Whole language does teach phonics, but not explicitly. It teaches phonics only as needed in relation to why certain words are pronounced in certain ways. Choices (A) and (D) are legitimate criticisms because some children poorly utilize context and picture clues when reading. Choice (B) is a legitimate criticism because many children have weak auditory and visual memory skills and cannot effectively use this approach.

33. **The correct answer is (A).** This is the only legitimate statement in support of whole language. Choice (B) is incorrect because whole language instruction usually commences in kindergarten. Choice (C) is incorrect because state legislatures (California) have earmarked money and textbooks to convert back to phonics instruction. Choice (D) is incorrect because tests for higher education presuppose that a student already knows how to read fluently.

34. **The correct answer is (A).** *Why Johnny Can't Read* outlined a sophisticated marketing plan carded by Scott Foresman to sell this "look say" approach to reading—an approach devoid of nonbiased research proving its effectiveness. Choice (B) is wrong because Silberman is in favor of progressive approaches to reading instruction, such as phonics. Choices (C) and (D) are incorrect because these two choices are associated with whole language, not phonics.

35. **The correct answer is (D).** Choice (C) is wrong because whole language is a general reading methodology, not just for remedial instruction. Choice (B) is incorrect because whole language depends upon students reading

literary passages appropriate for their ages. Choice (A) is wrong because phonic skills are often separated from the teaching of language skills.

36. **The correct answer is (C).** The richness of the vocabulary being used will not enhance phonic skills. On the other hand, a controlled vocabulary should be used to teach phonics. Options I, II, and III are an eclectic synthesis of whole language and phonetic elements in the development of the school's reading program.

37. **The correct answer is (D).** This choice is not appropriate because phonics should not be taught in total isolation; it should be taught and applied to realistic reading situations. Choices (A), (B), and (C) are all pieces of literature that enhance phonic skills and sight vocabulary development.

38. **The correct answer is (C).** In a directed reading lesson, reading should be guided, not independent. Developing needed concepts, choice (D), enhances comprehension skills prior to reading the material. With choice (A), students learn and apply a variety of skills to meet the challenge of decoding unknown words. With choice (B), interpretation of the story should be extended through supplemental and follow-up activities.

39. **The correct answer is (B).** The students are drawing conclusions in their own words from indirect information in the story. Choice (A) is incorrect because these questions are not predicting upcoming events. Choices (B) and (D) are both inappropriate because these questions are neither finding a cause and effect nor sequencing the information given.

40. **The correct answer is (A).** Students should not read in a round-robin fashion because many students do not read along. Reading should be silent, and oral reading should be used only to obtain answers to questions posed prior to silent reading and to analyze the material. Choices (B), (C), and (D) are all necessary components of guided reading.

41. **The correct answer is (B).** The teacher is poorly utilizing academic learning time because

he is engaged in so many off-task activities. Choice (A) is incorrect because we do not know how the students are focusing on the task. We cannot determine choice (C) from this question, and choice (D) is wrong because structure is really not defined in this question.

42. **The correct answer is (B).** Based upon his ability, the student should remain in regular education with adaptations.

43. **The correct answer is (D).** At this grade level, penmanship is secondary to the ability to spell and write using a variety of adaptations (which include a computer). Choices (A), (B), and (C) are appropriate recommendations within a 504 plan.

44. **The correct answer is (D).** A regular education teacher must implement a 504 plan—a plan that allows for adaptations for a student within regular education. Choices (A) and (B) are wrong because a teacher can be cited for discrimination if he does not implement the plan. Choice (C) is wrong because this plan's purpose is to prevent a student from receiving a direct special educational service.

45. **The correct answer is (C).** Options I and II are appropriate strategies to prevent fatigue with visual materials and for the child to hold his place. Option III is flawed because we cannot define "improved." Option IV is out of the question because the teacher must implement the adaptations.

46. **The correct answer is (D).** The latest research states that all remediation must be relevant to the classroom tasks. Choice (A) is wrong because the tracking and visual acuity tasks are not relevant to the classroom. Choice (B) is wrong because students with normal comprehension skills should remain in a regular classroom environment. Choice (C) is incorrect because the test profile of these students usually exhibits academic achievement that is close to grade level.

47. **The correct answer is (B).** The student needs concrete strategies to organize himself visually. Options II and IV help the student keep his place and write in the correct place. Options I

and III do not specifically tell the student how to structure his work in a visual manner.

48. **The correct answer is (C).** This is a skill that is usually taught at the first-grade level. Roman numerals, rounding, and place value are third-grade-level skills.

49. **The correct answer is (D).** The concepts of odd and even are second-grade-level skills. The other skills are usually taught in fifth grade.

50. **The correct answer is (B).** Categorizing is one procedure by which information is analyzed. Choice (A) represents knowledge according to Bloom's *Taxonomy*. Choice (C) represents evaluation according to Bloom's *Taxonomy*. Choice (D) represents synthesis according to Bloom's *Taxonomy*.

51. **The correct answer is (C).** This represents the use of the kinesthetic approach to teaching. Choice (A) represents visual approaches to learning, while choice (B) represents auditory approaches to learning. Choice (D) represents a tactile approach to learning.

52. **The correct answer is (C).** Many of the students have decoding problems and will not be able to find or understand specific information. Choice (A) is an appropriate strategy because all the students will hear the play and gain comprehension through the expressions being used. Choice (B) is an appropriate strategy to increase comprehension by previewing the information. Choice (D) is a good strategy because comprehension will increase if the students gain understanding of many vocabulary words.

53. **The correct answer is (A).** This is the best method with which to clarify complex plots and character development because it reinforces the text using the visual modality. Choice (B) is incorrect because many of these low-achieving students may not have the writing skills necessary to develop an outline. Choice (C) is busy work. Looking up words will not enable the students to apply words that represent different characters to the text. Choice (D) will not help the students if they cannot analyze the story's events and characters.

54. **The correct answer is (D).** This is probably an answer to an application type question in which the student sees a common yet modern theme in the play. Choices (A) and (B) represent answers to analysis-type questions. Choice (C) is an answer to a comprehension type of question.

55. **The correct answer is (A).** The students will not only hear the play, but they will also understand various nonverbal expressions. Choices (B) and (C) are incorrect because, by offering help with the teaching of specific skills, the teacher will focus less on comprehension. Choice (D) is incorrect because only the best readers will comprehend some of the more complex material.

56. **The correct answer is (A).** This represents few consequences for breaking minor rules. Choice (B) is wrong because the whimsical nature of administration does not often lead to administrative control. The event is objective, so choice (C) is incorrect. Choice (D) is wrong because a structure is set up even though there is little follow-through.

57. **The correct answer is (B).** This encourages the students to write more than simple sentences. Choices (A) and (D) will not improve the writing skills of the students; they are rote workbook exercises. Choice (C) is incorrect; the sentences may not convey different meanings of the same word because of the students' immature writing skills.

58. **The correct answer is (B).** The teacher will explain his rationale for the lesson in an objective manner to the parent. As long as the teacher was not favoring any particular view, critical thinking is a legitimate skill to teach in a classroom. Choices (A) and (C) are both examples of censorship. The teacher should not bring a union representative to such a meeting because it will create a confrontational atmosphere.

59. **The correct answer is (C).** The response is positive, and the teacher is also taking ownership of the situation. This may result in the students helping the teacher pick up the paper. Choices (A) and (B) are very

confrontational. Choice (D) may not be a feasible punishment if students are not allowed to be kept from their next class.

60. **The correct answer is (D).** At the beginning of the school year, few students are concerned about who will work with them in cooperative projects. They are more interested in what the projects are going to be. Lower-achieving students are more concerned with choice (B); they want to determine the fairness of the teacher. Choices (A) and (C) are good examples of classroom management that can be modeled by others.

61. **The correct answer is (D).** Students must understand that the teacher, not the bell, dismisses them. Choices (A), (B), and (C) are appropriate classroom procedures for the first day of school.

62. **The correct answer is (D).** This is an attention rule. Choice (A) is an entry rule. Choices (B) and (C) are classroom-specific rules.

63. **The correct answer is (A).** This is ineffective because the student is not doing any type of reading activity. Choices (B), (C), and (D) all involve some type of reading activity that working parents can fit into their busy lifestyles.

64. **The correct answer is (C).** Poetry often uses rhyming and phonic patterns along with nursery rhymes. In addition, many types of songs rhyme or make a play on words. Myths do not provide any type of rhyming elements. In addition, many myths contain very difficult vocabulary concepts.

65. **The correct answer is (C).** Identifying and pronouncing words from foreign origin is a higher-level structural analysis skill taught in the upper grades. Discussing consonant blends and more advanced vowels, choices (A), (B), and (D) are skills taught in the second and third grades.

66. **The correct answer is (D).** Research shows that teachers should read aloud to model reading with expression and to expose children to different types of literature they may not

read on their own. Options III and IV are inappropriate responses because reading should not be used as a management tool.

67. **The correct answer is (B).** The teacher is engaging the students in structured comprehension by asking the same question in different ways. In this example, she is asking main idea questions in different ways. Choice (C) is wrong because these are not drawing-conclusion questions. Choices (A) and (D) offer no valid reason for why these questions are being asked.

68. **The correct answer is (D).** This approach is most strongly associated with the Discovery method of Jerome Bruner. Choices (B) and (C) are mostly associated with different theories of child development, while choice (A) is mostly associated with the diagnosis and instruction of children with autistic behavior.

69. **The correct answer is (B).** Bruner stated that every concept need not be discovered by the student. Option I is false because students usually do better on standardized tests using this approach. Option III is false because this approach is used to help students make connections. Option IV is false because simple household materials can be used for this method.

70. **The correct answer is (B).** This is an example of deductive thinking because the students formulate hypotheses and then deduce what their effects would be in a situation. With propositional thinking, choice (A), the teacher proposes a problem involving several factors, and the student makes propositions. With reflexive thinking, choice (C), the teacher presents a problem and asks students to reflect on their thinking and reasoning. With evaluative thinking, choice (D), the teacher asks questions requiring students to make value judgments.

71. **The correct answer is (D).** Predicting is one of the cognitive processes of discovery. The other processes are observing, classifying, measuring, and inferring. Choices (A), (B), and (C) are all examples of scientific inquiry.

72. **The correct answer is (A).** This is an example of the heuristics of discovery. Choice (B) occurs when an individual only learns and develops his mind by using it. Choice (C) is incorrect because this occurs when students receive a satisfactory intellectual thrill. Choice (D) is incorrect because this definition has nothing to do with improved short-term memory.

73. **The correct answer is (A).** This is an example of guided discovery and inquiry in which the teacher outlines much of the planning for the experiment. In free discovery, choice (B), the student originates the problem and determines how to resolve it. In modified discovery, choice (C), the teacher presents the problem, but the student resolves it. This is no such method as experimental discovery and inquiry, choice (D).

74. **The correct answer is (D).** This sentence requires the students to construct mental concepts about what they have learned. This culminating activity helps students to summarize their learning experiences. Choices (A) and (B) foster divergent thinking, and choice (C) is convergent.

75. **The correct answer is (B).** This is an example of an analysis question. Choice (A) is an evaluation question. Choice (C) is a knowledge question, and choice (D) is a comprehension question.

76. **The correct answer is (B).** This taps into divergent thinking because there are many possible answers. With the other choices, only a limited amount of answers exist; therefore, their answers are convergent.

77. **The correct answer is (C).** This question is teleological because it implies that natural phenomena have an end in mind. Choice (A) is wrong because the question is a knowledge-type question and is not too abstract. Choice (B) is incorrect because it does not give a concept of human characteristics. Choice (D) is wrong because with this question there may be more than one answer; therefore, it may have divergent elements.

78. **The correct answer is (C).** He is being taught how to visually reinforce stories that he reads or that are read to him. Option I is incorrect because the student is writing a composition in isolation that is not related to the lesson. Option II is wrong because if a student is reading silently, it is impossible to tell whether that student is losing her place. Option IV is also wrong because this drill may be unrelated to the lesson.

79. **The correct answer is (B).** A consultant teacher can work with up to eight children in a classroom, even if they are not classified. Choices (A), (C), and (D) are wrong because there is too little time to work individually with students at the junior high school level.

80. **The correct answer is (D).** This is an incorrect modification because the student has problems with auditory sequencing. He needs visual reinforcement. The other three choices are correct for this student, who seems to have potential difficulties with attention. He needs more time, a less distracting environment, and the ability to respond in an alternate manner.

ESSAY RESPONSE

Several months into the school term, my sixth-grade social studies class was making little progress in developing meaningful concepts. It became clear to me that this class was having difficulty comprehending their social studies textbook. The students were having difficulty answering the summary questions for each chapter. Many gave word-for-word responses to conceptual and application questions. When tests were given, the students had uneven skills answering multiple-choice and essay questions.

The first strategy I would utilize in developing content area comprehension is to teach them how to develop concept maps. Concept maps are visual representations of information in a chapter. Many different strategies can be utilized to teach this skill. One method is through the use of the herringbone technique. Information is presented in the form of a herringbone. The main idea is written on a central line that represents the backbone of a fish. To this central line are attached oblique lines representing supporting details. This technique can be used for a whole chapter or for part of a chapter. It can also be used in preplanning answers to essay questions, either at the end of a chapter or on a test.

Another mapping method is to divide a paper into six boxes. Each box has the following labels: *who*, *what*, *when*, *where*, *how*, and *why*. Key words and phrases from each chapter are placed into the individual boxes. For example, all the *who* information is placed into the first box. This means that the important names mentioned in a chapter are placed into this box. This method helps students organize information conceptually, and helps them focus on key words when multiple-choice tests are given.

A second method used to increase content area comprehension is the use of SQ3R: Survey, Question, Read, Recite, and Review. This method enables students to summarize and outline important information within a chapter. Using this method, a student surveys or previews the information in a chapter by looking over summary questions, chapter subheadings, illustrations, captions, maps, charts, and similar information. Next, subheadings are turned into questions and the student reads the chapter to answer the questions. Then the student recites the important information in the chapter. Finally, the student reviews this information by placing the relevant material in outline form.

The skills mentioned here do not develop overnight. The instructor must offer the students a great deal of practice by incorporating the techniques into many different lessons. However, through constant reinforcement, students will eventually use these strategies to enhance their metacognitive ability-identifying important conceptual information while reading and writing about content area material.

ABOUT THE AUTHORS

Authors **Joan U. Levy** and **Norman Levy** are the founders of NJL College Preparation & Learning Center, a private tutoring, test preparation, and college guidance service. Joan and Norman are co-authors of 20 books, software, and videos on test preparation.

Joan, Director of NJL, has a Bachelor of Arts from City College of New York, a Master of Science in Guidance and Counseling from Fordham University, and a Ph.D. in Behavioral Science.

Norman is the Executive Director of NJL and has a Bachelor of Education from City College of New York, a Master of Science in Operations Research from New York University, and a Ph.D. in Educational Administration.

NOTES

NOTES

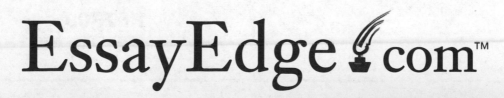

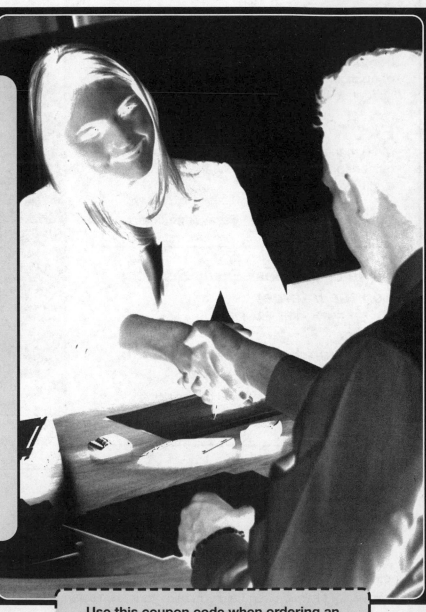